T0186141

Lecture Notes in Computer Science   12985

More information about this subseries at http://www.springer.com/series/7407

Dalibor Klusáček · Walfredo Cirne ·
Gonzalo P. Rodrigo (Eds.)

Job Scheduling Strategies for Parallel Processing

24th International Workshop, JSSPP 2021
Virtual Event, May 21, 2021
Revised Selected Papers

 Springer

Editors
Dalibor Klusáček
CESNET
Prague, Czech Republic

Walfredo Cirne
Google
Mountain View, CA, USA

Gonzalo P. Rodrigo
Apple
Cupertino, CA, USA

ISSN 0302-9743   ISSN 1611-3349   (electronic)
Lecture Notes in Computer Science
ISBN 978-3-030-88223-5   ISBN 978-3-030-88224-2   (eBook)
https://doi.org/10.1007/978-3-030-88224-2

LNCS Sublibrary: SL1 – Theoretical Computer Science and General Issues

This Springer imprint is published by the registered company Springer Nature Switzerland AG
The registered company address is: Gewerbestrasse 11, 6330 Cham, Switzerland

Preface

This volume contains the papers presented at the 24th Workshop on Job Scheduling Strategies for Parallel Processing (JSSPP 2021) that was held on May 21, 2021, in conjunction with the 35th IEEE International Parallel and Distributed Processing Symposium (IPDPS 2021). The proceedings of previous workshops are also available from Springer as LNCS volumes 949, 1162, 1291, 1459, 1659, 1911, 2221, 2537, 2862, 3277, 3834, 4376, 4942, 5798, 6253, 7698, 8429, 8828, 10353, 10773, 11332, and 12326.

This year 17 papers were submitted to the workshop, of which we accepted 10. All submitted papers went through a complete review process, with the full version being read and evaluated by an average of 3.4 reviewers. Additionally, one invited keynote paper was included in the workshop. We would like to especially thank our Program Committee members and additional reviewers for their willingness to participate in this effort and their excellent, detailed, and thoughtful reviews.

For the second time in its history the JSSPP workshop was held fully online due to the worldwide COVID-19 pandemic. Despite the obvious logistic problems, all talks were presented live, allowing the participants to interact with the authors of the papers. We are very thankful to the presenters of accepted papers for their participation in the live workshop session. Recordings from all talks at the 2021 edition can be found at the JSSPP's YouTube channel: https://bit.ly/3mXyT8F.

This year, the workshop was organized into three major parts: a keynote, a session containing two papers discussing open scheduling problems and proposals, and a session containing eight technical papers.

The keynote was delivered by Dror Feitelson from the Hebrew University, Israel. In his keynote, Feitelson presented resampling with feedback, a performance evaluation method for job scheduling. The method builds upon previous methods in the field. First works on evaluation used accounting logs as workload data for simulations. These logs were precise, but would only provide data on specific situations and would not allow simulating scenarios different to the original logs. These challenges were solved by workloads models, but models are usually limited to workload insights that researchers know in advance. Resampling combines characteristics of both, partitioning real workloads in different components (job streams from different users) and generating new workload by sampling from the pool of basic components. These workloads keep most of the original structure while adjusting them to simulate desired scenarios. However, they lack realism as patterns in the workloads do not change depending on the behavior of the scheduler. This is solved in resampling with feedback, a model where users are modeled and their behavior adapts to the resulting scheduling decisions, e.g., jobs must start in a particular order, or jobs are not submitted till others complete or start. Resampling with feedback provides the realism of logs while eliminating many of their drawbacks and enables evaluations of throughput effects that are impossible to observe with static workloads.

Papers accepted for this year's JSSPP cover several interesting problems within the resource management and scheduling domains and include two open scheduling problems (OSP). This year's OSPs focus on the artifacts and data formats needed to perform scheduling research. Soysal et al. highlight the lack of availability of source code from past work on runtime prediction. As a consequence, evaluating new methods includes re-implementing past methods and frameworks numerous times. The authors present a framework to describe, evaluate, and store runtime prediction methods within an openly available online collection that will help future research.

In the second OSP, Corbalan et al. discuss the challenge of simulating systems using standard formats that cannot capture characteristics of current systems and workloads. The paper proposes to extend the Standard Workload Format (SWF) with the Modular Workload Format (MWF). MWF allows new semantics to be defined as modules in the header and referred to as units of workload or part of jobs.

The first full technical paper was presented by Minami et al., who proposed over-committing scheduling systems to enable interactive workloads in HPC systems. The paper analyzes the impact of resource and proposes performance prediction when over commitment is not present. These methods reliably predict the performance degradation of collocated applications, becoming a valid source for future collocation of HPC schedulers.

Rao et al. propose a placement scheme to map containers of a micro service within a node to maximize performance by taking into account the architecture of the hardware. Their mechanism reduces the latency and increases throughput of hosted services. At the same time, it coalesces services to increase performance even further.

The third paper presents a learning-based approach to estimate job wait times in high-throughput computing systems. Such systems are usually governed by fair-share schedulers that do not provide estimations on the expected wait times. To correct this, Gombert et al. analyzed the correlation between job characteristics and wait time in real workloads. Based on this study, they evaluated machine learning algorithms to train on the past workloads and produce wait time prediction models based on the more promising job characteristics.

Souza et al. describe a co-scheduler for HPC systems that relies on reinforcement learning to determine the best collocation patterns to increase utilization in some long running HPC workloads. This scheduler applies decision trees to collocate jobs and learns from low and high quality past decisions to improve its collocation logic. This scheduling system increases utilization and reduces wait time together with overall makespan.

In the fifth paper, Jaros et al. propose a set of methods to determine the right resource request for moldable jobs. The methods rely on genetic algorithms that evolve on historical data while aiming to reduce makespan, computation cost, and idling resources. The methods were tested with a set of established workflows, improving their makespan.

The last section of the workshop started with a presentation on methods to to optimize task placement for streaming workloads on many-core CPUs with DVFS. Kessler et al. argue that performance and energy usage can be optimized by taking into account the thermal impact of task placing decisions, the physical structure of a CPU, and its heat propagation patterns. In particular, they show that alternating task executions between disjoint "buddy" cores avoids long term overheating of cores, and thus allows for higher throughput.

In the seventh paper, Zhang et al. show that future clusters will suffer large variations in their available resources due to power constraints or non-predictable supply from cloud providers. The authors modeled this variability and its impact on cluster performance governed by current scheduling systems. They conclude with some ideas on scheduling techniques to reduce the impact of capacity variability.

Last but not least, Hataishi et al. present GLUME, a system that reduces workflow execution times. This system divides the workflow subsections aiming for the shortest combination of runtime and estimated inter wait times, thus providing the shortest makespan. GLUME also re-evaluates its plan when the completion of each job is near. As each job completes, the remaining workflow is shorter and estimations are more precise, reducing the makespan even further.

We hope you can join us at the next JSSPP workshop, this time in Lyon, France, on June 3, 2022. Enjoy your reading!

August 2021

Dalibor Klusáček
Gonzalo P. Rodrigo
Walfredo Cirne

Organization

Program Chairs

Dalibor Klusáček	CESNET, Czech Republic
Gonzalo P. Rodrigo	Apple, USA
Walfredo Cirne	Google, USA

Program Committee

Amaya Booker	Facebook, USA
Stratos Dimopoulos	Apple, USA
Hyeonsang Eom	Seoul National University, South Korea
Dror Feitelson	Hebrew University, Israel
Jiří Filipovič	Masaryk University, Czech Republic
Liana Fong	IBM T. J. Watson Research Center, USA
Bogdan Ghit	Databricks, The Netherlands
Eitan Frachtenberg	Facebook, USA
Alfredo Goldman	University of Sao Paulo, Brazil
Cristian Klein	Umeå Univeristy/Elastisys, Sweden
Bill Nitzberg	Altair, USA
Christine Morin	Inria, France
P-O Östberg	Umeå University, Sweden
Larry Rudolph	Two Sigma, USA
Lavanya Ramakrishnan	Lawrence Berkeley National Lab, USA
Uwe Schwiegelshohn	TU Dortmund, Germany
Leonel Sousa	Universidade de Lisboa, Portugal
Ramin Yahyapour	University of Göttingen, Germany

Additional Reviewers

Ganesh Kamath Nileshwar	TU Dortmund, Germany
Joao C. Martins	Polytechnic Institute of Beja, Portugal
Ricardo Nobre	INESC-ID, Portugal
Abel Souza	Umeå University, Sweden
Diogo Marques	Tecnico Lisboa, Portugal

Contents

Keynote

Resampling with Feedback: A New Paradigm of Using Workload Data for Performance Evaluation
(Extended Version)

Dror G. Feitelson[✉][ID]

School of Computer Science and Engineering, The Hebrew University of Jerusalem,
91904 Jerusalem, Israel
feit@cs.huji.ac.il

Abstract. Reliable performance evaluations require representative workloads. This has led to the use of accounting logs from production systems as a source for workload data in simulations. But using such logs directly suffers from various deficiencies, such as providing data about only one specific situation, and lack of flexibility, namely the inability to adjust the workload as needed. Creating workload models solves some of these problems but creates others, most notably the danger of missing out on important details that were not recognized in advance, and therefore not included in the model. Resampling solves many of these deficiencies by combining the best of both worlds. It is based on partitioning real workloads into basic components (specifically the job streams contributed by different users), and then generating new workloads by sampling from this pool of basic components. The generated workloads are adjusted dynamically to the conditions of the simulated system using a feedback loop, which may change the throughput. Using this methodology analysts can create multiple varied (but related) workloads from the same original log, all the time retaining much of the structure that exists in the original workload. Resampling with feedback thus provides a new way to use workload logs which benefits from the realism of logs while eliminating many of their drawbacks. In addition, it enables evaluations of throughput effects that are impossible with static workloads.

This paper reflects a keynote address at JSSPP 2021, and provides more details than a previous version from a keynote at Euro-Par 2016 [18]. It summarizes my and my students' work and reflects a personal view. The goal is to show the big picture and the building and interplay of ideas, at the possible expense of not providing a full overview of and comparison with related work.

1 Introduction

Performance evaluation is a basic element of experimental computer science [3]. It is used to compare design alternatives when building new systems, to tune parameter values of existing systems, and to assess capacity requirements when

© Springer Nature Switzerland AG 2021
D. Klusáček et al. (Eds.): JSSPP 2021, LNCS 12985, pp. 3–32, 2021.
https://doi.org/10.1007/978-3-030-88224-2_1

setting up systems for production use. Lack of adequate performance evaluations can lead to bad decisions, which imply either not being able to accomplish mission objectives or inefficient use of resources. A good evaluation study, on the other hand, can be instrumental in the design and realization of an efficient and useful system.

It is widely accepted that the performance of a computer system depends on its design and implementation. This is why performance evaluations can be used to judge designs and assess implementations. But performance also depends on the workload to which the system is subjected. Evaluating a system with the wrong workload will most probably lead to erroneous results, that cannot be relied upon [10,17]. It is therefore imperative to use representative and reliable workloads to drive performance evaluation studies. However, workloads can have complicated structures and distributions, so workload characterization can be a hard task to perform [5].

The problem is exacerbated by the fact that workloads may interact with the system and even with the performance metrics in non-trivial ways [12,13]. Thus it may not be enough to use a workload model that is generally correct, and it may be important to get minute details correct too. But it is not always clear in advance which details are the important ones. This suggests that the workload should be comprehensive and include *all* possible attributes [26].

In the field of parallel job scheduling, the workload is the sequence of jobs submitted to the system. Early research in this field, in the 1980s, lacked data on which to base workloads. Instead studies were based on what were thought to be reasonable assumptions, or compared possible distributions—for example, a uniform distribution of job sizes, a distribution over powers of 2, and a harmonic distribution [23,24]. But it was not known which of these is the most realistic.

Since the mid 1990s workload logs became available (starting with [22]) and were collected in the Parallel Workloads Archive [28,34]. This enabled the substitution of assumptions with hard data [14,16]. In particular, using logged data to drive simulations became the norm in evaluations of parallel job schedulers. But experience with this methodology exposed problems, especially in the context of matching the workload to the simulated system. This is described below in Sect. 3.

The suggested solution to these problems is to use resampling with feedback, as described in Sect. 4. The idea is to partition the workload into basic components, specifically the individual job streams produced by different users, and sample from this pool of components to create multiple alternative workloads [49]. At the same time, feedback from the simulated system is used to pace the workload generation process as would occur in reality [19,37,39,51]. In practical terms, this means that we no longer just simulate the behavior of the system under study—rather, we study the dynamics of how the system interacts with its environment, and in particular, with its users.

The fact that jobs are submitted by simulated users might seem innocuous at first, but in fact it has major implications. The feedback effect works in both directions. On the one hand, the volume of the workload can grow as far as the system capacity allows. But on the other hand we also have a stabilizing *negative* feedback, where extra load causes the generation of additional load to be throttled [19]. This reduces the risk of system saturation.

The resulting methodology enables evaluations that are not possible when using logs as they were recorded—and in particular, evaluations of how system design may affect throughput and utilization. This is extremely important, as low utilization of large-scale systems translates to the loss of a sizable fraction of the investment in the system. Notably, this methodology applies to any system type, not only to the context of parallel job scheduling.

2   Background

Our discussion is couched in the domain of parallel job scheduling. Parallel jobs are composed of multiple interacting processes which run on distinct processors. They can therefore be modeled as rectangles in *processors × time* space, where the height of a rectangle represents the number of processors used, and its width represents the duration of use. This representation rests on the assumption that processors are allocated to jobs on an exclusive basis, and jobs are run to completion on dedicated processors. This enables the parallel processes which constitute the job to communicate with each other efficiently using the machine's high-speed network, and avoids memory contention problems.

Scheduling parallel jobs is the decision of when each job will run. This can be considered as packing the rectangles which represent the jobs. An important goal is to create a dense packing, and minimize the space between job rectangles, because such spaces represent resources that are not utilized. Note that scheduling is an on-line problem: at each instant we do not know of future job arrivals, and even once a job arrives, we do not know for sure how long it will run.

The simplest scheduling algorithm is First-Come-First-Serve (FCFS), which simply schedules the jobs in the order that they are submitted to the system (Fig. 1). An alternative is EASY, named after the Extensible Argonne Scheduling sYstem which introduced it [31,33]. The idea here is to optimize the schedule by taking small jobs from the back of the queue, and using them to fill in holes that were left in the schedule, an operation known as *backfilling*. This reduces fragmentation and improves throughput.

But note that the utility of backfilling depends on the workload. For example, if all the jobs require more than half the processors, two jobs can never run at the same time, and backfilling cannot be used. Thus if EASY is evaluated with such a workload, the result would be that the backfilling optimization is useless. But if real workloads actually do include many small jobs, then this conclusion would be wrong. Therefore workloads used in evaluations must be representative of real workloads. In particular, we need to correctly specify the job arrival patterns, and the job resource demands (processors and runtime).

An important observation is that, in the context of job scheduling (as opposed to task scheduling), there is a human in the loop. Jobs are submitted by human users of the system, and they often wait for the results of one job before submitting another job. This creates a feedback loop from the system performance to

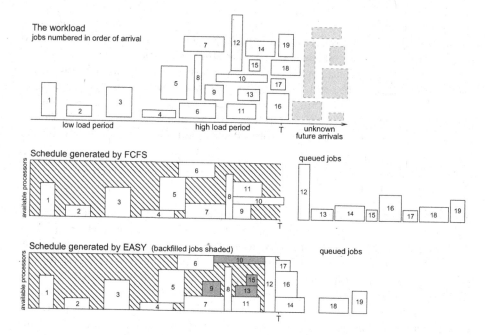

Fig. 1. Illustration of a sequence of parallel jobs (the workload) and how it would be scheduled by FCFS and EASY up to time T. Hatched areas represents wasted resources.

the job submittal process. Our work is about how to achieve representativeness, and at the same time, how to incorporate this feedback.

3 Using Workload Logs and Models to Drive Simulations

There are two common ways to use a logged workload to analyze or evaluate a system design: (1) use the logged data directly to drive a simulation, or (2) create a model from the log and use the model for either analysis or simulation. As we'll show, both have deficiencies that may lead to problems in evaluations. The idea of resampling can be thought of as combining the two in order to enjoy the best of both worlds.

3.1 Workload Modeling

The generation of a workload model proceeds as follows:

1. Identify the workload attributes that need to be modeled. These are the important attributes that are expected to influence the outcome, for example the job arrival times and resource requirements.
2. Collect data, namely workload logs from production systems.
3. Fit the data regarding the identified workload attributes to mathematical distributions.

The model is then the description of the workload using these distributions. It can be used for random variate generation as input to simulations, or else the mathematical distributions can be used directly in a mathematical analysis.

Workload models have a number of advantages over logs. Some of the most salient ones are [17, Sect. 1.3.2]:

- The modeler has full knowledge of workload characteristics. For example, it is easy to know which workload parameters are correlated with each other because this information is part of the model. Such knowledge increases our understanding, and can lead to new designs based on this understanding. Workload logs, on the other hand, may include unknown features that nevertheless have a significant influence on the results. These cannot be exploited and may lead to confusion.
- It is possible to change model parameters one at a time, in order to investigate the influence of each one, while keeping other parameters constant. This allows for direct measurement of system sensitivity to the different parameters. In particular, it is typically easy to check different load levels. It is also possible to select model parameters that are expected to match the specific workload at a given site.
- A model is not affected by policies and constraints that are particular to the site where a log was recorded. For example, if a site configures its job queues with a maximum allowed duration of 4 h, it forces users to break long jobs into multiple short jobs. Thus, the observed distribution of durations in a log will be different from the "natural" distribution users would have generated under a different policy, and the log—despite being "real"—is actually unrepresentative. In a model we can recreate the postulated real distribution.
- Logs may be polluted by bogus data. For example, a log may include records of jobs that were killed because they exceeded their resource bounds. Such jobs impose a transient load on the system, and influence the arrival process. However, they may be replicated a number of times before completing successfully, and only the successful run represents "real" work. In a model, such jobs can be avoided (but they can also be modeled explicitly if so desired).
- Models have better statistical properties: they are usually stationary, so evaluation results converge faster [9], and they allow multiple statistically equivalent simulations to be run so as to support the calculation of confidence intervals. Logs, on the other hand, provide only a single data point, which may be based on an unknown mixture of conditions.

These advantages have led to the creation and use of several workload models (e.g. [2,4,30,32]), and even a quest for a general, parameterized workload model that can serve as a canonical workload in all evaluations [25].

3.2   Problems with Models

By definition, models include only what you know about in advance, and decide to incorporate in the model. As the result they do not include workload features that you think are not important, or that you don't know about. But such workload features may actually be important, in the sense that they have an effect on scheduler performance.

Over the years several examples of important attributes that were not anticipated in advance have been discovered. Three interesting ones are the following.

User Runtime Estimates: Perhaps the most interesting feature of parallel job workloads—in terms of its unexpected importance—is user runtime estimates. Many schedulers (including EASY) require users to provide estimates of job runtime when submitting a job; these estimates are then used by the scheduler to plan ahead. Simulations often assumed that perfect estimates are available, based on the assumption that users are motivated to provide them: shorter estimates increase the chances to backfill, but too short estimates would cause the job to be killed when it overruns its allocated time. This turned out to be wrong on two counts: first, estimates are actually very inaccurate, and second, it actually matters.

Typical runtime estimate accuracy data is shown in Fig. 2 [33]. These are histograms of the fraction of the user runtime estimates that was actually used (that is, of the quotient of the true runtime divided by the user's estimate). Ideally we would like to see all jobs near 100%, implying near-perfect estimates. But the actual peak at 100% is due to jobs that were killed because they exceeded their estimate. For other jobs except the very shortest ones the histogram is flat, implying that the estimates provide little information about the actual runtimes.

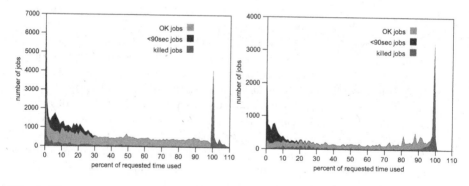

Fig. 2. Histograms of user runtime estimate accuracy, from logs from the CTC and KTH SP2 machines [33].

The effect of these inaccurate estimates is that unnecessary holes are left in the schedule. These holes allow for backfilling, and in particular, short holes allow for the backfilling of short jobs [45]. This leads to a shortest-job-first like effect, which improves scheduling metrics like the average response time. As a result it appears that worse estimates lead to better performance [20,33,52].

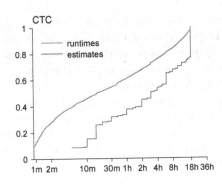 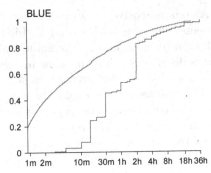

Fig. 3. Comparison of the CDFs of the distributions of user estimates and actual runtimes, from logs from the CTC and BLUE machines [42].

In order to achieve more reliable evaluations we need a better model of user runtime estimates and their (in)accuracy. This turned out to be highly non-trivial [42]. As shown in Fig. 3, users tend to use round figures such as 30 min or 2 h as their estimates. And they tend to over-estimate by a large amount, often using the maximal allowed estimate, so as to avoid the risk of having their jobs killed. Together, this means that estimates provide much less information than they could.

In retrospect we now have a good model of user runtime estimates [42], and a good understanding of the interactions between estimates and other features of the workload, and the conditions under which one scheduler is better than another [13, 45]. But the more important result is the demonstration that performance evaluation results may be swayed by innocent-looking workload details, and that a very detailed analysis is required in order to uncover such situations.

The Daily Cycle of Activity: Another example is that real workloads are obviously non-stationary: they have daily, weekly, and even yearly cycles. In many cases this is ignored in performance evaluations, with the justification that only the high load at prime time is of interest. While this is reasonable in the context of network communication, where the individual workload items (packets) are very small, it is very dubious in the context of parallel jobs, that may run for many hours.

Consider the "user-aware" scheduler, which attempts to promote interactive work by prioritizing short jobs that have been submitted recently [39, 51]. This idea is based on the observation that short response times are correlated with short think times [38]: if a job's response time is short, chances are that the user will submit another job soon after. But if the response time is long, the think time till the next job will also be long, implying that the user may leave the system and take a break. Consequently, by prioritizing recent short jobs, we better support users' workflows and facilitate the extension of their active sessions.

A comprehensive evaluation of this idea turned out to require two unusual elements. One was a user model which responds to feedback from the system performance, and adjusts the submittal of jobs based on their response time. This is discussed at length below in Sect. 4.3. The other was that the workload include a daily cycle of activity, as described at the end of Sect. 4.4.

Note that we did not explicitly design the user-aware scheduler to exploit the daily cycle of activity. But its performance turned out to depend on the existence of such a cycle [26]. The reason was that the prioritization of recent short jobs led to the starvation of long and non-recent jobs. If the workload exhibited a daily cycle, the non-critical jobs submitted during prime time were delayed and executed later during the night hours. As a result the system backlog was drained, and the full capacity was available for the interactive work of the next day. But if the workload did not have a daily cycle, there was no non-prime time, and thus no alternative time to execute the non-critical jobs. They therefore had to compete, and interfere with, the interactive workload—making it seem that the user-aware scheduler provides no benefits.

Workload Locality: Yet another effect that is prevalent in logs but usually absent from models is locality [15]. The locality properties of real workloads are especially important for the evaluation of adaptive and predictive systems (for example, it may be possible to predict job runtimes and compensate for inaccurate estimates [43]). Such features are becoming more commonplace with the advent of self-tuning and self-management. The idea is that the system should be able to react to changing conditions, without having to be reconfigured by a human operator [21]. But in order to study such systems, we need workloads with changing conditions as in real workload logs. A model based on random sampling from a distribution will not do, as it creates a stationary workload. This can be solved by employing "localized sampling" from the distribution [15], but a better solution is to use user-based modeling (or resampling), as described below.

3.3   Using Logs Directly

The perception that workload models may be over-simplified and unjustified has led many researchers to prefer real workload logs. Logs are used to generate the workload for simulations in a straightforward manner: jobs just arrive according to the timestamps in the log, and each job requires the number of processors and runtime as specified in the log.

The advantage of using a traced log directly as the input to a simulation is that it is the most "real" test of the simulated system: the workload reflects a real workload precisely, with all its complexities, even if they are not known to the person performing the analysis [10, 17]. Consequently, this is the current best practice and is widely used.

The first such log to be made available came from the iPSC/860 hypercube machine installed at NASA Ames Research Center, and included all jobs executed on the system in the fourth quarter of 1993 [22]. This provided a wealth of hitherto unknown information regarding the distributions of job sizes and run-times and patterns of user activity. Over the years many additional logs have been collected in the Parallel Workloads Archive [28,34]. This resource is widely used as shown in Fig. 4.

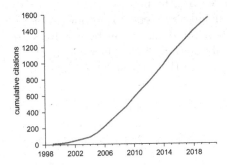

Fig. 4. Number of citations to the parallel workloads archive on Google Scholar.

Contributing to the popularity of the Parallel Workloads Archive is the fact that each log is accompanied by copious metadata concerning the system and the logged data. In addition, all the logs are converted to a "standard workload format" [1]. Thus if a simulator can read this format, it can immediately run simulations using all the logs in the archive.

3.4   Drawbacks of Using Logs

While using logs "as is" avoids the problems associated with models, logs too have their drawbacks. Three major issues are the following.

Evaluation Flexibility: Each log reflects only one specific workload, and can only provide a single data point to the evaluation. But evaluations often require multiple simulations with related workloads. For example, the calculation of confidence intervals is best done by running multiple simulations with distinct but statistically identical workloads. This is easy with a workload model but impossible with a log.

More specifically, it is not possible to manipulate logs to adjust the workload to the simulated system and conditions, and even when it is possible, it can be problematic. In particular, it is often desirable to evaluate the performance of a system under different load conditions, e.g. to check its stability or the maximal load it can handle before saturating. Thus a single load condition (as provided by a log) is not enough, and we need a tunable parameter that allows for the generation of different load conditions.

In log-based simulations it is common practice to increase the load on the system by reducing the average interarrival time. For example, if a log represents a load of 70% of system capacity, multiplying all interarrival times by a factor of $7/8 = 0.875$ will increase the load to 80%. But this practice has the undesirable consequence of shrinking the daily load cycle as well. The alternative of increasing the runtime to increase the load is not much better: jobs that originally came one after the other, and maybe even depended on each other, may now overlap. And increasing the number of processors to increase load is even worse. For example, if job sizes tend to be powers of 2 (which they are) then they pack well together. Increasing them by say 10% is not always possible (a 4-processor job can only be increased in increments of 25%), and when possible it has detrimental effects on the packing of the jobs onto processors.

Dirty Data: While logged data represents real activity, it is dubious whether *all* real data is worth using. Potential problems include errors in data recording, workload evolution and non-stationarity, multi-class workload mixtures, and abnormal activity.

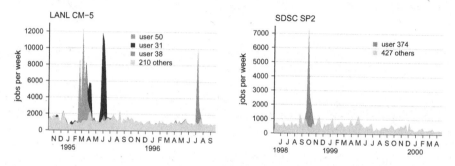

Fig. 5. Arrivals per week on two parallel supercomputers, showing flurries of activity due to single users [27, 44].

One type of unrepresentative activity is huge short-lived surges of activity by individual users, called flurries (Fig. 5). Such flurries may single-handedly affect workload statistics, especially the statistics of job arrivals, and perhaps also job attributes (a flurry with numerous similar jobs will create a mode in the distribution). While the existence of flurries is not uncommon (many logs exhibit them up to a few times a year), they are very different from the normal workload between them, and also different from each other. They should therefore be removed from the workload logs before they are analyzed and used in simulations [27, 44].

An example of the effect of a workload flurry is shown in Fig. 6. This is a rather small flurry that occurred in the CTC SP2 log. The log records data about 79,302 jobs submitted by 678 users over the course of 11 months. One of these users, user no. 135, had a flurry of 2080 jobs, nearly all of them during one day. The log was used in simulations of the EASY scheduler for different load conditions, where the load was changed in steps of 1% by modifying the job

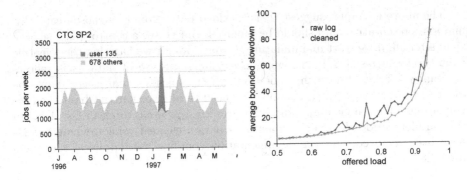

Fig. 6. The effect of the CTC flurry on slowdown results.

interarrival times as described above. Surprisingly, the results where erratic: the average bounded slowdown showed considerable fluctuations between neighboring load conditions. Even more surprisingly, these fluctuations disappeared when user 135's flurry was removed from the log, leaving a curve similar to what is expected in queueing analysis results [44]. In other words, a flurry that contained just 2.6% of the jobs and existed largely during a single day out of 11 months led to unreliable results.

A different type of example is shown in Fig. 7. This is not a short-lived flurry, but rather the voluminous activity of a single user throughout the recorded log. In fact, user no. 2 in the HPC2N log accounted for no less than 57% of the jobs that appear in the log. Thus, if this log is used to analyze schedulers, we risk optimizing the scheduler to the behavior of a single user on a certain cluster in Sweden. An alternative interpretation is that this is not a real user, but rather represents a funnel for jobs from some external source, e.g. a multi-national grid system. This is just as bad, as it means that all data about individual users is lost.

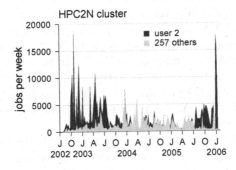

Fig. 7. Arrivals per week on the HPC2n cluster, showing voluminous activity by user no. 2.

The above examples suggest that workload data should be chosen carefully, and unrepresentative data should be removed. But this is a controversial suggestion: after all, if we start manipulating the data, aren't we harming the scientific validity of the results? In my opinion extolling the use of data as is reflects ignorance. Workload data that does not reflect typical system usage should be identified and removed [27]. However, we need to be transparent about the considerations for such cleaning, and what exactly was done to clean the data. In the parallel workloads archive, many logs have a cleaned version where flurries have been removed, and the documentation contains the details of the filters used [28].

Signature of the Logged System: At a deeper level, we find that logged workloads actually contain a "signature" of the logged system. In other words, there is no such thing as a "real" workload which is the right one for general use: *every workload observed on a real system is the result of the interaction between that particular system and its users.* If the system behaves differently, for example if we decide to use a different scheduler, the users change their behavior as well.

This has major implications. It means that using a workload from one system to evaluate a different system is wrong, because the workload will not fit the simulation conditions [37–39]. We demonstrated this using a pair of cross-simulations of the two schedulers described above (Fig. 1) [37]. The first is the well known FCFS scheduler, which is inefficient and leads to wasted resources, because processors are left idle until the first queued job can run. The second is the optimizing EASY scheduler, which optimizes the schedule by taking small jobs from down the queue and backfilling them into holes left between earlier jobs. This allows EASY to sustain a heavier load. Using these schedulers, we conducted a site-level simulation of each one, namely a full simulation of the interaction between the scheduler and its users (this is explained below in Sect. 4.3). Importantly, in these simulations the workload is generated on-the-fly. These generated workloads were recorded, creating logs like those that are obtained from real supercomputer sites.

We then used each log as the input to a conventional simulation of the other scheduler (Fig. 8). As expected, the simulation of FCFS using a workload generated by an EASY simulation led to system saturation and overloading: FCFS could not handle the load that was generated when users interacted with EASY. Conversely, simulation of EASY using a workload generated by an FCFS simulation failed to show that EASY had a significant advantage, because the workload was not challenging enough.

Taken together, all these problems seem to imply that workload logs are actually not any better than workload models. Resampling and feedback are designed to solve these problems and facilitate reliable evaluations.

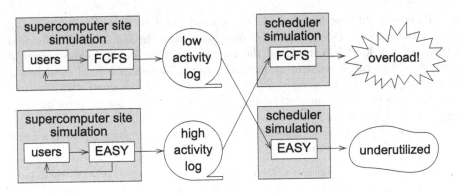

Fig. 8. Experimental setup to demonstrate the effect of a system's signature on the workload.

4   Resampling and Feedback

The root cause of many of the problems with using logs is that a log represents unique conditions that were in effect when it was recorded, and may not be suitable for the desired evaluation. At the same time logs contain significant structure that we want to retain. Resampling is a way to provide flexibility while preserving the structure. And feedback adds just the necessary level of adjustment to the conditions that hold during the evaluation.

4.1   Before Resampling: Input Shaking and User-Based Modeling

The idea of resampling grew out of the ideas of input shaking and user-based modeling.

Input shaking was also an innovative use of logs in simulations [46]. The idea was to "shake" the job stream, meaning that in general the workload remained the same as in the log, but some of the jobs were adjusted to a small degree. For example, their arrival time could be changed by a small random amount. This enabled many simulations with similar but not identical workloads, and facilitated the identification of situations where the original results were actually due to some artifact and therefore not representative.

User-based modeling is based on the observation that the workload on a multi-user system is composed of the workloads by multiple individual users [5,8]. The idea is then to *turn this into a generative approach* to creating workloads: first create independent workloads representing the different users, and then combine them together.

This idea was first proposed as a mechanism to generate locality of sampling [11], based on the fact that different users submits jobs with different characteristics [5,8]. Since the community of active users changes over time, the number of active users in a given week—and the number of different programs they run— will be relatively small. The short-term workload will therefore tend to include repetitions of similar jobs, and will consequently tend to have more locality and be more predictable. But over a longer period this will change, because the set of active users has changed.

The essence of user-based modeling is an attempt to capture this structure using a multi-level model of the user population and the behavior of individual users. The top level is a model of the user population, including the arrival of new users and the departure of previous users. The second level models the activity of individual users as a sequence of sessions synchronized with the time of day (again based on data extracted from logs [48]). The lowest level includes repetitions of jobs within each session.

Remarkably, user-based modeling makes significant progress towards solving the problems outlined above:

- The workload will naturally have locality provided that the job models of different users are different from each other. During the tenure of each set of users the job stream will reflect the behavior of those users.
- The load on the system can be modified by changing the number of active users, or in other words, by changing parameters of the user population model. More users would generate higher load, but do it "in the right way".
- The generated workload can include non-stationary elements such as a daily cycle, by virtue of the model of when users engage in sessions of activity [39].
- As a special case, unique events such as workload flurries can be included or excluded at will, by including or excluding users with such unique behaviors.
- By using heavy-tailed session durations (and inter-session breaks) one can generate self similarity [47], which has been found in many types of workloads including parallel jobs [41, 49].

The drawback of this approach is the need to collect data and construct all these models. But maybe all this modeling takes us too far from the original log data? Resampling was designed to retain the original data as much as possible, and modify only whatever is needed for a specific purpose.

4.2 Resampling from a Log

Resampling is a powerful technique for statistical reasoning in situations where not enough empirical data is available [6, 7]. The idea is to use the available data sample as an approximation of the underlying population, and resample from it. Applying this to workloads, we can create workloads using the following procedure [49]:

1. Partition a workload log into its basic components, taken to be the individual job streams submitted by different users.
2. Sample from this pool of users.
3. Combine the job streams of the selected users to create a new version of the workload.

When looking at individual user traces, we find that some of them are active throughout much of the log's duration, while others are active only during a relatively short interval (a few weeks or months). We therefore distinguish between long-term users and temporary users (Fig. 9), and use them differently in the resampling. Users whose entire activity is too close to either end of the log are excluded.

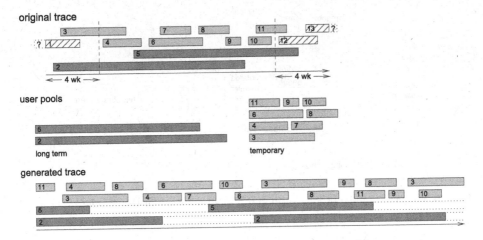

Fig. 9. Conceptual framework of dividing users into long-term and temporary, and reusing them in a generated workload [49]. Each rectangle represents the full extent of activity by a certain user.

Given the pools of temporary and long-term users, the resampling and generation of a new workload is done as follows:

- **Initialization:** We initialize the active users set with some temporary users and some long-term users. The defaults are the number of long-term users in the original log, and the average number of temporary users present in a single week of the original log. Users are not started with their first job from the trace, because we are trying to emulate a workload that was recorded over an arbitrary timespan, and there is no reason to assume that the beginning of the logging period should coincide with the beginning of a user's activity. Therefore each user is started in some arbitrary week of his traced activity. However, care is taken that jobs start on the same day of the week and time of the day in the simulation as in the original log.
- **Temporary users:** In each new week of the simulation, a certain number of new temporary users are added (and a similar number are expected to leave, on average). The exact number is randomized around the target number, which defaults to the average rate at which temporary users arrived in the original log. The selected users are started from their first traced jobs. A user can be selected from the pool multiple times, but care is taken not to select the same user twice in the same week.
- **Long-term users:** The population of long-term users is constant and consists of those chosen in the initialization. When the traced activity of a long-term user is finished, it is simply regenerated after a certain interval. Naturally the regenerations are also synchronized correctly with the time and day.

Each active user submits jobs to the system exactly as in the log (except that their timing may vary to reflect feedback as explained below). The flow of the simulation is shown in Fig. 10.

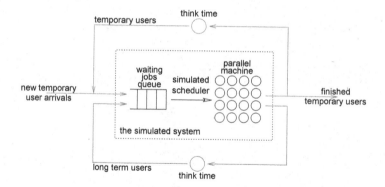

Fig. 10. Queueing model of long term and temporary users in the simulation, leading to a semi-open system [51].

Using resampled workloads enjoys all the benefits listed above for user-based workloads. In addition to that, it has the following advantages over using a log directly:

- We can create multiple different workloads with the same underlying structure and statistics, and
- We can extend the workload by continued resampling beyond the original length of the log.

However, recall that logs contain a signature of the interaction between the users and the scheduler (Sect. 3.4). In addition, each user's job stream contains a signature of interactions with the activity of other users: when one user loads the system, others tend to back off (Fig. 11). So if we just remix them randomly we might create unrealistic conditions. To solve these problems we need to add feedback.

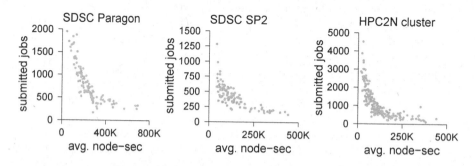

Fig. 11. Evidence of interactions between users. In these scatter plots, each dot represents a week's activity. In weeks with jobs that require a lot of resources, there are relatively few jobs. When there are many jobs, all of them, by all users, are small.

4.3   Adding Feedback

Conventional simulations that replay a log to recreate the workload essentially assume an open systems model: they assume the jobs arrive from an external, large user population, which is insensitive to the system's performance. As a result the jobs' arrivals are independent of each other. However, real computer systems are often more like closed systems [35,36]: They have a limited user population, and new jobs are submitted only after previous ones terminate. This leads to a feedback from the system's performance to the workload generation.

We therefore suggest that it is not enough to simulate the computer system in isolation—we should also simulate the system's environment, namely the users who interact with the system, create its input, and wait for its response [37]. With resampling we introduce this explicitly by including a changing user community in the simulation. It is these (simulated) users who create the (simulated) jobs submitted to the (simulated) system. We need to add a feedback effect to these users' behavior.

Another way to look at the resulting system dynamics is as follows. Conventional performance evaluations, whether based on simulations or queueing analysis, attempt to assess the system's performance as a function of the offered load. But at the same time, the additional load generated by the users depends on the system's performance. By studying both effects together we can find the equilibrium point where workload generation and performance match each other (Fig. 12) [10]. This is the actual expected performance for this system and these users.

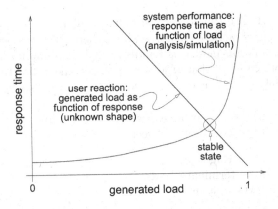

Fig. 12. The observed workload on a system reflects the equilibrium between generating more jobs when performance is better and reduced performance when there are more jobs.

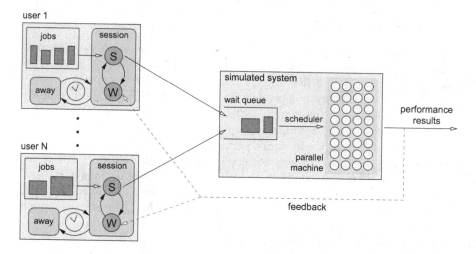

Fig. 13. Illustration of a user-based simulation with feedback. When users are in session, they alternate between submitting jobs (S) and waiting for feedback regarding previous jobs (W). The sessions themselves often depend on (simulated) time of day.

The fact that realistic workloads need to be paced according to system performance has also been noted in the context of computer networks [29]. In this case the feedback is caused by link congestion, which may not be readily visible in packet traces.

User Models with Feedback: The way that feedback is incorporated into the simulations is via user models. As noted above there are three such models. The top level, the population model, is handled by the resampling as explained in Sect. 4.2. The bottom level, that of jobs, is actually taken directly from the logs. The middle model, which concerns user activity patterns, is where the feedback comes in.

The way this works is shown in Fig. 13. In its simplest form, each user's activity is modeled by transitions between three states:

- Thinking and submitting a job,
- Waiting for a job to terminate, and
- Being away from the system.

When a job is submitted the user transitions to the waiting state. The feedback signal informs the user that the job has terminated, causing a transition back to the think and submit state. Alternatively, if the wait is too long, a transition to the "away" state may occur. Such a transition can also occur due to the passage of time. Returning to the system is also usually associated with the passage of time, e.g. simulating coming to work in the morning.

Recovering Dependencies from Logs: The idea of feedback is to pace the job submittal rate. Additional jobs will be submitted (by the simulated users) only after the jobs that they depend on have terminated (on the simulated system).

In other words, when we want to evaluate a new scheduling policy using a representative workload, the workload should reflect the user-level logic and not just parrot a previous workload. The logic is embodied in the dependencies between jobs. Note that there is a tradeoff involved: the traditional approach is to replay the log using the exact timestamps of job arrivals as recorded in the log. This may violate the user logic if jobs are delayed in the simulated system. the alternative is to retain the logical dependencies, at the expense of losing the recorded timestamps. We argue that *it is more important to preserve the logic of the users' behavior than to repeat the exact timestamps that appear in the original log.*

The problem is that accounting logs used as data sources do not include explicit information regarding the dependencies between jobs. We therefore need to identify user sessions and extract dependencies between the jobs in each session [37,50]. Two types of dependencies have been suggested [50]:

- Order constraint: jobs should start in the same order in the simulation as in the original log. In any log, the arrival times of all the jobs submitted by the same user form a sequence. Each job in the sequence should therefore depend on the previous job.
- Potential dependence constraint: every job potentially depends on all the jobs that have terminated before it started to run. As the jobs in each session form a sequence, it is enough to enforce dependencies on the last terminated job in each previous session.

These dependencies are illustrated in Fig. 14.

The way to integrate such considerations into log-driven simulations is by manipulating the timing of job arrivals. In other words, the *sequence* of jobs submitted by each user stays the same, but the *submittal times* are changed [50]. Specifically, each job's submit time is adjusted to reflect feedback from the system performance to the user's behavior.

However, a job cannot arrive immediately when all its constraints are removed. Rather, its arrival should reflect reasonable user behavior (for example, users often go to sleep at night). One possible model of user behavior is the "fluid" user model. The idea of this model is to retain the original session times of the users, but allow jobs to flow from one session to another according to the feedback. To do this, we keep each session's start and end timestamps from the original log. The think times between successive jobs are also retained from the original log. But if a job's execution is delayed in the simulation, leading to the next arrival falling beyond the end of the session, the next job will be delayed even more and arrive only at the beginning of the next session [50]. Contrariwise, if jobs terminate sooner in the simulation, jobs that were submitted originally in the next session may flow forward to occur in the current one.

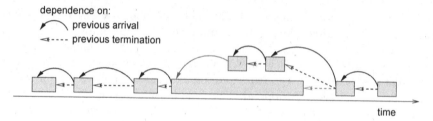

Fig. 14. Dependencies on previous job arrivals and terminations. The ones shown in red show that the two types are not redundant.

4.4   Applications and Benefits

So what can we do with this new tool of workload resampling with feedback? Here are some results that would be hard or impossible to achieve with conventional simulations that just replay an existing log.

Validation: The first and foremost is to validate simulation results. Simulating with a given log provides a single data point. But with resampling we can get a distribution based on statistically similar workloads. In most cases the value which is obtained using a conventional simulation is within the body of this distribution, and the result is verified (Fig. 15). The width of the distribution can then be used to estimate the result's accuracy. But in some cases (e.g. the Blue log on the right) the distribution is shifted, indicating a mismatch between the behavior of the users in the original log and the expected behavior in the simulated system. This is a warning that a direct simulation with the original log may not be suitable for an evaluation of this scheduler.

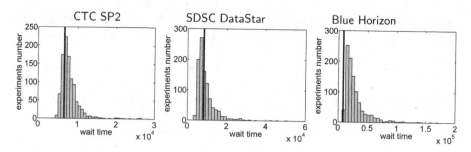

Fig. 15. Histograms of the average waiting time in a thousand simulations of EASY on resampled workloads, compared to a simulation using the original logs (vertical line).

Enhanced Simulations: Other benefits are more technical in nature. One of them is the ability to extend a log and create a longer workload, with more jobs in total, so as to facilitate better convergence of the results and reduce the detrimental effects of the initial "warmup" period. This is easy to achieve: we just continue resampling on and on for as long as we wish.

In principle it may seem that we can also change the load on the system by increasing or decreasing the number of active users. This is done by changing the number of long-term users in the initialization, and the number of new temporary users which arrive in each simulated week. Such a manipulation facilitates the study of how the system responds to load, and enables the generation of response curves similar to those obtained from queueing analyses. However, as noted above, increasing the load on the system is at odds with the throttling effect that comes with feedback. This is further discussed below.

Nevertheless, adding users to increase the load does work as long as the system does not saturate. This has the benefit of making low-load logs usable. Some logs were recorded on very low-load systems, with a utilization of only 25% of capacity or so. These workloads are not interesting as they do not tax the system to any appreciable degree. But by using resampling to increase their load they become interesting.

Finally, we note that once we partition the workload into individual users we can also look at different user classes in isolation. One example noted before is the workload flurries occasionally produced by some users. We can then evaluate the effect of such flurries by oversampling these users, and thus causing more and more flurries to occur (Fig. 16).

Throughput and Capacity Evaluation: Using results from resampling and feedback for verification hinges on the claim that such simulations are more valid to begin with. As noted above, using a log to drive a simulation suffers from the possible mismatch between the behavior of the users in the logged system and the behavior that would be observed for the simulated system. In particular, if the simulated system is more powerful, the users would be expected to submit more jobs, and vice versa. In simulations with feedback this indeed happens automatically, as demonstrated in Fig. 17. Note that this result is impossible

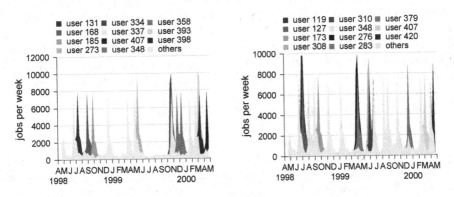

Fig. 16. Examples of workloads with repeated flurries based on the SDSC SP2 workload from Fig. 5.

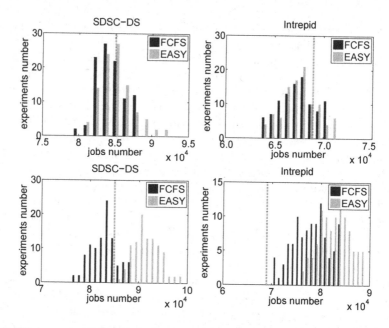

Fig. 17. Histograms of the throughput achieved in one hundred simulations of the EASY and FCFS schedulers using the SDSC DataStar and Intrepid logs [51]. Top: in simulation without feedback the throughput is determined by the input, and a better scheduler has no effect. Bottom: in simulation with feedback EASY is seen to support a higher throughput than FCFS. The vertical line represents the throughput in the original log.

to achieve using conventional log-based simulations. The ability of EASY to support a higher load is only observable when using feedback-based simulations.

However, note that increasing the load on the system is at odds with the throttling effect that comes with feedback. As the load increases, the system will naturally take longer to process each job. Simulated users who are waiting for a job to terminate before submitting their next job will therefore be delayed. So having more users will eventually cause each of these users to produce additional work at a slower rate, and the load will cease to increase! This is good because it is assumed that such an effect exists in real systems, where users abandon the system if it is too slow. But it frustrates our attempt to control the load and increase it at will.

Importantly, as a result of these dynamics we also have the additional benefit of being able to measure the maximal load that the system is expected to support. Resampling and user-based modeling facilitate the use of throughput as a performance metric, because the users become part of the simulation. But every system has a maximal capacity, and if the load exceeds this capacity the system saturates. In real systems this hardly happens, because of the feedback, and the system settles into a slightly lower load. Identifying this maximal expected load is an important part of a performance evaluation. Likewise, if we add system abandonment to the user behavior model, we can add the metric of the number of frustrated users.

Simulating User Aware Schedulers: Given that simulations based on resampling and feedback can exhibit changes in throughput, they can specifically be used to evaluate adaptive systems that are designed to enhance throughput (and thus productivity) rather than response time [39,51].

For example, we can design a scheduler that prioritizes jobs based on their expected response time (mentioned above in Sect. 3.2). The idea is that if the response time is short, there is a good chance that the user will continue to submit more jobs. Note, however, that this depends on a model of what users care about. Regrettably, we typically do not have any explicit information about a user's motivation and considerations. But still some information can be gleaned by analyzing logs. For example, the question of what annoys users more and causes them to abort their interactive work has been investigated by tabulating the probability to submit another job as a function of the previous job's response time or its slowdown [38]. The result was that response time was the more meaningful metric (Fig. 18).

Based on this insight, we define think times of 20 min to be the boundary between continuously submitting jobs in the same session (short think times and rapid additional jobs) and session breaks (a long time before the next job, so the user probably took a break). With this definition, we find that the longer a job's response time, the lower the probability that the session will continue—namely, that the think time till the next job is submitted will be shorter than 20 min [38,39].

With this background we can design schedulers that prioritize jobs that are expected to have short response times [39,51]. To avoid starvation this is balanced with prioritizing based on waiting time. At one extreme all the weight is placed on responsiveness, accepting the risk of starvation. At the other extreme all the weight is placed on waiting time and none on responsiveness, which is equivalent to EASY. Different mixes lead to a spectrum of algorithms.

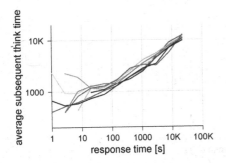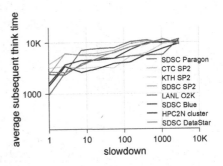

Fig. 18. A job's performance as measured by the response time is a better predictor of subsequent user behavior (think time till the next job) than the job's slowdown.

Trying to evaluate this idea with conventional workloads and simulations is useless—such simulations cannot evaluate productivity, and might even show that average response time is actually increased. But with a dynamic user-based simulation we can compare the resulting dynamics as the competition for resources intensifies. The results are shown in Fig. 19. When priority is given to the interactive jobs, sessions retain their length despite increasing load and the overall system throughput increases.

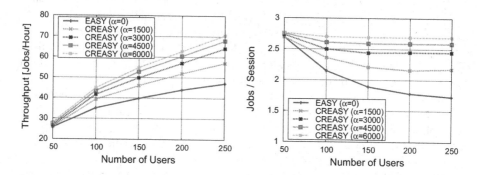

Fig. 19. Average job throughput and session length are higher the more emphasis is placed by the scheduler on responsiveness (as reflected by the parameter α; CREASY is a version of EASY with priority to critical interactive jobs).

It is also interesting to see how these results are achieved. Figure 20 shows an analysis of the performance achieved by different job classes, where the classification is based on runtime: short is up to 1 min, medium is 1 to 10 min, and long is above 10 min. As seen in the graph, the user-aware scheduler achieves a significant reduction in response time for short and medium jobs, which are prioritized, while suffering a significant increase in response time for the long jobs, which were delayed.

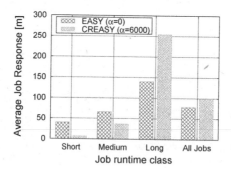

Fig. 20. The improved performance of short jobs comes at the expense of long jobs, which are delayed.

Interestingly, this only worked when the simulation included a daily cycle of activity [26]. In retrospect, the reason is simple: the daily cycle allows the jobs that were delayed to run later, when the load on the system abates. A comparison of the (simulated) scheduler queue lengths is shown in Fig. 21. For both EASY and the user aware scheduler the queue builds up in the morning. But with EASY it quickly drains in the evening, leaving the system idle during the night. The user-aware scheduler, in contradistinction, overcommits during the day. As a result it has much more work left for the night, and utilizes the resources that EASY leaves idle. In simulations without daily cycles this effect cannot occur, and both schedulers display the same level of performance.

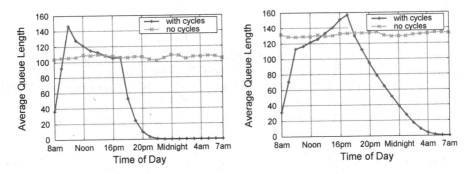

Fig. 21. Queue lengths in simulations with and without daily cycles; EASY on the left and user-aware on the right. The simulation used a simple model where jobs arrive only between 8 AM and 6 PM.

5   Conclusions

Resampling with feedback provides a new way to use workload logs in simulations, enabling the generation of varied and dynamically adjusted workloads that are specifically suited to evaluate the simulated system. This combines the realism of real log data with the flexibility of models. Basing the simulations as closely as possible on real logs reflects the importance of using hard data rather than assumptions. Adjusting the workload to the specific conditions during the simulation reflects the importance of the interaction between the users and the system. Without this, evaluation results are of unknown relevance, and might pertain to only irrelevant situations which do not occur in practice.

Particularly, by applying resampling and feedback to real workloads we achieve the following:

- Retain all important (including possibly unknown) details of the workload as they exist in logs recorded from production systems, with as little modifications as possible. At the same time, avoid the "signature" of the system on which the log was recorded.

- Enable evaluations of throughput and user satisfaction in addition to (or instead of) being limited to the response time and slowdown metrics. This also leads to natural support for assessing the saturation limit of the system.
- Provide a new interpretation of the goal of "comparing alternatives under equivalent conditions": this is not to process exactly the same job stream, but rather to face the same workload generation process (users). This acknowledges the realization that there is no such thing as a generally correct workload—rather, the workload depends on system.

Table 1. Performance metrics under oblivious workloads and workloads with resampling and feedback.

Metric	Oblivious	Resampling+feedback
Load	Compared with offered load to find the threshold beyond which the system saturates	Measured to find the maximum utilization achievable—a performance Metric
Throughput	If not saturated, throughput is completely determined by the workload	Achieved throughput is the main metric of system performance
Response time	Response time is the main metric of system performance	Quoting response time is misleading without taking into account the throughput and user frustration
User satisfaction	Assumed to be measured by the response time or slowdown	Measured directly by the feedback model, e.g. in the form of frustrated user departures

The shift to using resampling with feedback has very significant implications. First, performance metrics change (Table 1). The new interpretation of good performance is that a better scheduler facilitates the execution of more jobs. Therefore the most important metric becomes the throughput. This can not be measured using conventional log-based simulations, where the workload is oblivious to the simulated system conditions, because in that context the throughput is dictated by the log and does not change in the simulation. Moreover, a consequence of achieving higher throughput may be that the average response time is also somewhat higher. In conventional simulations this would be taken as indicating that performance is worse, but now it is a side-effect of an improvement.

Related to this change in metrics is a change in simulation dynamics. In conventional oblivious simulations one must worry about system saturation. If the system is saturated, the simulation results are unreliable. A thorough methodology then has to check various load conditions to find the system capacity limit.

But with resampling and feedback we do not need to do this any more. The feedback counteracts our efforts to increase the load by adding users and jobs, and leads to stability. The simulation then naturally settles to the throughput that reflects the correct balance between user behavior and system performance.

Workload manipulations such as those embodied in resampling with feedback are important tools in the performance analyst's toolbox, that have not received due attention in terms of methodological research. As a result, inappropriate manipulations are sometimes used, which in turn has led to some controversy regarding whether *any* manipulations of real workloads are legitimate. By increasing our understanding of resampling-based manipulations we hope to bolster the use of this important tool, allowing new types of manipulations to be applied to workload logs, and enabling researchers to achieve better control over their properties, as needed for different evaluation scenarios.

Naturally, there are many opportunities for additional research regarding resampling and feedback. One element that is still largely missing is the user population model, and especially the issue of leaving the system when performance is inadequate. Another is the distribution of user types and behaviors. Resolving these issues requires not only deep analysis of workload logs, but also a collaboration with researchers in psychology and cognition [40]. After all, computer systems are used by humans.

Acknowledgments. The work described here was by and large performed by several outstanding students, especially Edi Shmueli, Netanel Zakay, and Dan Tsafrir. Our work was supported by the Israel Science Foundation (grants no. 219/99 and 167/03) and the Ministry of Science and Technology, Israel.

References

1. Chapin, S.J., et al.: Benchmarks and standards for the evaluation of parallel job schedulers. In: Feitelson, D.G., Rudolph, L. (eds.) JSSPP 1999. LNCS, vol. 1659, pp. 67–90. Springer, Heidelberg (1999). https://doi.org/10.1007/3-540-47954-6_4
2. Cirne, W., Berman, F.: A comprehensive model of the supercomputer workload. In: 4th Workshop on Workload Characterization, pp. 140–148 (2001). https://doi.org/10.1109/WWC.2001.990753
3. Denning, P.J.: Performance analysis: experimental computer science at its best. Comm. ACM **24**(11), 725–727 (1981). https://doi.org/10.1145/358790.358791
4. Downey, A.B.: A parallel workload model and its implications for processor allocation. Cluster Comput. **1**(1), 133–145 (1998). https://doi.org/10.1023/A:1019077214124
5. Downey, A.B., Feitelson, D.G.: The elusive goal of workload characterization. Perform. Eval. Rev. **26**(4), 14–29 (1999). https://doi.org/10.1145/309746.309750
6. Efron, B.: Bootstrap methods: another look at the jackknife. Ann. Statist. **7**(1), 1–26 (1979). https://doi.org/10.1214/aos/1176344552
7. Efron, B., Gong, G.: A leisurely look at the bootstrap, the jackknife, and cross-validation. Am. Stat. **37**(1), 36–48 (1983). https://doi.org/10.2307/2685844
8. Feitelson, D.G.: Memory usage in the LANL CM-5 workload. In: Feitelson, D.G., Rudolph, L. (eds.) JSSPP 1997. LNCS, vol. 1291, pp. 78–94. Springer, Heidelberg (1997). https://doi.org/10.1007/3-540-63574-2_17

9. Feitelson, D.G.: Metrics for parallel job scheduling and their convergence. In: Feitelson, D.G., Rudolph, L. (eds.) JSSPP 2001. LNCS, vol. 2221, pp. 188–205. Springer, Heidelberg (2001). https://doi.org/10.1007/3-540-45540-X_11

10. Feitelson, D.G.: The forgotten factor: facts on performance evaluation and its dependence on workloads. In: Monien, B., Feldmann, R. (eds.) Euro-Par 2002. LNCS, vol. 2400, pp. 49–60. Springer, Heidelberg (2002). https://doi.org/10.1007/3-540-45706-2_4

11. Feitelson, D.G.: Workload modeling for performance evaluation. In: Calzarossa, M.C., Tucci, S. (eds.) Performance 2002. LNCS, vol. 2459, pp. 114–141. Springer, Heidelberg (2002). https://doi.org/10.1007/3-540-45798-4_6

12. Feitelson, D.G.: Metric and workload effects on computer systems evaluation. Computer **36**(9), 18–25 (2003). https://doi.org/10.1109/MC.2003.1231190

13. Feitelson, D.G.: Experimental analysis of the root causes of performance evaluation results: a backfilling case study. IEEE Trans. Parallel Distrib. Syst. **16**(2), 175–182 (2005). https://doi.org/10.1109/TPDS.2005.18

14. Feitelson, D.G.: Experimental computer science: the need for a cultural change (2005). http://www.cs.huji.ac.il/~feit/papers/exp05.pdf

15. Feitelson, D.G.: Locality of sampling and diversity in parallel system workloads. In: 21st International Conference Supercomputing, pp. 53–63 (2007). https://doi.org/10.1145/1274971.1274982

16. Feitelson, D.G.: Looking at data. In: 22nd IEEE International Symposium on Parallel and Distributed Processing (2008). https://doi.org/10.1109/IPDPS.2008.4536092

17. Feitelson, D.G.: Workload Modeling for Computer Systems Performance Evaluation. Cambridge University Press, Cambridge (2015)

18. Feitelson, D.G.: Resampling with feedback — a new paradigm of using workload data for performance evaluation. In: Dutot, P.-F., Trystram, D. (eds.) Euro-Par 2016. LNCS, vol. 9833, pp. 3–21. Springer, Cham (2016). https://doi.org/10.1007/978-3-319-43659-3_1

19. Feitelson, D.G., Mu'alem, A.W.: On the definition of "on-line" in job scheduling problems. SIGACT News **36**(1), 122–131 (2005). https://doi.org/10.1145/1052796.1052797

20. Feitelson, D.G., Mu'alem Weil, A.: Utilization and predictability in scheduling the IBM SP2 with backfilling. In: 12th International Parallel Processing Symposium, pp. 542–546 (1998). https://doi.org/10.1109/IPPS.1998.669970

21. Feitelson, D.G., Naaman, M.: Self-tuning systems. IEEE Softw. **16**(2), 52–60 (1999). https://doi.org/10.1109/52.754053

22. Feitelson, D.G., Nitzberg, B.: Job characteristics of a production parallel scientific workload on the NASA Ames iPSC/860. In: Feitelson, D.G., Rudolph, L. (eds.) JSSPP 1995. LNCS, vol. 949, pp. 337–360. Springer, Heidelberg (1995). https://doi.org/10.1007/3-540-60153-8_38

23. Feitelson, D.G., Rudolph, L.: Distributed hierarchical control for parallel processing. Computer **23**(5), 65–77 (1990). https://doi.org/10.1109/2.53356

24. Feitelson, D.G., Rudolph, L.: Evaluation of design choices for gang scheduling using distributed hierarchical control. J. Parallel Distrib. Comput. **35**(1), 18–34 (1996). https://doi.org/10.1006/jpdc.1996.0064

25. Feitelson, D.G., Rudolph, L.: Metrics and benchmarking for parallel job scheduling. In: Feitelson, D.G., Rudolph, L. (eds.) JSSPP 1998. LNCS, vol. 1459, pp. 1–24. Springer, Heidelberg (1998). https://doi.org/10.1007/BFb0053978

26. Feitelson, D.G., Shmueli, E.: A case for conservative workload modeling: parallel job scheduling with daily cycles of activity. In: 17th Modelling, Analysis & Simulation of Computer and Telecommunication Systems (2009). https://doi.org/10.1109/MASCOT.2009.5366139

27. Feitelson, D.G., Tsafrir, D.: Workload sanitation for performance evaluation. In: IEEE International Symposium on Performance Analysis of Systems and Software, pp. 221–230 (2006). https://doi.org/10.1109/ISPASS.2006.1620806

28. Feitelson, D.G., Tsafrir, D., Krakov, D.: Experience with using the parallel workloads archive. J. Parallel Distrib. Comput. **74**(10), 2967–2982 (2014). https://doi.org/10.1016/j.jpdc.2014.06.013

29. Floyd, S., Paxson, V.: Difficulties in simulating the Internet. IEEE/ACM Trans. Netw. **9**(4), 392–403 (2001). https://doi.org/10.1109/90.944338

30. Jann, J., Pattnaik, P., Franke, H., Wang, F., Skovira, J., Riordan, J.: Modeling of workload in MPPs. In: Feitelson, D.G., Rudolph, L. (eds.) JSSPP 1997. LNCS, vol. 1291, pp. 95–116. Springer, Heidelberg (1997). https://doi.org/10.1007/3-540-63574-2_18

31. Lifka, D.A.: The ANL/IBM SP scheduling system. In: Feitelson, D.G., Rudolph, L. (eds.) JSSPP 1995. LNCS, vol. 949, pp. 295–303. Springer, Heidelberg (1995). https://doi.org/10.1007/3-540-60153-8_35

32. Lublin, U., Feitelson, D.G.: The workload on parallel supercomputers: modeling the characteristics of rigid jobs. J. Parallel Distrib. Comput. **63**(11), 1105–1122 (2003). https://doi.org/10.1016/S0743-7315(03)00108-4

33. Mu'alem, A.W., Feitelson, D.G.: Utilization, predictability, workloads, and user runtime estimates in scheduling the IBM SP2 with backfilling. IEEE Trans. Parallel Distrib. Syst. **12**(6), 529–543 (2001). https://doi.org/10.1109/71.932708

34. Parallel Workloads Archive. http://www.cs.huji.ac.il/labs/parallel/workload/

35. Prasad, R.S., Dovrolis, C.: Measuring the congestion responsiveness of internet traffic. In: Uhlig, S., Papagiannaki, K., Bonaventure, O. (eds.) PAM 2007. LNCS, vol. 4427, pp. 176–185. Springer, Heidelberg (2007). https://doi.org/10.1007/978-3-540-71617-4_18

36. Schroeder, B., Harchol-Balter, M.: Web servers under overload: how scheduling can help. ACM Trans. Internet Technol. **6**(1), 20–52 (2006)

37. Shmueli, E., Feitelson, D.G.: Using site-level modeling to evaluate the performance of parallel system schedulers. In: 14th Modelling, Analysis & Simulation of Computer and Telecommunication Systems, pp. 167–176 (2006). https://doi.org/10.1109/MASCOTS.2006.50

38. Shmueli, E., Feitelson, D.G.: Uncovering the effect of system performance on user behavior from traces of parallel systems. In: 15th Modelling, Analysis & Simulation of Computer and Telecommunication Systems, pp. 274–280 (2007). https://doi.org/10.1109/MASCOTS.2007.67

39. Shmueli, E., Feitelson, D.G.: On simulation and design of parallel-systems schedulers: are we doing the right thing? IEEE Trans. Parallel Distrib. Syst. **20**(7), 983–996 (2009). https://doi.org/10.1109/TPDS.2008.152

40. Snir, M.: Computer and information science and engineering: one discipline, many specialties. Comm. ACM **54**(3), 38–43 (2011). https://doi.org/10.1145/1897852.1897867

41. Talby, D., Feitelson, D.G., Raveh, A.: Comparing logs and models of parallel workloads using the co-plot method. In: Feitelson, D.G., Rudolph, L. (eds.) JSSPP 1999. LNCS, vol. 1659, pp. 43–66. Springer, Heidelberg (1999). https://doi.org/10.1007/3-540-47954-6_3

42. Tsafrir, D., Etsion, Y., Feitelson, D.G.: Modeling user runtime estimates. In: Feitelson, D., Frachtenberg, E., Rudolph, L., Schwiegelshohn, U. (eds.) JSSPP 2005. LNCS, vol. 3834, pp. 1–35. Springer, Heidelberg (2005). https://doi.org/10.1007/11605300_1

43. Tsafrir, D., Etsion, Y., Feitelson, D.G.: Backfilling using system-generated predictions rather than user runtime estimates. IEEE Trans. Parallel Distrib. Syst. **18**(6), 789–803 (2007). https://doi.org/10.1109/TPDS.2007.70606

44. Tsafrir, D., Feitelson, D.G.: Instability in parallel job scheduling simulation: the role of workload flurries. In: 20th International Parallel & Distributed Processing Symposium (2006). https://doi.org/10.1109/IPDPS.2006.1639311

45. Tsafrir, D., Feitelson, D.G.: The dynamics of backfilling: solving the mystery of why increased inaccuracy may help. In: IEEE International Symposium on Workload Characterization, pp. 131–141 (2006). https://doi.org/10.1109/IISWC.2006.302737

46. Tsafrir, D., Ouaknine, K., Feitelson, D.G.: Reducing performance evaluation sensitivity and variability by input shaking. In: 15th Modelling, Analysis & Simulation of Computer and Telecommunication Systems, pp. 231–237 (2007). https://doi.org/10.1109/MASCOTS.2007.58

47. Willinger, W., Taqqu, M.S., Sherman, R., Wilson, D.V.: Self-similarity through high-variability: statistical analysis of Ethernet LAN traffic at the source level. In: ACM SIGCOMM Conference, pp. 100–113 (1995)

48. Zakay, N., Feitelson, D.G.: On identifying user session boundaries in parallel workload logs. In: Cirne, W., Desai, N., Frachtenberg, E., Schwiegelshohn, U. (eds.) JSSPP 2012. LNCS, vol. 7698, pp. 216–234. Springer, Heidelberg (2013). https://doi.org/10.1007/978-3-642-35867-8_12

49. Zakay, N., Feitelson, D.G.: Workload resampling for performance evaluation of parallel job schedulers. Concurr. Comput. Pract. Exp. **26**(12), 2079–2105 (2014). https://doi.org/10.1002/cpe.3240

50. Zakay, N., Feitelson, D.G.: Preserving user behavior characteristics in trace-based simulation of parallel job scheduling. In: 22nd Modelling, Analysis & Simulation of Computer and Telecommunication Systems, pp. 51–60 (2014). https://doi.org/10.1109/MASCOTS.2014.15

51. Zakay, N., Feitelson, D.G.: Semi-open trace based simulation for reliable evaluation of job throughput and user productivity. In: 7th IEEE International Conference on Cloud Computing Technology & Science, pp. 413–421 (2015). https://doi.org/10.1109/CloudCom.2015.35

52. Zotkin, D., Keleher, P.J.: Job-length estimation and performance in backfilling schedulers. In: 8th International Symposium on High Performance Distributed Computing, pp. 236–243 (1999). https://doi.org/10.1109/HPDC.1999.805303

Open Scheduling Problems and Proposals

Collection of Job Scheduling Prediction Methods

Mehmet Soysal[✉] and Achim Streit

Steinbuch Centre for Computing, Karlsruhe Institute of Technology,
Hermann-von-Helmholtz-Platz 1, Eggenstein-Leopoldshafen, Germany
{mehmet.soysal,achim.streit}@kit.edu

Abstract. For more than two decades, researchers have been developing methods to predict HPC job run times. The methods vary from simple rule-based solutions to modern methods using machine and deep learning libraries. These studies are often developed for scientific publications and the sustainability after publication is often neglected. It is also often difficult to compare a solution with previously published, because the focus can be slightly different and missing the availability of source code. With this work, we want to start a collection of different wall time prediction methods to better compare new solutions and to promote sustainability. Therefore, this paper is submitted as a Open Scheduling Problem. The collection of source codes and results are going to be published on GitHub: https://hpc-job-scheduling-repo.github.io.

Keywords: Job scheduling · Job prediction · Job walltime

1 Introduction

For the execution of applications on HPC systems, a so-called job is created and submitted to a queue [1]. A job describes the application, needed resources, and requested wall time. A HPC Job Scheduler manages the queue and orders the jobs for efficient use of the resources. To plan the future usage of resources, job schedulers typically use a wall time that corresponds to the maximum execution time for each job. This wall time, also known as estimated job run time or wall (clock) time, is crucial for accurate planning. Nevertheless, users tend to request more time to prevent jobs being canceled too early. Accurate estimates of job wall time are important for many purposes, such as making better predictions about when waiting jobs will start. In addition, this information is needed when data should be staged in advance on the compute nodes [2]. There is also a online prediction system available for the XSEDE [3] resources – KARNAK [4]. Karnak uses machine learning to provide a prediction for users either when their job will start, or how long a hypothetical job would wait before being started.

Without accurate job wall time estimation, it is almost impossible to make any preparation of the system for future job requirements. This challenge is more important if the HPC systems become larger. For future exascale systems,

© Springer Nature Switzerland AG 2021
D. Klusáček et al. (Eds.): JSSPP 2021, LNCS 12985, pp. 35–42, 2021.
https://doi.org/10.1007/978-3-030-88224-2_2

this can help to improve the overall efficiency significantly. For these reasons, there are always attempts to predict the wall time more accurately. There are many different approaches and solutions. With this work we would like to start a collection of these solutions. The source code and the results will be made available on a website as a repository. Thereby, we want to ensure sustainability and if needed, the results can be reproduced by other scientists. Moreover, a better comparison of the own solution with the existing ones is easier. This repository is initially for job wall time prediction, but can be extended for other problem cases.

The remainder of this paper is structured as follows: In Sect. 2 we give a brief introduction to the background of job wall time predictions. We show in Sect. 3 what is needed to make the solutions better comparable. In Sect. 4 we finish with a conclusion and outlook on future work.

2   Background

The background of this work covers two areas. On the one hand, the approaches to predict job wall times and on the other hand, historical job workload logs. As a source for historical job workloads, the Parallel Workload Archive (PWA) is well established [5,6]. However, it happens from time to time that logs are used for publications which are not publicly available. The reasons for this can be manifold, e.g., to show how privacy sensitive data like directories and job names can be used for better predictability [7]. Unfortunately, this complicates the ability to compare different approaches or reproduce the work. Therefore, only a comparable and reproducible solution should be accepted into the collection.

There are several approaches to improve wall time estimates, and we can only give a brief overview in this section. The different methods can be divided into 2 different areas. One is the traditional methods and the "new" ones with the use of machine or deep learning libraries. As representatives for traditional methods, the solutions of Gibbons [8,9] and Downey [10] or also the built-in functionality of the ALEA Scheduling simulator [11]. Gibbons and Downey used historical workloads to predict job wall times. The prediction was performed based on templates. Previously collected metadata was analyzed and grouped according to similarities. Alea determines the deviation between the user estimated wall time and the used wall time is determined and applied to new jobs. It is working on a per-user basis. A new run-time estimation for a new job is computed using information about previous jobs of that user.

In recent years, **new methods** like machine and deep learning methods were used to predict resource consumption in studies [8,12–15]. As an example, Smith [16] is using genetic and greedy search methods to estimate job run times and queue wait times. This solution is used by XSEDE to predict queue wait time [3]. Other popular methods are using linear regression for predictions [17, 18], Nearest Neighbors [19,20], Regression Trees [21], or Instance Learning [16, 22,23]. Matsunga [24] used a combination of multiple machine learning methods to predict the execution time of two bioinformatics applications: BLAST [25] and RAxML [26]. These methods rely on domain experts in the machine learning discipline to preprocess the input data and to select the correct model including the optimization of parameters. Therefore, in the recent time, automatizing the machine learning process also gained attraction for predicting walltimes [7].

The examples given here show that there are many approaches and solutions. There are repeatedly publications in this area, but there is often a lack of comparisons with the corresponding metrics.

3 Predictions

For a sustainable and reproducible collection of tools, several conditions must be met. A source for job workloads as test data is needed. Different metrics and conditions should be specified to better compare the different solutions. Of course, the different solutions with their results should be available in a repository.

3.1 Job Workloads and Metadata

The Parallel Workload Archive offers job workload logs in SWF format [27]. It contains detailed workload logs collected from large-scale parallel systems. Every job in these data sets are represented by a sequence of lines (one job per line) containing 18 columns (job metadata). Available job metadata is listed below and Table 1 show all 40 available logs.

1. Job Number – Unique job identifier, also called JobID.
2. Submit Time – seconds starting from workload log time.
3. Wait Time – difference between Submit Time and Start Time in seconds.
4. Run Time – the actual time in seconds the job was running
5. Number of Allocated Processors – integer value of allocated cores or CPU, depends on configuration
6. Average CPU Time Used – both user and system, in seconds.
7. Used Memory – average used memory per core in kilobytes.
8. Requested Number of Processors
9. Requested Time – Wall time requested for job
10. Requested Memory – requested memory per processor in kilobytes
11. Status – a number indicating the reason why job has finished. 1 = job was completed normal, 0 = failed, and 5 = canceled. If this field can not be provided it is −1.
12. User ID – a number identifying a user.
13. Group ID – a number identifying a group.
14. Executable (Application) Number – a number to identify the application. If not available then −1.
15. Queue Number – a number identifying configured queues. It is suggested to use 0 for interactive jobs.
16. Partition Number – a number identifying configured partitions.

Table 1. Selected workloads and available metadata. * (Req. Number of Processors equals Allocated Number of Processors.)

	Job Number	Submit Time	Wait Time	Run Time	# of Alloc. Processors	Average CPU Time Used	Used Memory	Req. # of Processors	Req. Time	Req. Memory	Status	User ID	Group ID	Exe. Number	Queue Number	Partition Number	Preceding Job Number	Think Time Preceding Job
ANL-Intrepid-2009-1	Y	Y	Y	Y	Y	n.A.	n.A.	*	Y	n.A.	n.A.	n.A.	n.A.	n.A.	Y	n.A.	n.A.	n.A.
CEA-Curie-2011-2	Y	Y	Y	Y	Y	n.A.	n.A.	*	Y	n.A.	Y	Y	Y	n.A.	n.A.	Y	n.A.	n.A.
CIEMAT-Euler-2008-1	Y	Y	Y	Y	Y	Y	Y	*	Y	n.A.	Y	Y	Y	Y	Y	Y	n.A.	n.A.
CTC-SP2-1995-2	Y	Y	Y	Y	Y	Y	n.A.	n.A.	Y	n.A.	Y	Y	Y	Y	Y	n.A.	n.A.	n.A.
CTC-SP2-1996-3	Y	Y	Y	Y	Y	Y	n.A.	n.A.	Y	n.A.	Y	Y	n.A.	Y	Y	n.A.	n.A.	n.A.
DAS2-fs0-2003-1	Y	Y	Y	Y	Y	Y	n.A.	*	Y	n.A.	Y	Y	Y	Y	Y	n.A.	n.A.	n.A.
DAS2-fs1-2003-1	Y	Y	Y	Y	Y	Y	n.A.	*	Y	n.A.	Y	Y	Y	Y	Y	n.A.	n.A.	n.A.
DAS2-fs2-2003-1	Y	Y	Y	Y	Y	Y	Y	*	Y	n.A.	Y	Y	Y	Y	Y	n.A.	n.A.	n.A.
DAS2-fs3-2003-1	Y	Y	Y	Y	Y	Y	Y	*	Y	n.A.	Y	Y	Y	Y	Y	n.A.	n.A.	n.A.
DAS2-fs4-2003-1	Y	Y	Y	Y	Y	Y	Y	*	Y	n.A.	Y	Y	Y	Y	Y	n.A.	n.A.	n.A.
HPC2N-2002-2	Y	Y	Y	Y	Y	Y	n.A.	*	n.A.	n.A.	Y	Y	Y	n.A.	n.A.	n.A.	n.A.	n.A.
Intel-NetbatchA-2012-1	Y	Y	Y	Y	Y	Y	Y	n.A.	n.A.	n.A.	Y	Y	Y	Y	n.A.	n.A.	Y	Y
Intel-NetbatchB-2012-1	Y	Y	Y	Y	Y	Y	Y	n.A.	n.A.	n.A.	Y	Y	Y	Y	n.A.	n.A.	Y	Y
Intel-NetbatchC-2012-1	Y	Y	Y	Y	Y	Y	Y	n.A.	n.A.	n.A.	Y	Y	Y	Y	n.A.	n.A.	Y	Y
Intel-NetbatchD-2012-1	Y	Y	Y	Y	Y	Y	Y	n.A.	n.A.	n.A.	Y	Y	Y	Y	n.A.	n.A.	Y	Y
KIT-FH2-2016-1	Y	Y	Y	Y	Y	n.A.	n.A.	*	Y	n.A.	Y	Y	Y	n.A.	n.A.	Y	n.A.	n.A.
KTH-SP2-1996-2	Y	Y	Y	Y	Y	n.A.	n.A.	*	Y	n.A.	Y	Y	Y	Y	Y	Y	n.A.	n.A.
LANL-CM5-1994-4	Y	Y	Y	Y	Y	Y	Y	*	Y	n.A.	Y	Y	n.A.	Y	n.A.	n.A.	n.A.	n.A.
LANL-O2K-1999-2	Y	Y	Y	Y	Y	Y	Y	*	n.A.	Y	Y	Y	Y	Y	Y	n.A.	n.A.	n.A.
LCG-2005-1	Y	Y	Y	Y	Y	n.A.	n.A.	*	n.A.	n.A.	Y	Y	Y	Y	n.A.	Y	n.A.	n.A.
LLNL-Atlas-2006-2	Y	Y	n.A.	Y	n.A.	n.A.	n.A.	n.A.	n.A.	n.A.	n.A.	Y	Y	Y	Y	Y	n.A.	n.A.
LLNL-T3D-1996-2	Y	Y	n.A.	Y	Y	n.A.	n.A.	n.A.	n.A.	n.A.	Y	Y	n.A.	Y	n.A.	Y	n.A.	n.A.
LLNL-Thunder-2007-1	Y	Y	n.A.	Y	Y	n.A.	n.A.	*	n.A.	n.A.	Y	Y	Y	Y	n.A.	n.A.	n.A.	n.A.
LLNL-uBGL-2006-2	Y	Y	n.A.	Y	n.A.	n.A.	n.A.	n.A.	n.A.	n.A.	Y	Y	n.A.	Y	n.A.	Y	n.A.	n.A.
LPC-EGEE-2004-1	Y	Y	n.A.	Y	Y	Y	n.A.	*	Y	n.A.	Y	Y	Y	n.A.	Y	n.A.	n.A.	n.A.
METACENTRUM-2009-2	Y	Y	Y	Y	Y	n.A.	Y	n.A.	n.A.	n.A.	Y	Y	n.A.	n.A.	Y	Y	n.A.	n.A.
METACENTRUM-2013-3	Y	Y	Y	Y	Y	Y	Y	*	Y	n.A.	Y	Y	Y	Y	Y	Y	n.A.	n.A.
NASA-iPSC-1993-3	Y	Y	n.A.	Y	Y	n.A.	n.A.	n.A.	n.A.	n.A.	n.A.	Y	n.A.	n.A.	n.A.	n.A.	n.A.	n.A.
OSC-Clust-2000-3	Y	Y	Y	Y	Y	n.A.	n.A.	*	n.A.	n.A.	n.A.	Y	Y	n.A.	n.A.	n.A.	n.A.	n.A.
PIK-IPLEX-2009-1	Y	Y	Y	Y	Y	Y	Y	*	Y	Y	Y	Y	Y	Y	Y	n.A.	n.A.	n.A.
RICC-2010-2	Y	Y	Y	Y	Y	n.A.	n.A.	*	Y	n.A.	Y	Y	Y	Y	Y	n.A.	n.A.	n.A.
Sandia-Ross-2001-1	Y	Y	Y	Y	Y	Y	Y	*	Y	n.A.	Y	Y	n.A.	n.A.	Y	n.A.	n.A.	n.A.
SDSC-BLUE-2000-4	Y	Y	Y	Y	Y	Y	n.A.	*	Y	n.A.	Y	Y	Y	Y	Y	Y	n.A.	n.A.
SDSC-DS-2004-2	Y	Y	Y	Y	Y	Y	n.A.	*	Y	n.A.	Y	Y	Y	n.A.	Y	n.A.	n.A.	n.A.
SDSC-Par-1995-3	Y	Y	Y	Y	Y	n.A.	n.A.	n.A.	n.A.	n.A.	Y	Y	n.A.	n.A.	Y	n.A.	n.A.	n.A.
SDSC-Par-1996-3	Y	Y	Y	Y	Y	Y	n.A.	n.A.	n.A.	n.A.	Y	Y	n.A.	n.A.	Y	Y	n.A.	n.A.
SDSC-SP2-1998-4	Y	Y	Y	Y	Y	n.A.	n.A.	*	Y	n.A.	Y	Y	Y	Y	Y	Y	n.A.	n.A.
SHARCNET-2005-2	Y	Y	Y	Y	Y	Y	Y	n.A.	n.A.	n.A.	Y	Y	n.A.	Y	n.A.	n.A.	n.A.	n.A.
SHARCNET-Whale-2006-2	Y	Y	Y	Y	Y	Y	Y	n.A.	n.A.	n.A.	Y	Y	Y	Y	Y	Y	n.A.	n.A.
UniLu-Gaia-2014-2	Y	Y	Y	Y	Y	Y	Y	*	Y	n.A.	Y	Y	Y	Y	Y	n.A.	n.A.	n.A.

17. Preceding Job Number – a previous Job Number (JobID) which is the job is waiting to finish. With this a dependency between jobs can be established.
18. Think Time from Preceding Job – a value indicating how long a job has to wait after a preceding job has finished before the job is started.

If more metadata is available then defined by the SWF format, these additional metadata could be published as a additional log. As an example for such a log, the historical log for the Gaia system offers a companion log with accumulated I/O for each job [28].

3.2 Metrics

To better compare the solutions, the same metrics should be used. The metrics proposed here should rather be seen as initial metrics and could change after discussion with the community. The Sci-kit library offers many different metrics to compare the quality of predictions. Thereby, the real used wall time (y) and the predicted wall time $(\hat{y})$ is passed to the corresponding function. Sci-kit offers several metrics and the metrics below are a selection of them, which might change in the future.

The mean absolute error (MAE) and the median absolute error (MedAE) measure the difference between predicted and used wall time [29, 30]. MAE is the mean over all pairs of predicted and used wall times,

$$\text{MAE}(y, \hat{y}) = \frac{1}{n_{\text{samples}}} \sum_{i=0}^{n_{\text{samples}}-1} |y_i - \hat{y}_i|, \tag{1}$$

where y_i is the real used walltime and $\hat{y}_i$ is the predicted value of the i-th sample, and MedAE is the median value of these pairs,

$$\text{MedAE}(y, \hat{y}) = \text{median}(|y_1 - \hat{y}_1|, \ldots, |y_n - \hat{y}_n|). \tag{2}$$

In contrast to MAE, MedAE is robust against outliers. These metrics are widely used and easy to understand. The result indicates the deviation in seconds and are therefore very well suited to compare solutions with each other. Another suitable metric could be the Mean absolute percentage error (MAPE) which expresses the accuracy as a ratio and therefore its very intuitive interpretation [31]

$$\text{MAPE}(y, \hat{y}) = \frac{100\%}{n} \sum_{i=1}^{n} \left| \frac{y_i - \hat{y}_i}{y_i} \right|. \tag{3}$$

Besides the accuracy of wall time predictions, there are other aspects that should be considered.

– Number of over- and under-estimates - An underestimation would be fatal in real scenarios, as the scheduler would cancel the job in these cases.

- Processing/Training time - In the case where methods are used to train a model, it should of course be recorded how much time is needed for the training.
- Training type - is a partial fit possible or does the model need to be trained from beginning.
- Cold start - what approach is used for the cold start.
- Prediction type - is the prediction done on a per-user basis.

Nevertheless, there are many points that impact the accuracy. However, a comparison becomes difficult if not the same dataset or metrics are used. Therefore, the data sets and metrics proposed here serve only as a starting point.

3.3 Repository

Only solutions that can be reproduced with published material should be included in the repository. This means also that solutions should be available under a free license. The solution can also be published on own pages, but it should be public so that the results can be reproduced. Preliminary repositories can be found on GitHub: https://hpc-job-scheduling-repo.github.io

4 Conclusion and Outlook

In this work, we propose a repository for HPC job wall time prediction approaches. This work shall serve as a starting point to collect scheduler predictions and metrics. With this, a comparison of the different solutions, approaches, and ideas should be possible. At the same time, sustainability is achieved by creating a repository for the approaches. The proposed metrics can change through feedback from the community. It is also conceivable to add further problem cases to the repository. The parallel workload archive and workload logs are a good source of HPC job workloads, but it shows that most workloads are very old and not all metadata are available. Here it might be useful to encourage the community to publish newer workloads to the archives.

Acknowledgement. We gratefully acknowledge funding by the Ministry of Science, Research and the Arts Baden-Württemberg and "Deutsche Forschungsgemeinschaft" (DFG).

References

1. Hovestadt, M., Kao, O., Keller, A., Streit, A.: Scheduling in HPC resource management systems: queuing vs. planning. In: Feitelson, D., Rudolph, L., Schwiegelshohn, U. (eds.) JSSPP 2003. LNCS, vol. 2862, pp. 1–20. Springer, Heidelberg (2003). https://doi.org/10.1007/10968987_1
2. Soysal, M., Berghoff, M., Klusáček, D., Streit, A.: On the quality of wall time estimates for resource allocation prediction. In: Proceedings of the 48th International Conference on Parallel Processing: Workshops, ICPP 2019, Kyoto, Japan, pp. 23:1–23:8. ACM, New York (2019)

3. Xsede. https://www.xsede.org/
4. Karnak start/wait time predictions. http://karnak.xsede.org/karnak/index.html
5. Feitelson, D.G., Tsafrir, D., Krakov, D.: Experience with using the parallel workloads archive. J. Parallel Distrib. Comput. **74**(10), 2967–2982 (2014)
6. Parallel workloads archive. http://www.cs.huji.ac.il/labs/parallel/workload/
7. Soysal, M., Berghoff, M., Streit, A.: Analysis of job metadata for enhanced wall time prediction. In: Klusáček, D., Cirne, W., Desai, N. (eds.) JSSPP 2018. LNCS, vol. 11332, pp. 1–14. Springer, Cham (2019). https://doi.org/10.1007/978-3-030-10632-4_1
8. Gibbons, R.: A historical profiler for use by parallel schedulers. Master's thesis, University of Toronto (1997)
9. Gibbons, R.: A historical application profiler for use by parallel schedulers. In: Feitelson, D.G., Rudolph, L. (eds.) JSSPP 1997. LNCS, vol. 1291, pp. 58–77. Springer, Heidelberg (1997). https://doi.org/10.1007/3-540-63574-2_16
10. Downey, A.B.: Predicting queue times on space-sharing parallel computers. In: Proceedings of the 11th International Parallel Processing Symposium 1997, pp. 209–218. IEEE (1997)
11. Klusáček, D., Tóth, Š., Podolníková, G.: Complex job scheduling simulations with Alea 4. In: Ninth EAI International Conference on Simulation Tools and Techniques (SimuTools 2016), pp. 124–129. ACM (2016)
12. Kapadia, N.H., Fortes, J.A.B.: On the design of a demand-based network-computing system: the Purdue university network-computing hubs. In: Proceedings of the Seventh International Symposium on High Performance Distributed Computing 1998, pp. 71–80. IEEE (1998)
13. Mu'alem, A.W., Feitelson, D.G.: Utilization, predictability, workloads, and user runtime estimates in scheduling the IBM SP2 with backfilling. IEEE Trans. Parallel Distrib. Syst. **12**(6), 529–543 (2001)
14. Nadeem, F., Fahringer, T.: Using templates to predict execution time of scientific workflow applications in the grid. In: Proceedings of the 2009 9th IEEE/ACM International Symposium on Cluster Computing and the Grid, pp. 316–323. IEEE Computer Society (2009)
15. Tsafrir, D., Etsion, Y., Feitelson, D.G.: Backfilling using system-generated predictions rather than user runtime estimates. IEEE Trans. Parallel Distrib. Syst. **18**(6) (2007)
16. Smith, W.: Prediction services for distributed computing. In: IEEE International Parallel and Distributed Processing Symposium, IPDPS 2007, pp. 1–10. IEEE (2007)
17. Lee, B.-D., et al.: Run-time prediction of parallel applications on shared environments. In: 2003 Proceedings IEEE International Conference on Cluster Computing, pp. 487–491. IEEE (2003)
18. Seneviratne, S., Levy, D.C.: Task profiling model for load profile prediction. Future Gener. Comput. Syst. **27**(3), 245–255 (2011)
19. Kapadia, N.H., Fortes, J.A.B., Brodley, C.E.: Predictive application-performance modeling in a computational grid environment. In: Proceedings of the Eighth International Symposium on High Performance Distributed Computing (Cat. No. 99TH8469), pp. 47–54. IEEE (1999)
20. Iverson, M.A., Ozguner, F., Potter, L.C.: Statistical prediction of task execution times through analytic benchmarking for scheduling in a heterogeneous environment. In: Proceedings of the Eighth Heterogeneous Computing Workshop (HCW 1999), pp. 99–111. IEEE (1999)

21. Miu, T., Missier, P.: Predicting the execution time of workflow activities based on their input features. In: 2012 SC Companion: High Performance Computing, Networking Storage and Analysis, pp. 64–72. IEEE (2012)
22. Li, H., Groep, D., Wolters, L.: An evaluation of learning and heuristic techniques for application run time predictions. In: Proceedings of 11th Annual Conference of the Advance School for Computing and Imaging (ASCI), Netherlands. Citeseer (2005)
23. Silva, R.F.D., Juve, G., Rynge, M., Deelman, E., Livny, M.: Online task resource consumption prediction for scientific workflows. Parallel Process. Lett. **25**(03), 1541003 (2015)
24. Matsunaga, A., Fortes, J.A.B.: On the use of machine learning to predict the time and resources consumed by applications. In: Proceedings of the 2010 10th IEEE/ACM International Conference on Cluster, Cloud and Grid Computing, pp. 495–504. IEEE Computer Society (2010)
25. Altschul, S.F., Gish, W., Miller, W., Myers, E.W., Lipman, D.J.: Basic local alignment search tool. J. Mol. Biol. **215**(3), 403–410 (1990)
26. Stamatakis, A.: RAxML version 8: a tool for phylogenetic analysis and post-analysis of large phylogenies. Bioinformatics **30**(9), 1312–1313 (2014)
27. The Standard Workload Format
28. The University of Luxemburg Gaia Cluster Log. https://www.cs.huji.ac.il/labs/parallel/workload/l_unilu_gaia/index.html
29. Scikit - Mean absolute error. http://scikit-learn.org/stable/modules/generated/sklearn.metrics.mean_absolute_error.html#sklearn.metrics.mean_absolute_error
30. Scikit - Median absolute error. http://scikit-learn.org/stable/modules/generated/sklearn.metrics.median_absolute_error.html#sklearn.metrics.median_absolute_error
31. de Myttenaere, A., Golden, B., Le Grand, B., Rossi, F.: Mean absolute percentage error for regression models. Neurocomputing **192**, 38–48 (2016)

Modular Workload Format: Extending SWF for Modular Systems

Julita Corbalan[1,2](✉)[iD] and Marco D'Amico[2][iD]

[1] Universitat Politecnica de Catalunya, Barcelona, Spain
`julita.corbalan@bsc.es`
[2] Barcelona Supercomputing Center (BSC), Barcelona, Spain

Abstract. This paper presents the Modular Workload Format (MWF), a proposal for extending the widely accepted Standard Workload Format (SWF) for job scheduling evaluation. David Talby and Dror Feitelson proposed the SWF in 1999, allowing to describe data center workload in a synthesized way. Its simplicity, representing each job by a single line in a text file and including details to make job scheduling evaluation quite accurate, was part of its success. Using these years' experience but considering new system and workload characteristics, we propose an extension to support multiple steps in a single job, heterogeneous jobs, and relevant inputs not covered by the SWF as energy/power references. The goal of this contribution is to adapt the SWF to current trends in architectures and workloads. Moreover, we propose a simple approach for converting any already existing SWF trace file into an MWF trace file to be able to reuse already existing traces.

Keywords: Workload traces · Job scheduling evaluation

1 Introduction and Motivation

Standard Workload Format (SWF) [9] is a widely accepted format in job scheduling research as a standard way to evaluate job scheduling policies. A repository of SWF traces provided by many HPC centers can be found at [8], and many research papers are using this format. There are also several proposals of workload models that generate job scheduling logs in SWF.

In the context of the DEEP-EST European project [1], we found some limitations when designing the job scheduling simulation methodology. Some workload characteristics, such as modular jobs, and some job features, such as power/energy data, were not considered, given they were not so relevant at the moment the SFW was proposed. A Modular System Architecture (MSA) [1] integrates compute modules (or sub-clusters) with different performance characteristics into a single heterogeneous system. Each module is a parallel, clustered

This work is partially supported from the European Union's Horizon 2020 under grant agreement No. 754304 (DEEP-EST Project) and the Spanish grant PID2019-107255GB-C21.

© Springer Nature Switzerland AG 2021
D. Klusáček et al. (Eds.): JSSPP 2021, LNCS 12985, pp. 43–55, 2021.
https://doi.org/10.1007/978-3-030-88224-2_3

system of potentially large size. A federated network connects the module-specific interconnects. A module differs from a partition because it is a hardware organization, whereas a partition is a software concept. Of course, nothing prevents describing a module as a partition, but we want to consider the scenario where even in MSA there is a single submission point, there could potentially be many sub-schedulers dealing with the same partition names referring to different configurations. This option already exists in some schedulers such as SLURM with the --clusters option, and we propose to have both options, partition, and module (or cluster), for flexibility.

A modular job in this context is a job with multiple sub-components, each running in different modules simultaneously. In this work, we will refer as *jobs* to a request sent to the scheduler that can be a traditional HPC job with a simple mapping, i.e., one-request-one-application, or something more complex such as one allocation including several sub-components, with or without internal dependencies, executed in the same or different modules. Similar use cases can be found in other systems, such as systems running Slurm that supports heterogeneous jobs, or jobs with multiple internal executions, steps executed with *srun*, or even MPI jobs executing different binaries as a single application part of the same allocation. The concept of dependency is already present in the SWF, but we propose to go one step forward and incorporate types of dependencies and dynamic dependencies. Finally, we propose incorporating in the trace files a list of runtime events associated with each component (not mandatory) to introduce actions to be passed to simulators to take into account when simulating or analyzing workload traces.

We decided to analyze the SWF in detail and extend it with a proposal as much compatible with SWF as possible for traces reusability and with the same philosophy, a text file with a fixed number of columns, with each row describing a *job component*, the minimum unit of execution in our proposal.

In our scenario, one job can be internally composed of several components, each consuming a piece of the allocation or the whole but using resources sequentially or in a non-exclusive way. Moreover, each component characteristic could be modeled with a high precision starting from collected related metrics such as the Cycles per Instruction (CPI) and the bandwidth. This kind of information is very valuable for complex scenarios where runtime decisions are also simulated and not only the initial resource allocation. However, given this information is not provided by users at submission time and most of the schedulers do not automatically collect them, we avoided including all these metrics in the proposal to keep the number of columns to a reasonable value. However, it is advisable to include additional data related to components in separate files that allow more precise modeling. The additional data could be linked to MWF data using the component ID as an identifier.

MWF is compatible with SWF. SWF traces can be directly re-used by simply considering that each job in the SWF is one MWF job with a single component. All the extra fields in the MWF can be set to null values if the information is not available.

In the rest of this document, Sect. 2 analyses the SWF in deep and proposes the granularity of the fields, either job or component. Based on this analysis, Sect. 4 presents our proposal for MWF. To make our proposal more comprehensive, Sect. 6 presents, in a simplified way, few examples showing how the MWF can be used to represent different scenarios and some experiments already done using this format. Finally, Sect. 7 presents some conclusions and lessons learned.

2   Standard Workload Format

The SWF was defined in order to ease the use of workload logs and models. SWF allows simple workload analysis and or system's job scheduling simulation since they only need to parse a common standard format applied to multiple workloads. The SWF files are portable and easy to parse:

- Each workload is stored in a single ASCII file.
- Each job is represented by a single line in the file.
- Lines contain a predefined number of fields, which are mostly integers, separated by whitespace(s).
- Fields that are irrelevant for a specific log or model appear with a value of -1.
- Comments are allowed, and identified by lines that start with a ';'. In particular, files are expected to start with a set of header comments that define the environment or model.
- The same format is used for logs and model outputs.
- The format is completely defined, with no scope for user extensibility.

This last point is what we would like to reconsider after many years using the same format.

Current Fields in SWF. We have analysed fields to identify which ones are job-specific (J) or potentially component-specific (C). Those fields referring components will be replicated the MWF. Fields marked as (W) are used to specify job dependencies, i.e., workflows.[1]

1. (J) Job Number – a counter field, starting from one.
2. (J) Submit Time – in seconds. The earliest submit time in the log is zero, and usually, it is the submit time of the first job. The lines in the log are sorted by ascending submit times. It makes sense for jobs to also be numbered in this order.
3. (J/C) Wait Time – in seconds. The difference between the job's submit time and the time at which it actually started its execution. It is only relevant to real logs, not to models.

---

[1] The fields description comes from the SWF web page.

4. (J/C) Run Time – in seconds. The total execution time of the job, i.e., end time minus start time. We decided to use "wait time" and "run time" instead of the equivalent "start time" and "end time" because they are directly attributable to the scheduler and application, and are more suitable for models where only the run time is relevant. Note that when values are rounded to an integral number of seconds (as often happens in logs) a run time of 0 is possible and means the job ran for less than 0.5 s. On the other hand it is permissible to use floating point values for time fields.

5. (C) Number of Allocated Processors – an integer. In most cases this is also the number of processors the job uses; if the job does not use all of them, we typically don't know about it.

6. (C) Average CPU Time Used – both user and system, in seconds. This is the average over all processors of the CPU time used, and may therefore be smaller than the wall clock runtime. If a log contains the total CPU time used by all the processors, it is divided by the number of allocated processors to derive the average.

7. (C) Used Memory – in kilobytes. This is again the average per processor.

8. (C) Requested Number of Processors.

9. (C) Requested Time. This can be either runtime (measured in wallclock seconds), or average CPU time per processor (also in seconds) – the exact meaning is determined by a header comment. In many logs this field is used for the user runtime estimate (or upper bound) used in backfilling. If a log contains a request for total CPU time, it is divided by the number of requested processors.

10. (C) Requested Memory (again kilobytes per processor).

11. (J) Status 1 if the job was completed, 0 if it failed, and 5 if cancelled. If information about checkpointing or swapping is included, other values are also possible.

12. (J) User ID – a natural number, between one and the number of different users.

13. (J) Group ID – a natural number, between one and the number of different groups. Some systems control resource usage by groups rather than by individual users.

14. (J/C) Executable (Application) Number – a natural number, between one and the number of different applications appearing in the workload. in some logs, this might represent a script file used to run jobs rather than the executable directly; this should be noted in a header comment.

15. (J/C) Queue Number – a natural number, between one and the number of different queues in the system. The nature of the system's queues should be explained in a header comment. This field is where batch and interactive jobs should be differentiated: we suggest the convention of denoting interactive jobs by 0.

16. (J/C) Partition Number – a natural number, between one and the number of different partitions in the systems. The nature of the system's partitions should be explained in a header comment. For example, it is possible to use partition numbers to identify which machine in a cluster was used.

17. (W) Preceding Job Number – this is the number of a previous job in the workload, such that the current job can only start after the termination of this preceding job.
18. (W) Think Time from Preceding Job – this is the number of seconds that should elapse between the termination of the preceding job and the submission of this one.

3 Heterogeneous Systems Requirements

Modular architectures term comes from the DEEP-EST projects and stands for multiple clusters, or modules, with different specialized architectures working together as a single homogeneous system. The system software hides the complexity existing in this proposal. Even though our motivation comes from this complex scenario, heterogeneous systems already exist in many data centers as a simplified version of this use case. As an example, it is a common strategy in the current data center to have some computational nodes with specific characteristics such as extra memory of GPUs.

The SWF was designed in a context where jobs were considered as a whole and systems with multiple clusters were not usual. In recent years, having multiple clusters in a single data center became a typical scenario, but in many cases, the system workload was a set of disjoint workloads given the architecture differences. The only flexibility in terms of submission was the possibility to specify multiple partitions but always referring to the same HW characteristics.

With potentially highly specialized modules, or sub-clusters, this new hardware context opens to the possibility of considering new job profiles and use cases to be evaluated:

- Jobs asking for resources in a specific module.
- Jobs asking for resources in more than one module at the same time.
- Jobs asking for resources in more than one module but not at the same time, i.e., asking for additional resources dynamically.
- Jobs asking for not only the classical computing resources, e.g. GPUs, memory devices.
- Jobs with dependencies among them, i.e., workflows.

4 Modular Workload Format (MWF) Proposal

We define a modular job as a scheduling unit belonging to a single user containing a single or multiple binaries. At submission time, the job will include an N ($N \geq 1$) list of requirements for allocation and components submission. All these allocations will be validated before any of these components start. These allocations could refer to different modules. Some components can be specified with different submission times representing the case where job allocation is dynamically increased.

The MWF includes the resource requirements and the resources allocated as it was proposed in SWF. Requirements represent the job scheduler's input, while resource allocation fields will be used for its output.

Each line will describe one component from one modular job. Dependencies can be specified between components of different modular jobs or the same job. Each workload trace file can include a system description, e.g., the available modules, the resources at each module, in the same way SFW did in the headers. The Component_Job_Id is a unique number and can be seen as the job_id in the SWF. The N potential components being part of the same job will share the same Modular_Job_Id.

Next subsections include the list of fields and a brief description of the semantic and valid values following a similar approach as in the SWF.

4.1   Modular Workload Format Fields

Modular Fields

1. **Modular_Job_Id** – An ID common to all the components of the modular job.
2. **Total_Components** – Number of components in the modular job (minimum one)
3. **Modular_Job_Name** – Text . Max of 16 chars. Job names is an user provided input and there can be more than one job name for the same executable.
4. **Submit_Modular_Job_Time** – in seconds. Submission time for the first set of components
5. **Wait_Modular_Job_Time** – in seconds. The difference between the job's submit time and the time at which it actually began to run (some of its components). It is not needed for evaluation, only for comparison between results.
6. **Modular_Requested_Time** – in seconds. Limit for the modular job. -1 if this value is not provided. In that case, the partition limit will be used
7. **Num_Components_At_Submit_Time** – Integer. This field is the number of components submitted together at modular submit time
8. **User_ID** – Integer
9. **Group_ID** – Integer

Job Component Fields

10. **Component_Job_Id: Modular_Job_Id+ Offset** – This JOB ID is unique. It goes from Modular_Job_Id to Modular_Job_Id+(Total_Components-1).
11. **Component_Job_Name** – text . Max of 16 chars. Components names is an user provided input and there can be more than one job name for the same executable.

12. **Component_Wait_Time** – in seconds. The difference between the job's submit time and the time at which it actually began to run. It is not needed for evaluation, only for comparison between results
13. **Component_Run_Time** – in seconds. Integral number of seconds.
14. **Status** – 0 means COMPLETED with success. Values different from 0 will represent errors.

Job Component Resource Requirements Description. The job scheduler receives job component requirements, applies the job scheduler and resource selection policy, and reports a set of resources allocated. Resource allocation is reported for comparison, but it is not part of the input. One component will run in a single module. If one job needs more than one module, one component per module will be specified.

15. **Executable_Number** – a natural number, between one and the number of different applications appearing in the workload. in some logs, this might represent a script file used to run jobs rather than the executable directly; this should be noted in a header comment
16. **Requested_Partition_Name** – Text with the partition name; NA, if no specific partition is requested
17. **Requested_Nodes** – an integer. Number of nodes requested
18. **Requested_Processes_Per_Node** – an integer
19. **Requested_Cores_Per_Process** – an integer
20. **Requested_Cores_Per_Node** – an integer
21. **Requested_Memory_Per_Node** – In KB
22. **Requested_GPUS_Per_Node** – an integer
23. **Requested_Freq** – Requested frequency in Gigahertz, Format is min[-max]
24. **Reference Power** – Input average power in Watts. Input by user or a power model.
25. **Extra_requirements** – A set of keywords, potentially with & or | special characters. These constraints must be specified in the different modules to simplify resource selection. For instance, based on sbatch manual [12] $intel\&gpu, intel|amd$. This field can be used as a wildcard field to cover those new cases that could appear in the future.
26. **Licenses** – a comma separated list of requested licenses. name[:how_many, name2:]. Default 1

Component Resource Allocation Description. One component will run in a single Module. If one job needs more than one module, one component per module will be specified.

27. **Component_Module_Id** – 0 - Number of Modules (One component will run in a single module). Module ID where this component is executed
28. **Partition_Name** – Text with the partition name selected
29. **Nodes** – Number of allocated nodes

30. **Processes_Per_Node** – an integer
31. **Cores_Per_Process** – an integer
32. **Cores_Per_Node** – an integer
33. **Memory_Per_Node** – In KB (0 if not requested)
34. **GPUS_Per_Node** – an integer
35. **Average_CPU_Time** – an integer
36. **Freq** – frequency in Gigahertz
37. **Average Power** – measured average power in Watts
38. **Other_resources**

Dependencies

39. **After_Component_Job_Id** – This component must start after job ID. -1 if there is no dependency
40. **Dependency_Type** – -1=NO DEP/0=DYNAMIC/1=AFTER/ 2=AFTERANY/3=AFTEROK/4=AFTERNOTOK//5=SINGLE.
    This list of types of dependencies is inspired by Slurm dependencies. DYNAMIC is an additional type defined here.
    – -1 means there is no dependency.
    – DYNAMIC means the component must be started N seconds after AFTER_COMPONENT_JOB_ID. The number of seconds is defined in the next field, and in that case it is relative to the dependent job start time.
    – AFTEROK/AFTERNOTOK – This job can begin execution after the specified component_id have successfully/not successfully executed.
    – SINGLE is which job can begin execution after any previously launched component_id by the same user and sharing the same component_id name have terminated.
41. **Component_Think_Time** – in seconds. When DYNAMIC is selected, it corresponds to the requested delay from the start of the first component to the start of this component. Otherwise, it is related to the job finalization overhead, like the SWF *Think Time from Preceding Job* field.

Component-Level Events

42. **Sched_event_list** – in seconds. It models events called by the job that impact the job scheduling. It is a list of comma-separated *key:value* elements, with the key representing the event type, an ID or keyword, and value the number of seconds passed from the start of the job until the event. Keys depends on the specific simulator and it's a way to specify runtime actions. -1 means no events. E.g.: "ChangeDepToAfter:650".

4.2   Headers

The SWF includes a header section with comments describing workload and system characteristics. These headers describe the architecture where the trace was collected and are interpreted as comments when reading the trace file. These headers are **not mandatory** and are included to characterize the system at which the trace file was recorded.

We include here only new proposals and not all the headers already proposed in the SWF. Since this section is optional, it is not needed to be as exhaustive as with SWF fields. Two new headers are proposed to support having N modules. For each module, a module number will be provided together with headers referring to cluster characteristics.

- **(new)NumberModules**: Number of modules in the system, for each Module
- **(new)ModuleNumber**: from 0 to max modules

Headers will include then a common section Version..EndTime, NumberModules, $[ModuleNumber, Computer...Partition]$ repeated N times.

5   From SWF to MWF

Adapting SWF trace files to the new proposal is as easy as associating a job in the SWF with a job with one component in the MWF. Given we have defined all the new fields as optional, except IDs, they can be easily defined with NULL values, while the other fields are mapped with the following rules:

- Job Number is mapped to Modular Job ID.
- Submit Time, Wait Time, Run Time, Requested time are mapped to their Modular respective.
- Number of allocated Processors is mapped to Nodes and Cores Per Node by dividing its value by the node's number of cores.
- Used Memory and Requested Memory are mapped to Requested_Memory_Per _Node and Memory_Per_Node by dividing the total amount by the number allocated of nodes.
- Status, User ID, Group ID, Average CPU Time Used, and Executable Number exist in both formats, Partition Number is mapped to Partition_Name.
- Preeceding Job Number is mapped to Dependency_Type of type 3, Think Time from Preceding Job to Component_Think_Time.
- Queue Number can be mapped on Extra_requirements, or integrated in the partition mechanism as many center nowadays do.

An parser example is available in the BSC Slurm Simulator Github repository [16].

6   MWF Experiences

In this section, we present a list of use cases that can be represented using the MWF. We have included a subset of the fields to make it readable. The use cases focus on jobs with one or multiple components and some example with dependencies.

The main fields are presented in Table 1, showing the following use cases:

Fig. 1. Job with multiple steps.

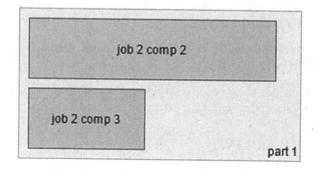

Fig. 2. Job with multiple parallel steps.

1. Jobs with a single step: a classical job submission is shown in job modular id 1.
2. Jobs with multiple steps: job 2, made up of two components, with id 2 and 3, represents a job with two sub-components. Component 3 starts after component 2 as shown in Fig. 1, because of the AfterCompJobID parameter set to 2. Using Slurm as an example, it represents two steps of a jobs. If component 3 does not set AfterCompJobID it means the components run in parallel, as represented in Fig. 2.
3. Jobs with multiple heterogeneous steps: similar to the example before, the steps request a different type of resources, for instance, different modules or partitions. In the case of job 12, also shown in Fig. 3, the first job asks for *part1* and the second and third job ask for *part2*.
4. Jobs with dependencies (workflows): job 4, made up of components 4 and 5, is a workflow in which component 5 only runs after component 4 starts. Job 6, made up of three components, models a dynamic dependency in which the third component starts 300 s after the start of the first component, as in Fig. 4. Finally, jobs 9, 10, and 11 in Fig. 5 represent another workflow, in which each job starts after the previous one terminates. Note that in this case jobs are not scheduled as a single entity, like the case of jobs with multiple steps, so, depending on the scheduling, there can be large delays between the end of a component end the start of the next.
5. Jobs with events to be processed by the scheduler: in the workflow in Fig. 5 made up of jobs 9, 10, and 11, job 10 uses Sched_event_time to run a change of its dependency, from AFTEROK to AFTER at time 600.
6. Job with extra resource requirements: jobs 11 and 12 request non CPU resources by specifying them in the Extra_Requirements field in the format

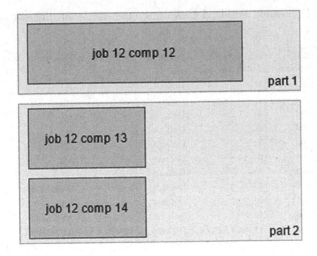

Fig. 3. Job with multiple heterogeneous steps.

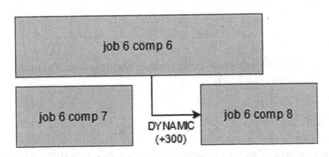

Fig. 4. Workflow with a dynamic dependency.

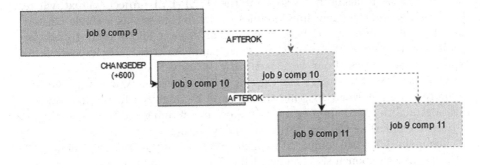

Fig. 5. Workflow using Sched_event_time to change dependency.

"type:value" or only "type" if the values is 1. Multiple requirements can be connected with logical operations or regular expressions. In the example, jobs are asking for one Field Programmable Gate Array (FPGA).

Table 1. MWF example workload presenting main fields for different categories of jobs.

Mod. JobID	Num Comp.	Mod. JobName	Comp. JobID	Exta. Requir.	Partition	AfterComp JobID	Dep Type	SchedEventList Time
1	1	job1	1	−	Default	−1	−1	−1
2	2	job2	2	−	Default	−1	−1	−1
2	2	job2	3	−	Default	2	−1	−1
4	2	job3	4	−	Default	−1	−1	−1
4	2	job3	5	−	Default	4	AFTER	−1
6	3	job4	6	−	Default	−1	−1	−1
6	3	job4	7	−	Default	−1	−1	−1
6	3	job4	8	−	Default	6	DYNAMIC	-1
9	1	job5	9	−	Default	−1	−1	−1
10	1	job6	10	−	Default	9	AFTEROK	changeDep:600
11	1	job7	11	FPGA	Default	10	AFTEROK	−1
12	2	job8	12	FPGA	part1	−1	−1	−1
12	2	job8	13	FPGA	part2	−1	−1	−1
12	2	job8	14	FPGA	part2	−1	−1	−1

For a better understanding of the example, we have used the text corresponding with the type of dependency rather than the number in column DepType and we have shortened the fields names.

7　Conclusions

This paper is a proposal for considering the extension of SWF to be adapted to new systems and workloads. We call this proposal the Modular Workload Format (MWF) because it has been developed in the DEEP-EST project context, where the scheduler manages multiple modules, i.e., sub-clusters, as a single cluster. This kind of architecture is becoming popular since it allows users to ask for specialized resources. However, given their characteristics, it is impossible to express the semantics of our workloads with the already existing format.

To make it possible to use the existing traces and models, our proposal is a compatible format where existing traces could be migrated to the new format with a straightforward approach. We propose maintaining the format as simple as possible, following the main criteria used when defining the SWF.

The main difference compared with the SWF is the possibility to define jobs with multiple components, each one with different requirements and potentially start times. We have also included additional fields to perform energy evaluations, and finally, some extra fields for demanding heterogeneous resources and dynamic workflow management.

This format has been used to evaluate job scheduling policies developed in the context of the DEEP-EST project. Workloads include job submission to multiple modules, new types of resource requirements specifics for some modules and components, and dynamic workflows. The current proposal is the result of four years of experience, and an intent to open a discussion to share and maintain tools and standards for the research community.

References

1. DEEP-EST project. http://www.deep-projects.eu/
2. DEEP-ER Deliverables. http://www.deep-projects.eu/project/deliverables.html
3. JUBE Online Documentation. https://apps.fz-juelich.de/jsc/jube/jube2/docu/index.html
4. MPI LinkTest. http://www.fz-juelich.de/ias/jsc/EN/Expertise/Support/Software/LinkTest/_node.html
5. SIONlib. http://www.fz-juelich.de/ias/jsc/EN/Expertise/Support/Software/SIONlib/_node.html
6. IOR. https://github.com/hpc/ior
7. HDF5 Group. https://support.hdfgroup.org/HDF5/
8. The Standard Workload Format. http://www.cs.huji.ac.il/labs/parallel/workload/swf.html
9. Chapin, S.J., et al.: Benchmarks and standards for the evaluation of parallel job schedulers. In: Feitelson, D.G., Rudolph, L. (eds.) JSSPP 1999. LNCS, vol. 1659, pp. 67–90. Springer, Heidelberg (1999). https://doi.org/10.1007/3-540-47954-6_4
10. Yoo, A.B., Jette, M.A., Grondona, M.: SLURM: simple linux utility for resource management. In: Feitelson, D., Rudolph, L., Schwiegelshohn, U. (eds.) JSSPP 2003. LNCS, vol. 2862, pp. 44–60. Springer, Heidelberg (2003). https://doi.org/10.1007/10968987_3
11. SchedMD: Slurm Workload Manager. https://slurm.schedmd.com/
12. sbatch: Submit a batch script to Slurm. https://slurm.schedmd.com/sbatch.html
13. Heterogeneous Resources and MPMD. https://slurm.schedmd.com/SLUG15/Heterogeneous_Resources_and_MPMD.pdf
14. SLURM: Heterogeneous job Support. https://slurm.schedmd.com/SLUG17/HeterogeneousJobs.pdf
15. DEEP-EST Deliverable 1.1 Application co-design input. https://www.deep-projects.eu/images/materials/D11.pdf
16. BSC Slurm Simulator code. https://github.com/BSC-RM/slurm_simulator_tools

Technical Papers

Measurement and Modeling of Performance of HPC Applications Towards Overcommitting Scheduling Systems

Shohei Minami[1,2]($\boxtimes$) (iD), Toshio Endo[2] (iD), and Akihiro Nomura[2] (iD)

[1] Fujitsu Limited, Kawasaki, Kanagawa, Japan
minami.shohei@jp.fujitsu.com
[2] Tokyo Institute of Technology, Meguro City, Tokyo, Japan
endo@is.titech.ac.jp, nomura@gsic.titech.ac.jp

Abstract. Recently, the use of interactive jobs in addition to traditional batch jobs is attracting attention in supercomputer systems. We expect overcommitting scheduling, in which multiple HPC jobs share computational resources, to accept them while keeping resource utilization higher and response time lower. In order to realize overcommitting scheduling, the following approaches are necessary: 1) to understand the impact on performance when various applications share resources, and 2) to predict the performance before overcommitting. With this knowledge, we will be able to optimize overcommitting scheduling that avoids performance degradation of jobs. In this paper, we describe the overall picture of overcommitting scheduling and took the two approaches shown above. We confirmed that overcommitting shows performance improvement of the overall system and also built a performance model that can be applied to job scheduling.

Keywords: Job scheduling · Overcommitting scheduling · Performance modeling

1 Introduction

Recently, the interactive use of supercomputers is attracting attention due to widespread of machine learning and deep learning, in addition to traditional interactive use including debugging and visualization. In such use cases, they need to allocate computing resources in real time, and they repeat execution and thinking; they sometimes execute computation, and see the results and consider what should be computed next. Such usages will be more popular in next generational supercomputer systems.

Well-known job schedulers allow interactive use by the `qrsh` command in Univa Grid Engine or by `salloc` in Slurm [13]. However, when interactive jobs

© Springer Nature Switzerland AG 2021
D. Klusáček et al. (Eds.): JSSPP 2021, LNCS 12985, pp. 59–79, 2021.
https://doi.org/10.1007/978-3-030-88224-2_4

and traditional batch jobs coexist in a system with a scheduler that is config-ured conservatively without any *overcommitting*, both users and system admin-istrators will see the following issues. For users, their interactive usage will not be started until some nodes become idle. For system administrators, the total resource utilization ratio, especially CPU utilization ratio, tends to be degraded since CPU utilization tends to be lower in interactive jobs, as illustrated in Fig. 1 (b).

From the above discussion, we consider that job schedulers in future super-computers should adapt overcommitting aggressively, where each computational resource (each compute node or each CPU core) is shared by two or more jobs. On the other hand, it is natural that overcommitting introduces slowdown of each job, which is inappropriate especially for batch jobs.

This paper demonstrates that the performance degradation ratio under over-committing depends on the characteristics of jobs, which include not only CPU utilization ratio, but also more microscopic ones like cache miss rates. Also this paper introduces a performance model to estimate performance degradation ratio by overcommitting, based on performance monitoring counters (PMCs). We expect these outcomes will be utilized towards future overcommitting job schedulers that realize high throughput and extremely lower response times for interactive jobs.

This paper is structured as follows: First, Sect. 2 overviews the system evalu-ation metrics and characteristics of interactive jobs. In Sect. 3, overcommitting is discussed in more detail. The expected overcommitting scheduling system is also mentioned here. Section 4 describes experiment settings and Sect. 5 describes the performance measurement results of application benchmarks under overcommit-ting to demonstrate the performance degradation ratio largely depends on job characteristics. In Sect. 6, we introduce the performance prediction model for applications under overcommitting and discuss the accuracy of the model. We mention related work in Sect. 7 and summarize the conclusions in Sect. 8.

2   Background

2.1   Evaluation Metrics for Scheduling

This section discusses two typical evaluation metrics for scheduling [5] required for discussion in this paper.

Utilization Ratio. From the viewpoint of administrators, supercomputers should indicate higher utilization ratio in order to utilize computing resources efficiently. In our context, it is insufficient to consider only periods when com-puting resources are occupied by any jobs, since interactive jobs may have lower CPU utilization ratio. Instead, we are more interested in total CPU utilization ratio of the entire system.

Slowdown. It is important for users to use the computing resources with smaller response times. Especially for interactive users, waiting time should be close to zero. Typical FIFO scheduling, however, tends to be more spiteful for short running or interactive jobs, since waiting time is relatively severer compared with length of running time [2,3]. To express the severeness, the slowdown, the ratio of time from submission to finish over time spent by actual execution, is often used [4].

2.2 Features of Interactive Jobs

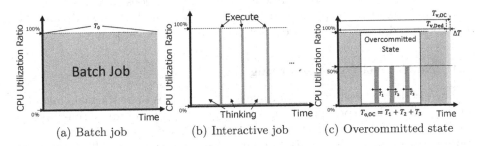

(a) Batch job   (b) Interactive job   (c) Overcommitted state

Fig. 1. The timeseries of CPU utilization. The horizontal axis is time, the vertical is CPU utilization ratio.

In traditional supercomputers, most jobs are batch jobs, whose CPU utilization are kept high as shown in Fig. 1 (a)[1]. On the other hand, interactive jobs use computing resources in real time, and CPU utilization fluctuates much more largely. Figure 1 (b) illustrates a simple model of the fluctuation.

In interactive usage, a user repeats execution and thinking: the user sometimes executes computation on computers, sees the results, and considers what should be computed next. While the user is thinking, the CPU utilization ratio is almost 0%. Note that for simplicity, the CPU utilization ratio due to key input is ignored here. When the execution starts, the CPU utilization ratio gets close to 100%. Thus the average CPU utilization ratio during interactive jobs depends on the ratio between thinking time and execution time. If the average ratio is very low, it is not desirable for system administrators.

Traditional scheduling methods like FIFO has two issues when interactive jobs are mixed with batch jobs. For system administrators, lower CPU utilization of interactive jobs decreases the entire CPU utilization ratio. For interactive users, longer waiting time prevents them from real time usage.

To mitigate the issues, some system administrators may decide to make an interactive queue and several nodes dedicated to interactive jobs. However, the

---

[1] Some batch jobs can have fluctuation of CPU utilization for file I/O or network. This paper omits discussion for such jobs for simplicity; however, overcommitting scheduling is expected to work efficiently for such jobs.

entire CPU utilization ratio of those nodes would still be low. Also it is hard to realize fairness between two types of jobs, since the demands for two types may change.

3   Overcommitting on Supercomputer Systems

From the discussion in the previous section, it is attractive to introduce over-committing scheduling, where multiple jobs share computing resources instead of letting each job occupy resources, in order to achieve both high utilization ratio and extremely short response time. In this paper, we define *overcommitting* as sharing a single computational resource with multiple jobs. It can be categorized by the type of computational resources to be shared. Here we discuss the categories and importance of processor core-level overcommitting.

3.1   Node-Level Overcommitting

A single node can be shared by multiple jobs. While jobs share the main memory of the node, each job occupies distinct processor cores. This is more conservative method than the next one and has been introduced in production supercomputers. For example, the TSUBAME3.0 supercomputer uses the Linux cgroups mechanism to split a single physical node into several virtual nodes [7].

The performance of each job is almost kept, since the processor cores dedicated to one of jobs. Also CPU utilization gets improved compared with when the entire node is occupied by a job. On the other hand, the CPU core utilization can be still low if there are jobs with low CPU utilization ratio, like interactive jobs. For such cases, core-level overcommitting would be preferable.

3.2   Processor Core-Level Overcommitting

Multiple jobs can share processor cores. It is expected to improve the total CPU utilization since the idle time of interactive jobs can be filled by other jobs as illustrated in Fig. 1 (c). In spite of this benefit, production supercomputers usually do not adopt this strategy mainly for the following issues.

- Each job may suffer from unpredictable performance degradation. A simple model of degradation is that throughput of a singe job is divided by the number of busy jobs sharing the same core. However, as shown in Sect. 5, the measured degradation largely depends on job characteristics. One of the reasons is that level 1 and 2 cache, attached to each core, are shared by multiple jobs. The cache may be polluted by other jobs and thus each job suffers from more cache misses than in dedicated cases.
- The performance degradation gets more critical for parallel jobs, many of which use synchronization among threads or processes. If one of threads (or processes) slows down by other jobs, the entire job speed may be degraded due to synchronization.

– Demands for the main memory capacity increase. If we do not permit over-committing of main memory capacity, the capacity for each job is further limited by the number of running jobs simultaneously.

Among the above issues, this paper mainly focuses on the first one and analyze performance degradation under core-level overcommitting in detail. For simplicity, this paper assumes that a demand for memory capacity per job is sufficiently small so that memory overcommitting is not needed.

In order to achieve core-level overcommitting, we require some mechanisms for process/thread preemption. The main choices are as follows:

Hardware level preemption: By using simultaneous multithreading, such as Intel's Hyper-Threading Technology, each physical core can provide multiple logical cores to accommodate multiple jobs. The scale of a time slice is clock frequency level, or nanoseconds level. The disadvantage is that the number of logical cores per physical core is limited to two in current server CPUs.

OS level preemption: When preemption is done by OS, the scale of a time slice is milliseconds level.

Software level preemption: In order to achieve coarser-grained preemption, some schedulers adopt preemption by software [2,3], which achieve job suspension and resume by using cgroups. In those schedulers, the time slice is configured as seconds or minutes level.

While shorter time slices are suitable for real time usage, each job suffers from heavier performance degradation. Section 5 mainly focuses on hardware level preemption, however, we will investigate trade off among different preemption mechanisms in detail in future.

Next we discuss performance degradation under overcommitting in detail using Fig. 1. Figure 1 (c) illustrates a case when a batch job and a interactive job share the same processor core. While the total CPU utilization is high and 100% in the figure, each job suffers from performance degradation. While the execution time of the batch job is $T_{v,Ded}$ on a dedicated core (Fig. 1 (a)), it is extended to $T_{v,OC} = T_{v,Ded} + \Delta T$ by overcommitting (Fig. 1 (c)). The degradation occurs mutually and the interactive job also suffers; but there is a difference from batch jobs since thinking periods of interactive jobs do not slow down, while execution periods suffer. In Sect. 4.3, we will define metrics to evaluate performance degradation that take this difference into account.

Let us repeat that performance degradation ratio depends not only on CPU utilization of each job but also on microscopic job characteristics like memory access frequency and access locality [8]. Therefore a future overcommitting scheduler, which is expected to improve the entire CPU utilization in the system, should work as follows. It takes information of plenty of jobs, including batch jobs and interactive jobs, coupled with information of job characteristics. When demands for processor cores are larger than physical cores in the system, it considers core level overcommitting. Here the scheduler should choose *well-matched* jobs to share computing resources, which have less negative impacts on performance of each other. We will define well-matched in Sect. 4.3 in detail.

3.3   Overcommitting Scheduling System

In order to make the motivation of this paper clearer, this section describes overview of the prototype design of an overcommitting scheduler that supports core-level overcommitting. This scheduler chooses well-matched jobs to share computing resources from the job pool in order to achieve higher CPU utilization ratio and smaller performance degradation. For this purpose, it obtains profile information of jobs. By combining those information and our performance prediction model described in the following section, this scheduler is designed to improve the performance of the entire system and each job.

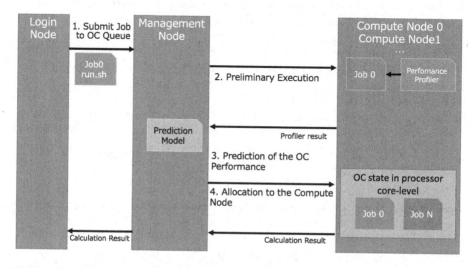

Fig. 2. The prototype design of the overcommitting scheduler. We assume the system includes a login node, a management node and compute nodes.

Figure 2 shows the flow of the overcommitting scheduling. When a user submits a batch job, the scheduler works as follows:

1. Job submission: The user accesses the login node and submits a job (called job 0 hereafter).
2. Preliminary execution: The job scheduler starts execution of job 0 in a dedicated environment as preliminary execution to obtain the job's performance profile. This execution is killed shortly.
3. Prediction of overcommitting performance: Using the profile obtained in step 2 as input, the scheduler scans running jobs on compute nodes and predicts the mutual performance degradation if job 0 is added on each node. The scheduler chooses a node, on which performance degradation is smallest.
4. Execution on the compute node: The scheduler starts job 0 on the node selected in step 3 under overcommitting.

From the viewpoint of batch job users, the above flow is transparent and same as usual schedulers. In obtaining the performance profile in step 2, it is better to use third-party measurement tools that does not need to modify the application binaries. For example, wrapping with `perf` command or attaching to a process using PAPI is considered. If it is in one measurement or short time, only initialization phase of the job may be measured. Thus, we plan to make several measurements during one preliminary execution, and adopt the value if we can judge that the trend has settled down. In step 3, we use the performance prediction model of a given jobs pair under overcommitting. We have previously developed a prototype model and verified its accuracy [8]. This paper largely modifies the model as described in Sect. 6. In this system, it is assumed that jobs can be resubmitted by the management side. In many supercomputer systems, when there is a failure of a compute node, the management side resubmits the job to another node. Therefore, we consider this to be a general assumption.

The usage of interactive jobs are similar, but there is a difference since killing preliminary execution in Step 2 significantly reduces the usability. Instead, we need to select nodes based on approximation as follows and start execution immediately.

- We can estimate the profiles of new jobs, if similar jobs have previously executed.
- Our prediction model can also detect "dangerous jobs", which tend to introduce heavier performance degradation with any coexisting jobs. In the current design, interactive jobs are scheduled so that they avoid nodes on which dangerous jobs are already running.

The above strategy is approximation of desirable method. If we can use light weight process migration mechanisms, the situation can be improved.

There are two main aims of this job scheduling system. One is to improve the efficiency of the overall system by overcommitting applications with different tendencies, as we have discussed. The other is to increase the number of concurrently executable jobs via overcommitting. For example, when the original number of concurrently executable jobs is N_j and overcommitting scheduling allows all computing resources M multiplicity, the number of concurrently executable jobs becomes MN_j. Thus waiting time that each job suffers from gets shorter, which should be ideally close to zero for interactive jobs.

4   Methodology for Evaluation Under Overcommitting

This paper focuses on performance of jobs under overcommitting. Evaluation results are shown in Sect. 5 and performance model is introduced in Sect. 6. Prior to those, this section describes methodology for evaluation and defines performance degradation ratio.

4.1   Target Workload

We are interested in the cases where batch jobs and interactive jobs share computing resources. For batch jobs, we use NAS Parallel Benchmarks (NPB) [1]. This benchmark set is provided by NASA and mimic various HPC applications. Table 1 summarizes the programs and classes (problem sizes), and the characteristics cited from [1]. In the following, when specifying a program including its class, we use the notation like "cg.B". In addition, we employed a simple matrix multiplication kernel (mm) as a CPU-intensive application. All the above applications are parallelized by OpenMP.

For interactive jobs, it is rather hard to collect plenty of profiles of real interactive jobs. Instead, we modify the NPB applications to mimic behaviors of interactive usage, by repeating execution periods and thinking periods. The details are described in Sect. 5.

Table 1. The specification of the workloads

Program	Class	Characteristic
ft	A-D	Discrete 3D fast Fourier Transform, all-to-all communication
mg	A-D	Multi-Grid on a sequence of meshes, long- and short-distance communication, memory intensive
sp	A-D	Scalar Penta-diagonal solver
lu	A-D	Lower-Upper Gauss-Seidel solver
bt	A-D	Block Tri-diagonal solver
ep	A-D	Embarrassingly Parallel
cg	A-D	Conjugate Gradient, irregular memory access and communication
mm	–	Simple matrix multiplication kernel

4.2   Experiment Environment for Overcommitting

The specification of the machines we used is shown in Table 2. The compiler and performance profiler we used are shown in Table 3. PAPI [10] and Score-P [6] were used to obtain the number of performance counters (PMCs) in Sect. 6.

On top of the above mentioned node, we evaluate performance of jobs when they share the same cores. In order to bind multiple application threads or processes to specific cores, we use the cgroup mechanisms.

As mentioned in Sect. 3.2, we mainly use hardware level overcommitting, based on simultaneous multithreading. Due to this choice, the number of jobs that shared resources (multiplicity) is two.

Table 2. The specification of the machine

Processor: Intel(R) Xeon(R) Gold 6140	
Num. of Cores	36
Num. of Cores per socket	18
Num. of Sockets	2
Level 1 Cache	32KB I + 32 KB D
Level 2 Cache	1024 KB
Level 3 Cache	25344 KB
Operating Frequency	2.30 GHz
Hyper-Threading Setting	Enabled

Table 3. A compiler and performance profiler

Software	
Compiler	gcc 9.3.0
Compiler Options	-O3 -fopenmp
Performance Profilers	PAPI 5.7.0.0 [10], Score-P 6.0 [6]

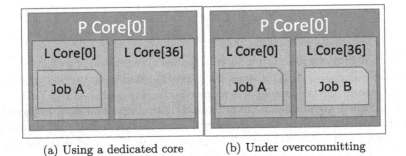

(a) Using a dedicated core   (b) Under overcommitting

Fig. 3. Overcommitted state with Hyper-Threading enabled

Figure 3 (b) shows the case where a single physical core is shared by two jobs. In our machine, logical core 0 and 36 share a single physical core 0. Thus each job process is bound to each logical core.

We currently evaluate only hardware level preemption and thus multiplicity is limited to two. However, our methodology can be extended to OS level or software level preemption to support larger multiplicity.

4.3 Definition of Performance Degradation Ratio

In the next section, we evaluate performance degradation of jobs by coexisting jobs on the same cores. We define degree of the degradation when multiplicity is two. While performance degradation occurs mutually among coexisting jobs, we define performance degradation ratio in an asymmetric style in order to capture that jobs may have different execution times and different CPU utilization ratios.

We assume that a batch job, which is called the *victim* job, is running for a long time. Then the other job, called the *opponent* job, starts execution using the same cores. While we assume the victim job keeps high CPU utilization ratio, the opponent's CPU utilization may or may not fluctuate; the opponent may be either a batch job or an interactive job.

Then we define several variables as follows. $T_{v,Ded}$ is the execution time of the victim on the dedicated cores (Fig. 3 (a)) and $T_{v,OC}$ is the execution time of the victim running with the opponent job.

We also define similar variables for the opponent, but we should take care of fluctuation of CPU utilization since it may repeat thinking and execution periods if it is an interactive job. $T_{o,ded}$ is the execution time of the opponent job on the dedicated cores, excluding of thinking periods. Thus it is the total time of execution periods[2]. Similarly, $T_{o,OC}$ is the total time of execution periods under overcommitting, which is illustrated in Fig. 1 (c).

Using these variables, we define performance degradation ratio E_v and E_o by the following equations:

$$E_v = \frac{T_{v,OC} - T_{v,Ded}}{T_{o,OC}} \tag{1}$$

$$E_o = \frac{T_{o,OC} - T_{o,Ded}}{T_{o,OC}} \tag{2}$$

Note that they are not simple relative values of extension of execution times, like $(T_{v,OC} - T_{v,Ded})/T_{v,Ded}$. Instead both have the denominator of $T_{o,OC}$ for the following reason. If the opponent is an interactive job with low CPU utilization (thinking periods are dominant), it is natural that relative extension of the victim is minor. However, we are more interested in characteristics of CPU utilization by the victim and execution periods in the opponent. To avoid underestimation of effects of the opponents, our definitions of degradation ratio are formulated as above.

It is reasonable that the threshold for performance evaluation is 0.5 both for the victim and the opponent. We can explain the reason for victim. First, $T_{v,OC}$ can be transformed as Eq. 3. The first term is dedicated execution time and the second is overcommitted execution time. Thus, Eq. 4 holds ideally between $T_{v,OC}$ and $T_{v,Ded}$. Equation 4 can be transformed as Eq. 5. We can gain $E_v = 0.5$ by using Eq. 1 and Eq. 5. We can explain in the same way for opponent, using Eq. 2 and Eq. 6.

$$T_{v,OC} = (T_{v,OC} - T_{o,OC}) + T_{o,OC} \tag{3}$$

$$T_{v,Ded} = (T_{v,OC} - T_{o,OC}) + T_{o,OC}/2 \tag{4}$$

$$T_{v,OC} = T_{v,Ded} + T_{o,OC}/2 \tag{5}$$

$$T_{o,OC} = 2T_{o,Ded} \tag{6}$$

---

[2] If the opponent is a batch job, it is same as the execution time.

From the above discussion, the expected degradation ratio is 0.5 for both if they do not suffer from effects of cache pollution or memory bandwidth contention. By harnessing this property, we can define well-matched job pairs for overcommitting. If the sum of ratio of the victim and the opponent, $E = E_v + E_o$, is smaller than 1.0, we call the pair of the two jobs well-matched. If E is larger, we should avoid overcommitting for that pair.

So far, we have discussed relationship between two jobs, one of which needs to be a batch job. In future, we extend the definitions to support more generic cases.

5   Performance Evaluation Under Overcommitting

This section evaluates how performance of jobs is affected by introducing overcommitting using the methodology described in the previous section. First, we show the results of the cases with two batch jobs, and then show the cases with a batch job and a mimicked interactive job.

5.1   Two Batch Jobs

The measurement has been done basically based on methodology in the previous section. Unlike the definition of degradation ratio, we have executed both the victim and the opponent repeatedly. As the results, both jobs are always affected by the coexisting job. This makes the measurement simpler than measuring $T_{o,OC}$ precisely.

We have measured cases when each job uses a single thread and cases when each job uses two threads.

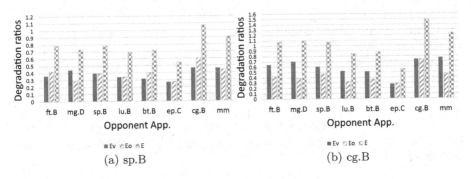

(a) sp.B   (b) cg.B

Fig. 4. The degradation ratio when two batch jobs share a physical core. Each job uses a single thread. We extract sp.B and cg.B as typical victim applications.

Table 4. The percentages of cases degradation ratio is less than (or more than) the threshold. Each job uses a single thread. It shows as a percentage. The threshold t is 0.5 for E_v and E_o, 1.0 for E.

	$\leq t$	$>t$
E_v	92%	8%
E_o	89%	11%
E	92%	8%

Table 5. The percentages of cases degradation ratio is less than (or more than) the threshold. Each job uses two threads. Threshold values are same as in Table 4.

	$\leq t$	$>t$
E_v	86%	14%
E_o	86%	14%
E	86%	14%

A Single Thread per Job. Two jobs share a single physical core as shown in Fig. 3 (b). The applications shown in Table 1 are used for the victim and opponent, and the number of measured combinations is 800, including different problem sizes. Among the measurement, Fig. 4 shows the results when the victim job is sp.B or cg.B. The horizontal axis indicates the opponent job, and the bars indicate the degradation ratio E_v, E_o, and $E = E_v + E_o$.

According to Fig. 4 (a), E_v of sp.B is less than 0.5, which indicates that overcommitting using hyper threading has advantageous in performance. On the other hand, Fig. 4 (b) shows E_v of cg.B is higher than 0.5, which indicates overcommitting incurs larger performance degradation on cg.B, thus this application should be excluded from overcommitting. We have observed that most of the NPB applications had E_v below 0.5 like sp.B. Table 4 shows the percentage of cases when the degradation ratio is less than the threshold that indicates whether a job pair is well-matched for overcommitting. We see that 89% or more pairs are well-matched.

Two Threads per Job. In these cases, four threads from two jobs are bound to two physical cores. Here core binding pattern is not unique as shown in Fig. 5. In our measurements, two jobs run like (b), where threads from different jobs share a single physical core. We have done this with an expectation that we could obtain better total performance when threads of different type share a single thread.

Figure 6 shows the results when the victim job is sp.B or cg.B, again. Also Table 5 indicates the percentages of well-matched job pairs. We observe the similar tendency to the case of one thread per job.

5.2   A Batch Job and an Interactive Job

In this experiment, we have used modified NPB applications to let them mimic behaviors of interactive jobs as the opponent, instead of collecting profiles of actual interactive jobs. The modifications to the program are shown in Listing 1. As an example, the case of sp is shown. The main loop of each application is

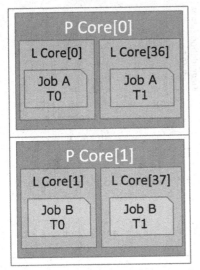

(a) A physical core per job

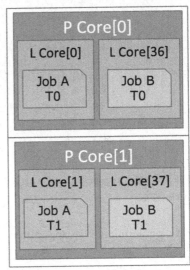

(b) Threads in each job are distributed

Fig. 5. The core bindings when two by two threads are sharing two physical cores

modified to sleep after a certain loop length (STEP) is calculated. sleepT in line 4 is generated by random number and different value for each time but we omit the part in the Listing for simplicity.

Contrarily, the victim job is same as the previous experiments. Each of the opponent and the victim uses a single thread.

Table 6. Differences in degradation ratio between batch versus interactive cases and batch versus batch cases ("bxb"). The Values correspond to mean and median among all tested job pairs.

Difference value	Mean	Median
$E_v - E_v(\text{bxb})$	0.04	0.02
$E_o - E_o(\text{bxb})$	0.15	0.16
$E - E(\text{bxb})$	0.19	0.19

Figure 7 shows the results when the victim job is sp.B or cg.B. The horizontal axis indicates the opponent job, and the bars indicate the degradation ratio. The graph also compares degradation ratio when both the victim and opponents are long batch jobs, as in the previous section ($E_v(bxb)$ and so on).

We observe that the degradation ratio in batch versus interactive cases tends to be larger than in batch versus batch cases. In order to discuss the difference, Table 6 shows statistics of the difference. From these results, we also see that the increase in E_o is larger than that of E_v.

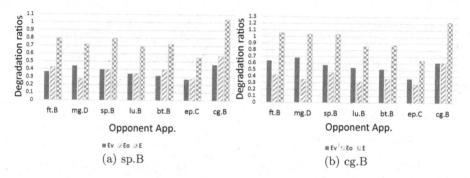

Fig. 6. The degradation ratio when two batch jobs share two physical cores. Each job uses two threads.

Listing 1. Mimic interactive application. By inserting `sleep` it behaves similarly to Figure 1 (c).

```
1 do step = 1, niter
2    call adi                    !! This is a compute kernel.
3    if (mod(step, STEP) .eq. STEP-1) then
4        call sleep(sleepT)      !! Call sleep at regular loop intervals.
5    endif
6 end do
```

We consider the reason for this asymmetric increase as follows. In all the cases under overcommitting, coexisting jobs interact with each other by evicting the other's data out of the cache. This effect is especially severe for a (mimic) interactive job, which repeats thinking and execution periods. During thinking periods, its data is mostly evicted out of the cache and thus it largely suffers from a large number of cache misses in the subsequent execution period.

6   Performance Modeling with Overcommitting

In Sect. 5, we have demonstrated that performance degradation introduced by overcommitting largely depends on the pair of coexisting jobs. Thus, when we conduct overcommitting scheduling in supercomputer systems as illustrated in Sect. 3.3, it is expected to choose compute nodes so that well-matched jobs with less performance degradation would share computing resources. However, it is unrealistic to collect the performance degradation ratio for all possible combinations of applications beforehand. Therefore, we have developed a model to predict the performance under overcommitting. The model takes information of performance monitoring counters (PMCs) of each application run on dedicated resources as input, instead of information of all possible application

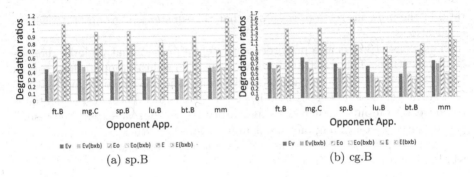

Fig. 7. The degradation ratio with a batch job as victim and a mimic interactive job as opponent. Also batch-batch cases are compared.

combinations. In Sect. 3.3, we have discussed how we obtain job's profile information (PMCs).

6.1 Overview of Prediction Model

The model we propose here is composed of two phases:

1. The model that detects applications whose performance will be degraded significantly (called "dangerous applications") by overcommitting
2. The model that predicts degradation for a given combination of applications

In phase 1, we take PMCs during each application as input, and classify applications using a clustering algorithm to pick up dangerous applications that should not be under overcommitting. This is based on an expectation that applications with similar PMCs are likely to show a similar degradation ratio.

Such dangerous applications are excluded and the rest applications are inspected by phase 2. Phase 2 estimates the prediction of degradation ratio for a given job pair. In the overcommitting scheduling, we could use the estimation to determine nodes for newly submitted jobs so that well-matched applications share computing resources.

6.2 Phase 1: Dangerous Application Detection Model

We adopt non-hierarchical cluster analysis as a statistical method to classify the applications. As a preliminary examination, we conducted a cluster analysis of applications using the PMCs on the dedicated cores as input. For this purpose, we have obtained around ten counters including the number of L1, L2 and L3 cache misses and branch instructions. The clustering results are shown in Fig. 8, where each application execution corresponds to a point, and the PMC space is mapped to two dimensional space.

In the right area, we see a cluster consisting of cg benchmarks with several problem sizes. Since we have observed that cg.B has a large degradation ratio in the previous section, we judge that this cluster is a group of dangerous applications.

This phase 1 works as a pre-processing step of phase 2 that excludes dangerous applications. This has two objectives: one is to reduce computation costs in phase 2, which considers all pairs of applications. The other is to exclude outliers from linear regression analysis used in phase 2. Generally, linear regression tends to be weak to inputs outside the explanatory space, thus we expect the results are improved by excluding dangerous applications as outliers.

The detailed validation of the model using non-hierarchical cluster analysis will be future work.

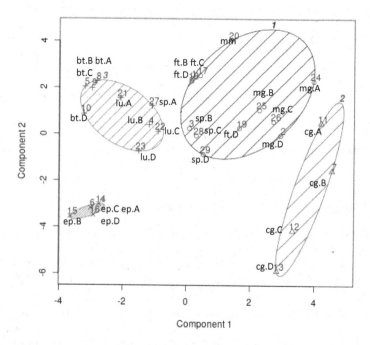

Fig. 8. The result of non-hierarchical cluster analysis. In this analysis, we set the number of cluster four. Each circle corresponds the cluster.

6.3   Phase 2: Degradation Prediction Model

We developed a model to predict the performance when a given applications share resources in overcommitting scheduling. This phase 2 is based on the linear logistic regression, which is known as a method for solving binary discriminant problems. The regression model returns the probability that binary value b equals 1 (True). Our strategy here is to estimate whether the pair of applications is well-matched or not, instead of estimating the degradation ratio directly.

In our model, the binary values correspond as follows:

1. If the degradation ratio of the victim application exceeds a certain threshold, the binary value b is 1 (True)
2. Otherwise, binary value b is 0 (False)

The threshold value of the degradation ratio t is 0.5 as we assume that multiplicity is two. The input data are the PMCs of the victim and opponent applications, which are already available in phase 1. The output is the probability. Here, the model is formulated as follows:

$$X = \sum_{k=1}^{n} (\alpha_{k,\text{vic}} C_{k,\text{vic}} + \alpha_{k,\text{opp}} C_{k,\text{opp}}) \tag{7}$$

$$Pr(E_v > t) = \pi = \frac{\exp(X)}{1 + \exp(X)} \tag{8}$$

where X is a linear combination of PMC values, n is the number of PMCs, $C_{k,\text{vic}}$ is k-th PMC value of a victim application measured in the dedicated state, $C_{k,\text{opp}}$ is that of an opponent application, and α_k is the regression coefficients.

Let us now estimate the match between two applications A and B. First, we take A as the victim and B as the opponent. Using the equation, we can predict the possibility of degradation of the victim, which is A now. Next, we swap A and B and repeat the computation to inspect B. If both calculated values are less than the threshold described below, the pair of A and B is judged well-match, which is suitable for overcommitting.

6.4   Validation of the Model

We use two different datasets for the validation of our model. One dataset consists of 800 records using 29 different applications shown in Table 1 (dataset1). The other dataset consists of 591 records, excluding the dangerous applications (dataset2). From the discussion in Subsect. 6.2, we assume the dangerous applications are cg.A, cg.B, cg.C, and cg.D. Also, among all PMCs obtained during dedicated executions, we have selected explanatory variables using a stepwise backward selection method. The number of selected counters are 31 and 11 for each dataset. By excluding the dangerous applications, we can build the model to capture the characteristic with fewer variables for dataset2. The selected counters for dataset2 are displayed in Table 7.

Here we conducted 3-fold cross-validation. In the validation, if the probability is greater than the threshold, the binary value is set to 1; otherwise, it is set to 0. The threshold value is set to 0.5.

We have compared the estimated results (well-matched or not) and the measurement results in Table 8. Generally, we observe the estimation by Phase 2 achieves good accuracy. When we compare dataset1 and dataset2, the latter shows even better accuracy, 96% or more. This result indicates the importance of excluding dangerous applications in Phase 1.

While the accuracy of the model is fairly good, we will discuss cases with misprediction below. Here we let b_t be true (measured) binary value and b_p be

Table 7. Performance counters selected for dataset2 by stepwise method. The suffix V(O) show the value of victim(opponent). The counters related to memory(cache) and branch are mainly selected.

Counter name	Value
(Intercept)	−8.8e1
PAPI_L3_TCM_V	−9.7e0
PAPI_PRF_DM_V	−4.7e0
PAPI_BR_UCN_V	−1.3e1
PAPI_BR_TKN_V	1.5e1
PAPI_L2_TCW_V	−1.1e1
PAPI_PRF_DM_O	4.9e1
PAPI_LST_INS_O	−2.4e1
PAPI_L3_LDM_O	−2e1
PAPI_BR_UCN_O	1.7e1
PAPI_BR_TKN_O	1.4e1
PAPI_BR_NTK_O	1.1e2

Table 8. Accuracy in three-fold cross validations.

	Fold1	Fold2	Fold3
dataset1	96%	92%	93%
dataset2	98%	96%	98%

the predicted value. Among the mispredicted cases, false negative cases with $b_t = 1$ and $b_p = 0$ are more critical than false positive cases with $b_t = 0$ and $b_p = 1$ for the overcommitting scheduler. This is because the scheduler determines resource allocation considering b_p, and thus mispredicted jobs may suffer from large performance degradation by undesirable overcommitting.

Table 8 shows the detail of all mispredicted cases with dataset2. Among them, cases 2, 305, 318, 462 are the false negative cases. Some of them can be corrected by changing configuration of the threshold. If we want to be more conservative, we can choose a smaller threshold. For example, if we set the threshold to 0.3 considering safety factor, cases 305 and 318 would be correct. On the other hand, such configuration can increase false positive cases, however, they are relatively harmless as discussed above.

7   Related Work

A classic survey for job scheduling techniques is [5]. Although reducing waiting time using job preemption has been discussed here, preemption is rarely used in production supercomputers for the reasons discussed in Sect. 3.2. In this work,

Table 9. The detail of all wrong cases with dataset2

Case no.	Fold	Victim	Opponent	True E_v	b_t	π	b_p
2	1	ft.B	mg.D	0.50	1	0.14	0
305	1	ft.A	mg.D	0.53	1	0.42	0
318	1	ft.A	ft.D	0.57	1	0.42	0
448	2	mg.A	mg.D	0.41	0	0.61	1
472	2	mg.B	mg.D	0.43	0	1.00	1
477	2	mg.B	mm	0.44	0	1.00	1
486	2	mg.B	ft.D	0.37	0	1.00	1
490	2	mg.B	mg.A	0.40	0	1.00	1
491	2	mg.B	mg.C	0.42	0	1.00	1
534	2	sp.A	ft.D	0.43	0	1.00	1
323	3	ft.A	mg.B	0.50	0	1.00	1
329	3	ft.C	mg.D	0.47	0	1.00	1
462	3	mg.A	ft.D	0.60	1	0.00	0

one of the largest issues, performance degradation has been analyzed in detail. The above survey paper also mentions the importance of job migration, which will improve scheduling, especially for interactive jobs in our context.

Wong et al. [11] conducted the experiment where multiple MPI applications share the computing resources, which is the almost same situation as overcommited state. They showed the performance was degraded, and the trend was various according to the communication and computation patterns. This is the opposite trend to ours possibly because they didn't adopt hardware preemption. In addition, they considered the combination of a parallel application and a sequential application. The overcommiting scheduling is expected to be beneficial to the combination because the slowdown of the sequential application will improve.

There are several prior studies on job scheduling algorithms considering overcommitting. Chen et al. [2] and Delgado et al. [3] evaluated the case of preemption implementation using public workload traces of data centers. Both show that waiting time can be reduced by preemption. In the former study, preemption is conducted by suspending long jobs with long execution times in order to maintain fairness between long jobs and short jobs. The latter shows that when resuming a long job from preemption, selecting a job with a short execution time up to suspension can further improve the slowdown. Since these are systems using the YARN scheduler, we would need adaptation of the techniques for schedulers in supercomputers.

Yabuuchi et al. used workload traces on a GPU cluster to evaluate preemption [12]. They propose an algorithm to select the job with the least resources when choosing a preemption victim from a long (best-effort) jobs.

Tau et al. measured the performance of HPC applications in Hyper-Threading environment [9]. They compared the performance of HT enabled and HT disabled when using the same number of physical cores. They pointed out that the performance of cache-friendly applications degrades when HT is enabled. This is in common with the properties confirmed in this paper.

8   Conclusion and Future Work

Overcommitting scheduling is expected to lead to efficient resource utilization and schedule improvement, especially for interactive realtime jobs. Towards such scheduling, we conducted the following two examinations. First, we measured the performance of jobs under overcommitting. It is natural that each job suffers from performance degradation, however, total throughput can be improved with well-matched application combinations. In our experiments, we considered the case of interactive jobs as well as conventional batch jobs. Next, we built a model to predict the performance under overcommitting, which shows high accuracy. These results will be harnessed to improve overcommitting scheduling.

Towards realization of the overcommitting scheduling shown in this paper, we consider future work as follows:

Performance measurement of other parallelization methods: Since we have already investigated the performance degradation of applications parallelized with OpenMP, we need to investigate other common parallelization methods in the HPC field, such as intra-node and inter-node MPI.

Performance measurement of more various interactive jobs: It is necessary to consider interactive jobs rather than the mimic interactive jobs used in this work. As for the workload, in addition to debugging and visualization of results, we should also consider Jupyter Notebook and VScode, which are getting more common in recent years.

Analysis of wider types of preemption: While this work has focused on hardware preemption using simultaneous multithreading, we are going to investigate more generally including OS level preemption and software level preemption.

Improving the dangerous application detection model: In this paper, we used non-hierarchical cluster analysis to detect dangerous applications, but we have not sufficiently validated or automated the process. It is an important issue because we confirmed that the accuracy of the degradation prediction model could be improved by detecting dangerous applications as shown in Sect. 6.3.

Implementation and evaluation of the overcommitting scheduler: To confirm the proposed scheduling method's effect, we evaluate it on the simulator using the existing workload trace of the supercomputer system.

Acknowledgements. This work was supported by JSPS KAKENHI Grant Number JP19H04121.

References

1. Bailey, D., et al.: The NAS parallel benchmarks. Int. J. Supercomput. Appl. **5**(3), 63–73 (1991). https://doi.org/10.1177/109434209100500306
2. Chen, W., Rao, J., Zhou, X.: Preemptive, low latency datacenter scheduling via lightweight virtualization. In: 2017 USENIX Annual Technical Conference (USENIX ATC 2017), pp. 251–263 (2017)
3. Delgado, P., Didona, D., Dinu, F., Zwaenepoel, W.: Kairos: preemptive data center scheduling without runtime estimates. In: Proceedings of the ACM Symposium on Cloud Computing, pp. 135–148 (2018)
4. Feitelson, D.G.: Metrics for parallel job scheduling and their convergence. In: Feitelson, D.G., Rudolph, L. (eds.) JSSPP 2001. LNCS, vol. 2221, pp. 188–205. Springer, Heidelberg (2001). https://doi.org/10.1007/3-540-45540-X_11
5. Feitelson, D.G., Rudolph, L., Schwiegelshohn, U., Sevcik, K.C., Wong, P.: Theory and practice in parallel job scheduling. In: Feitelson, D.G., Rudolph, L. (eds.) JSSPP 1997. LNCS, vol. 1291, pp. 1–34. Springer, Heidelberg (1997). https://doi.org/10.1007/3-540-63574-2_14
6. Knüpfer, A., et al.: Score-P: a joint performance measurement run-time infrastructure for Periscope, Scalasca, TAU, and Vampir. In: Brunst, H., Müller, M., Nagel, W., Resch, M. (eds.) Tools for High Performance Computing 2011, pp. 79–91. Springer, Heidelberg (2012). https://doi.org/10.1007/978-3-642-31476-6_7
7. Matsuoka, S., et al.: Overview of TSUBAME3.0, green cloud supercomputer for convergence of HPC, AI and big-data. TSUBAME e-Science J. **16**, 2–9 (2017)
8. Minami, S., Endo, T., Nomura, A.: Performance modeling of HPC applications on overcommitted systems (extended abstract). In: The International Conference on High Performance Computing in Asia-Pacific Region, pp. 129–132 (2021)
9. Tau Leng, R.A., Hsieh, J., Mashayekhi, V., Rooholamini, R.: An empirical study of hyper-threading in high performance computing clusters. Linux HPC Revolution **45** (2002)
10. Terpstra, D., Jagode, H., You, H., Dongarra, J.: Collecting performance data with PAPI-C. In: Müller, M.S., Resch, M.M., Schulz, A., Nagel, W.E. (eds.) Tools for High Performance Computing 2009, pp. 157–173. Springer, Heidelberg (2010). https://doi.org/10.1007/978-3-642-11261-4_11
11. Wong, F.C., Arpaci-Dusseau, A.C., Culler, D.E.: Building MPI for multi-programming systems using implicit information. In: Dongarra, J., Luque, E., Margalef, T. (eds.) EuroPVM/MPI 1999. LNCS, vol. 1697, pp. 215–222. Springer, Heidelberg (1999). https://doi.org/10.1007/3-540-48158-3_27
12. Yabuuchi, H., Taniwaki, D., Omura, S.: Low-latency job scheduling with preemption for the development of deep learning. In: 2019 USENIX Conference on Operational Machine Learning (OpML 2019), pp. 27–30 (2019)
13. Yoo, A.B., Jette, M.A., Grondona, M.: SLURM: simple Linux utility for resource management. In: Feitelson, D., Rudolph, L., Schwiegelshohn, U. (eds.) JSSPP 2003. LNCS, vol. 2862, pp. 44–60. Springer, Heidelberg (2003). https://doi.org/10.1007/10968987_3

Scheduling Microservice Containers on Large Core Machines Through Placement and Coalescing

Vishal Rao[1]([✉]) [iD], Vishnu Singh[1] [iD], K. S. Goutham[1],
Bharani Ujjaini Kempaiah[1], Ruben John Mampilli[1], Subramaniam Kalambur[1],
and Dinkar Sitaram[2]

[1] Department of Computer Science and Engineering, PES University,
Bangalore, India
subramaniamkv@pes.edu
[2] Cloud Computing Innovation Council of India (CCICI), Bangalore, India

Abstract. Current applications deployed on the cloud use the microservice programming model to enable rapid deployment. Due to the loosely coupled nature of the interactions between microservices, they are well suited for the distributed nature of cloud systems. However, we are seeing a trend of increasing core counts on newer server hardware and scheduling microservices agnostic to the local organization of cores and memory on these systems leads to sub-optimal performance. In this paper, we propose a placement scheme to map containers of a microservice to various cores on such machines to maximize performance. We further study the impact of various parameters such as packet sizes and database sizes on the placement scheme and demonstrate that our placement scheme increases throughput by 22% while simultaneously lowering tail latency. Finally, we propose a mechanism to dynamically coalesce services on commonly called paths into a single container and demonstrate a further 7.5% improvement in throughput.

Keywords: Microservices · Container-scheduling · Performance · NUMA

1 Introduction

A microservice has been defined as a cohesive, independent process interacting via messages [20] and a microservice-based architecture is a method of designing software where all the modules are microservices. This is in contrast to a monolithic application whose modules cannot be executed independently [20] and as a result, monolithic applications scale poorly. Microservice based deployments using containers are becoming more popular in today's world as they offer the following advantages over monolithic deployments-

– Each loosely coupled service scales independently.

D. Klusáček et al. (Eds.): JSSPP 2021, LNCS 12985, pp. 80–100, 2021.
https://doi.org/10.1007/978-3-030-88224-2_5

- The codebase is more modular and debugging is easier.
- Decoupled services are easier to reconfigure to serve different purposes.

Due to the many advantages, the most popular internet-based services such as Netflix [39] and Amazon [34] have adopted the microservice-based architecture. These microservice-based applications are deployed on a large number of servers to take advantage of the resources provided by a cluster of hosts. This has led to research on how optimally place the containers on a cluster of systems to maximize application performance [26–30, 35, 36, 45, 52, 53]. These efforts consider different factors such as hardware resource requirements, communication affinities, and resource contentions between containers to find the best placement of the containers on the set of available hosts.

Recent development in server hardware to deliver performance scalability has seen the introduction of high core-count server CPUs that are based on multi-chip module designs with multiple non-uniform memory access (NUMA) domains per socket. As a result, these CPUs behave like a mini-distributed system. On such systems, the performance impact of NUMA is more pronounced and a lack of knowledge of the underlying topology leads to a loss in performance [14]. This performance impact due to NUMA is significant for large scale web-service applications on modern multicore servers [48]. Previous work on process scheduling lays emphasis on minimizing resource contentions. Resource contentions cause concurrently executing workloads to interfere resulting in performance degradation as well as inefficient utilization of system resources [12, 19, 37, 38, 40, 41, 50]. In addition to minimizing resource contentions, minimizing communication overheads between tasks has been shown to benefit performance as well [13, 17, 23].

Similarly, in the case of container scheduling, minimizing resource contentions and communication overheads is very important. In a microservice-based architecture, large amounts of data are exchanged between services, and when deployed using Docker containers, there is a non-negligible overhead due to network virtualization [11, 21, 51]. Hence co-locating heavily communicating containers helps reduce the communication latency and benefits performance. In the case of high core-count systems, co-locating containers on the same core complex (CCX), i.e. a group of cores sharing an L3 cache (as illustrated in Fig. 1), results in faster communication with mean latencies that are 34% lower than that between containers located on adjacent CCXs. In Sect. 7, we show that co-located containers take advantage of the L3 cache to communicate and hence, communicate faster. In this research, we introduce the **'Topology and Resource Aware Container Placement and Deployment'** scheduler (TRACPAD). TRACPAD is a local container scheduler that strategically schedules multiple containers on a single system while reducing resource contentions and communication latencies between containers.

These latencies become very relevant in the case of end-to-end user-facing applications [44] such as social networks, search engines, and streaming services where overall application latency needs to be minimized to ensure smooth user experience. Hence, such applications have strict quality of service (QoS) con-

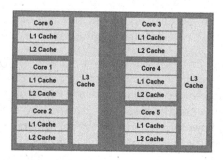

Fig. 1. AMD EPYC 7401 architecture with 2 CCXs

straints specified in the form of throughput and latency. As the number of users increases, tail latency becomes an extremely important factor in characterizing performance [18]. Hence, in our work we use throughput, mean latency, 95th percentile tail latency, and 99th percentile tail latency to measure application performance.

Most of the research on container scheduling is focused on how to schedule containers on a set of hosts and does not consider the topology of each server as a factor while placing a group of containers on a server. As today's servers act like mini-distributed systems, it becomes important to schedule containers in accordance with each system's underlying architecture. Recent research demonstrates that strategically placing containers on a large core count system improves application performance [14], but to the best of our knowledge, there is no automated scheduler that does the same. Our contributions are summarized as follows -

- A workload independent local scheduler – TRACPAD, that uses historical runtime data to find a CCX-container mapping that improves application performance and a detailed evaluation of our scheduler across 4 representative microservice applications. TRACPAD boosts application throughput by up to 22% and decreases mean latency by up to 80%.
- An understanding of how TRACPAD improves application performance and the factors that impact the scheduling policies generated by TRACPAD.
- An algorithm to strategically coalesce containers in order to eliminate the communication overhead and the performance benefits of using such a method. Coalescing containers significantly reduces application latencies. We show how our method reduces mean latency by up to 40% and 99th percentile tail latency by up to 60%.

The remainder of this paper is organized as follows. Section 2 goes over previous research and related work. Section 3 explains the implementation specifics of the TRACPAD scheduler and Sect. 4 outlines the experimental setup used for this study. Section 5 briefly introduces the microservice applications used in our study. Section 6 presents the evaluation of the scheduler and Sect. 7 explains why TRACPAD improves performance. Section 8 goes over two major factors that affect the scheduling policies generated by TRACPAD. Section 9 introduces the methodology to coalesce containers and goes over the performance impact of using this method. Finally, Sect. 10 concludes the paper and discusses further work.

2 Related Work

Virtual machines (VMs) have paved the way for containers in today's server ecosystem. Research on VM scheduling algorithms gives useful insights regarding what factors to consider while scheduling containers. Novaković et al.[41] and Nathuji et al. [40] emphasise on minimizing performance interference while co-locating VMs. Starling [46] and AGGA [15] show how performance can be improved by placing co-communicating VMs on the same hosts as this reduces the cost of network communication. This trade-off between scheduling heavily communicating processes, and trying to minimize resource contentions is also extremely valid in the case of container scheduling. Hu et al. [27] introduce a multi-objective container scheduler that generates deployment schemes that distribute the workload across servers to reduce resource contentions with the primary goal of providing multi-resource guarantees. They model the problem as a vector bin packing problem with heterogeneous bins. This scheduler also uses dependency awareness between containers to co-locate containers that heavily communicate. Many such schedulers that take into account container resource utilization affinity and resource contentions have been implemented [26,35,45].

Containerized microservice environments are sensitive to many operating system parameters [25] and hence the problem of container scheduling has also been tackled in many other ways using a large set of heuristics and a larger set of algorithms. Zhang et al. [53] propose a container scheduler that tries to minimize host energy consumption as one of its objectives. They use a linear programming based algorithm to schedule containers. ECSched [28] highlights the advantages of concurrent container scheduling over queue-based container scheduling. They model the scheduling problem as a minimum cost flow problem and incorporate multi-resource constraints into this model. Figure 2 illustrates a simple classification of the different types of schedulers surveyed as part of this research.

Kubernetes [4] and Docker Swarm [2] are the most commonly used container orchestration tools. These technologies do not factor in historical run-time data to analyze the characteristics of the application while scheduling containers on servers. Resource requirements of microservices vary with the workload they are servicing and historical runtime data is very useful while characterizing these dynamic workloads. Kubernetes placement algorithms schedule containers on nodes in a cluster based on the resource limits and tags preset by the developers. They do not consider the relationship between microservices while formulating a placement scheme. Kubernetes also recently added the topology manager [5] which tries to place containers on the same NUMA node based on different heuristics and user-specified criteria. However, this method does not consider previous runtime information to make an informed choice on which containers to co-locate on the same NUMA node whereas, the TRACPAD scheduler uses

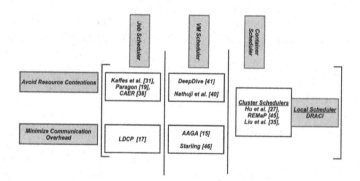

Fig. 2. Simple classification of schedulers

historical runtime data to make a more informed choice on which containers to co-locate.

REMaP [45] is another container scheduler that tries to solve some of the shortcomings of the common container management tools used today by using runtime adaptation. Each pair of microservices are assigned affinity scores based on the amount of data they exchange. REMaP tries to group microservices with high affinities on the same server to minimize the number of hosts while maximizing the affinity score of each host. The placement scheme also takes into account the amount of resources available on the server and approximates the amount of resources the microservice needs by using historical runtime data. It only co-locates a pair of microservices if the host has enough free resources to handle them. All these contributions present methods to schedule containers on a cluster of systems and do not consider the underlying topology of each server. This work presents a method that finds a placement scheme for containers that would benefit the application performance after taking into consideration the architecture of a server with a large core count. Previous works also shed light on how granular resource allocation can benefit performance. PARTIES [16] and CLITE [42] use fine-grained resource allocation to co-locate latency-critical jobs without violating their respective QoS targets. Sriraman [47] presents a method that uses A/B testing to tune configurable server parameters, such as core frequency and transparent hugepages, specifically for a microservice, so that it performs better on that server. Kaffes *et al.* [31] outline the benefits of a centralized core granular scheduler such as reducing interference. Octopus-Man [43] uses a core granular scheduling method to bind processes to cores in servers that have both brawny and wimpy cores in such a way that QoS constraints are not violated, throughput is improved and the energy consumption is reduced. The TRACPAD scheduler uses granular resource allocation to avoid resource contentions between containers while reducing the Docker network communication overhead.

3   Implementation of TRACPAD

This section explains how our method arrives at a partition and then allocates resources to containers dynamically based on the partition. This section is divided into 5 modules which describe how the whole scheduling process is automated.

3.1   The Container Resource Utilization Model

Figure 3 depicts a sample container resource utilization model for the 'Get Products' workload of the TeaStore application. The edge weights quantify the communication between two services while the node weights represent the CPU utilization of the service. In TRACPAD we use a bi-criteria approximation graph partitioning algorithm to [32] to partition the container resource utilization model based on two criteria -

- Minimization of the edgecut, i.e. the sum of the edge weights between partitions is minimized.
- Even distribution of node weights, i.e. the node weights are balanced across all partitions.

The edge weights in the model represent the amount of data transferred between the containers. The partitioning will, therefore, reduce network communication between the partitions. The node weights represent the CPU utilization of each container. Hence, each partition will have a balanced CPU utilization, thereby, reducing the CPU contentions in each partition. TRACPAD uses the 'Container Resource Utilization Model' to generate different partitioning schemes.

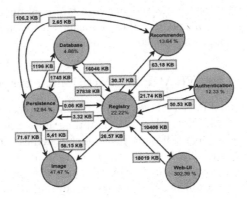

Fig. 3. Container resource utilization model - get products workload

3.2 Collection of Container Specific Data

Every container in an application requires adequate server resources for smooth functioning. This module identifies the CPU-intensive containers for a particular workload. Docker Stats is used to obtain container resource usage statistics for the duration of the workload. This is how TRACPAD uses historical run-time data to generate an informed placement scheme. TRACPAD uses this data to calculate average CPU utilization for every container. The CPU utilization metrics act as the node weights in the container resource utilization model.

3.3 Monitoring Network Traffic

This module establishes which sets of containers are communicating and the amount of data being transferred between them during any given workload. First, the ID of the Docker-bridge being used for communication is obtained. All network packets used to communicate between containers are sent on the Docker bridge. Tshark [10] is used to monitor the Docker bridge and records every packet that is transmitted. The packet headers contain the source container's IP address, destination container's IP address, and the payload size. TRACPAD uses the data in the packet headers to characterize container resource utilization patterns during the course of the workload.

A single request from the client may result in several packets being sent between containers. Different network protocols of the application layer and transport layer in the TCP/IP stack may be used to communicate between different containers and we need to capture all these packets. For example, in the social network application, Apache Thrift RPCs are used to communicate between the microservices only. To communicate with their respective databases, they use TCP, UDP, or Memcache protocols. The networkX library [7] is used to generate a container resource utilization model as illustrated in Fig. 3. TRACPAD aggregates all the data communicated between two containers in one direction irrespective of the protocol used for data transfer and assigns the sum of the payload sizes to the weight of that edge in the model.

3.4 Generation of the TRACPAD Partitioning Scheme

Algorithm 1 details the TRACPAD generates container placement schemes that map containers to CCXs. Note that this mapping is workload-specific. Thus, different workloads will have different placement schemes. Once the container resource utilization model has been partitioned, a Container-CCX mapping is generated. This mapping is invariant, i.e. it remains the same for the corresponding configuration of the application on that system and respective workload as long as the communication patterns for the workload do not change. Hence, it can be used to partition the application on the system multiple times in case the application needs to restart or if the server goes down. The next step is to affinitize the containers to the CPUs based on the mapping.

Algorithm 1: TRACPAD Partition Generator

Result: List of Tuples that map CCXs to Containers.
Require: Set of all Containers, CCXList
    /* List of CCXs allocated to application */
    Initialize CRM ← [] // Container Resource Utilization Model
    Initialize PartitionList ← []
    Initialize ContainerCCXMapping ← []
    Initialize NoOfPartitions ← Length(CCXList)

    NodeWeights$_i$ ← CPU-Util(C$_i$) ∀ C$_i$ ∈ ContainerSet
    Edges $_{i,j}$ ← BytesSent(C$_i$, C$_j$) ∀ C$_i$, C$_j$ ∈ ContainerSet
    CRM ← [NodeWeights, Edges]

    PartitionList ← generatePartitions(CRM, NoOfPartitions)
    /* PartitionList is a list of sets, All containers in a set belong to the same partition
    as shown in Fig. 9 */

    while !empty(PartitionList) **do**
        ContainerSet ← pop(PartitionList)
        CCX ← pop(CCXList)
        for all Container ∈ ContainerSet **do**
            push(ContainerCCXMapping, (Container, CCX))
        end for
    end while

3.5   Dynamic Provisioning of Resources

Once the Container-CCX mapping has been generated, TRACPAD redistributes server resources, in this case, CPUs, across all the containers according to the partitioning scheme. This is done on the fly, i.e., there is no need to stop and restart the containers. Since this redistribution of resources happens on the fly, the transition in performance is seamless. The cost of redistribution is system dependent. In our experiments, it took approximately 1.7 s to redistribute resources among the 30 containers spawned by the social-network application.

4   Experimental Setup

All our studies were conducted on a dual-socket AMD EPYC 7401 24-Core processor server with 128 GB of NUMA RAM and 2 TB Storage Capacity. The server consists of 16 core-complexes with each core-complex consisting of 3 cores (with 2-way SMT providing 6 logical CPUs) sharing an 8 MB L3 cache as illustrated in Fig. 1. Each physical core has a private 64 KB L1 instruction cache, 32 KB L1 data cache, and a 512 KB L2 cache.

The microservice-based applications were deployed on socket-0 and the HTTP workload generator on socket-1. We deployed both the client and the application on the same system to avoid any performance impact of network latency across multiple runs. The applications were allocated 24 Logical Cores across 4 CCXs and the TRACPAD algorithm was configured to generate four partitions, one per CCX. In the case of the Social Network Application and Media Service Application, the Nginx container was given access to all 24 logical cores in case of all scheduling policies so that the number of requests serviced by the application was not limited by the number of cores given to the Nginx server.

5   Microservice Benchmarks and Workloads

This section briefly introduces a variety of representative microservice benchmarks and workloads that have been used to evaluate the TRACPAD scheduler.

The DeathStar Bench Suite [22] provides two applications – a social network and a media service application. Workloads provided by both these applications are used to conduct our evaluations. These applications are heterogeneous, using C/C++, Java, Go, Scala, JavaScript, and many others. This makes the applications more representative as different functionalities are developed using different languages. The third application used is TeaStore [33] which is an end-to-end e-commerce application that is used to sell different types of tea and tea products. The last application used in this study is Sock Shop [9]. This is another end-to-end e-commerce application that sells socks to customers. All these applications have been used in previous microservices-based performance studies as suitable proxies for real-world applications [14,22,45,51]. Section 5.1 explains the social network application in detail to provide an example of the complexity and functioning of all these applications.

Table 1 summarizes the applications and lists the workloads that are used in this study.

Table 1. Summary of the applications and workloads

Application	Workload	No. of containers	Storage backends
Social network (DeathStarBench) [22]	Compose post Read home timeline Read user timeline	30	MongoDB, Redis, Memcached
Media service (DeathStarBench) [22]	Compose review	33	MongoDB, Redis, Memcached
TeaStore [33]	Get products Add to cart	7	MariaDB
Sock shop [9]	Get catalogue	15	MongoDB MySQL

5.1   The Social Network Application

It is an end-to-end application that implements a broadcast-style social network with unidirectional follow relationships. This application uses 14 microservices spawned across 30 containers. The microservices communicate with each other using Apache Thrift RPCs. This application uses Memcached and Redis for caching data and MongoDB for persistent storage of posts, profiles, and media. Each storage backend is implemented using an individual container. The Jaeger tracing application uses a Prometheus backend for storage and is a monitoring service implemented to trace packets. The architecture of the application is shown in Fig. 4.

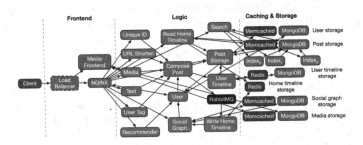

Fig. 4. Social network application architecture   Source: https://github.com/delimitrou/DeathStarBench

To test the impact of database load on the scheduling policy, we used two social network databases [3] to conduct our tests on the social network application.

- Reed 98 Social Network - 962 Users and 18812 Edges
- Penn Social Network - 43,000 Users and 1.3M Edges.

6   Evaluation of the TRACPAD Scheduler

To evaluate the TRACPAD scheduler, 6 workloads from four end-to-end microservice applications were used. Application performance was evaluated using four metrics -

- Application throughput
- Mean latency
- 95th percentile tail latency
- 99th percentile tail latency

These are the four important metrics that are commonly used to measure the performance of user-facing applications. The wrk HTTP workload generator [24] was used to measure application throughput and application latency was measured using the wrk2 HTTP workload generator [49].

First, all the partitions were generated after running the tool with each workload for 3–5 minutes. The tool collected all the required metrics and generated the partition. As the underlying graph partitioning algorithm is extremely parallelized, TRACPAD can generate partitions within a few milliseconds once the workload-specific runtime data points are collected.

As a baseline, we first measured these metrics for all the applications without any affinitization, i.e. all application containers could migrate between any of the 24 logical cores allocated to them. Figure 5a illustrates the relative gain in throughput observed for each workload.

The TRACPAD scheduler boosts the throughput by an average of 10.34% across all 6 workloads. Figure 5b illustrates the percentage reduction in latencies when the TRACPAD scheduler is used as compared to the naive policy of allocating all cores to all containers that Docker uses by default. Across all the workloads, on average, there is a 56.11% drop in mean latency, a 63.11% drop in 95th percentile tail latency, and a 68.15% drop in 99th percentile tail latency. As an example, Fig. 6 illustrates a comparison of the cumulative latency distributions between the naive policy and the policy generated by TRACPAD for the 'Get Products' workload of the TeaStore application. There is a drop in latencies throughout the latency percentile distribution demonstrating the ability of the TRACPAD scheduler to improve latencies by the strategic allocation of resources.

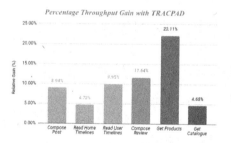 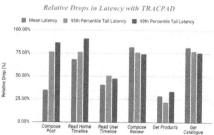

(a) Comparison of Baseline Throughput with TRACPAD Throughput

(b) Comparison of Baseline Latencies with TRACPAD Latencies

Fig. 5. Performance comparison between TRACPAD and baseline

These improvements in performance can be explained by the observations in Sect. 7. They are a result of lower communication latency between co-located containers, reduced resource contentions due to the graph partitioning, and reduced CPU migrations and context switches. There may be cases wherein a container needs more logical cores than provided by 1 CCX, like the Nginx container in our case, and in such cases, it is necessary to allocate more cores to the container. The TRACPAD scheduler has been developed with the aim of scaling up performance and can be implemented in tandem with schedulers that improve performance by using scale-out methodologies.

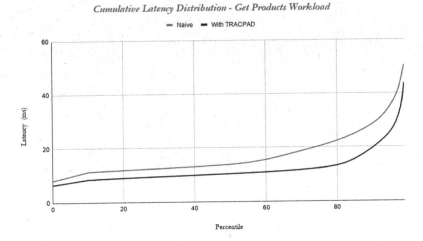

Fig. 6. Comparison of cumulative latency distribution of the get products workload

7 Analysis of TRACPAD

This section helps explain the factors that are responsible for the improvement in application performance. TRACPAD affinitizes containers to a set of cores belonging to the same CCX. We observed that this led to a reduction in both CPU thread migrations and context switches. CPU thread migrations can be very expensive on multi-socket systems with multiple NUMA domains in cases where threads migrate between NUMA domains as this either results in remote memory accesses, which have higher latencies than local memory accesses, or memory migration to the new node. Linux perf [8] was used to measure both metrics for the workloads listed in Table 1. Figure 7 illustrates the relative drop in these two metrics when the TRACPAD scheduler was used as compared to the naive case where containers have access to all cores allocated to the application.

TRACPAD also co-locates communicating containers on the same CCX. This helps reduces the communication latency between the containers and hence, improves performance. To illustrate this we used Netperf [6], which measures the network latency by sending packets between a client and a server. The server and client were containerized and the network latency was measured in 3 cases -

- Case 1: Server and client are placed on the same CCX.
- Case 2: Server and client are placed on adjacent CCXs on the same NUMA node.
- Case 3: Server and client are placed on adjacent NUMA nodes on the same socket.

Figure 8 compares the mean latencies, 90th percentile and 99th percentile tail latencies. It illustrates that there is a significant increase in all these metrics when the server and client are not placed on the same CCX. This happens because they can no longer use the L3 cache to communicate. To validate this,

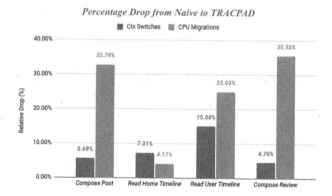

Fig. 7. Drop in context switches and CPU migrations by using TRACPAD

AMD μProf [1] was used to measure L3 miss rates for the CCX that the server and client were placed on for two packet sizes - 5 KB and 2 MB.

- A packet size of 5 KB is much smaller than the 8 MB capacity of the L3 cache and in this case, the L3 miss rates, as well as the network latencies, were extremely low.
- A packet size of 2 MB will exhaust the capacity of the L3 cache quickly and in this case, the L3 miss rate increased by 4 times as compared to the 5KB case and the network latencies shot up as well.

To explain the impact of cross CCX communication highlighted in Fig. 8, L3 miss rates were measured when the client and server were placed on the same CCX and when they were placed on different CCXs. AMD μProf showed that the L3 miss rate increased by 10 times when the server and client were placed on different CCXs. This points to the explanation that co-locating communicating containers on the same CCX reduces the communication latency between them as they use the shared L3 cache to communicate. TRACPAD takes this into account and creates placement schemes that co-locate heavily communicating containers on the same CCX to reduce the impact of the communication overhead induced by Docker. The placement schemes can be sensitive to factors like request packet sizes, database sizes, and data access patterns. Section 8 explores the impact of the request packet sizes and database sizes on the partitioning schemes.

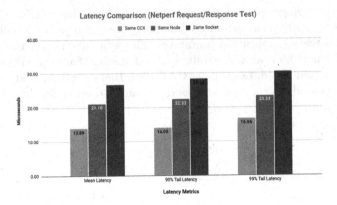

Fig. 8. Latency comparison using netperf

8 Factors Affecting the Scheduling Policy

This section investigates the impact of request packet size and database size on the scheduling policies generated by TRACPAD. Figure 9a and Fig. 9b depict the TRACPAD scheduling policies for different Request Packet Sizes for the Compose Post Workload on the same underlying database, i.e., The Reed98 Social Network. Figure 9c, which depicts the TRACPAD policy for a packet size of 256 bytes with the Penn Social Network as the underlying DB. The different TRACPAD policies improved application performance in each case after factoring in the changes in request packet size and database size.

8.1 Effect of Database Size on Scheduling Policy

TRACPAD scheduling policies can change with the size of the underlying database as evidenced by Fig. 9c and 9b. This may be because, as the database sizes increase, database operations like querying and sorting start utilizing more CPU. Therefore, the containers housing these databases also utilize resources differently. This alters the node weights in the container resource utilization model and hence, affects the scheduling policy.

8.2 Effect of Request Packet Size on Scheduling Policy

TRACPAD scheduling policies can change with the request packet size as evidenced by Fig. 9a and 9b. One of the reasons for this change is that a change in the request packet size can lead to a change in the amount of data processing done by the containers. If a container is performing compute-intensive operations (Ex. String Search) on the payload, then as the payload size increases, the container's CPU utilization will increase. This alters the node weights in the container resource utilization model and affects the scheduling policy. A change in the request packet size can also alter the edge weights of the container resource utilization model as this change can change the amount of data exchanged between application containers. This will also modify the scheduling policy. In the next section, we introduce a novel method to merge communicating containers so that the data exchanged between them is not routed through the Docker bridge and discuss how this method can be used along with TRACPAD to further improve performance.

(a) Request Packet Size 2 kB, Reed98 Database

(b) Request Packet Size 256 B, Reed98 Database

(c) Request Packet Size 256 B, Penn Database

Fig. 9. TRACPAD policies for different configurations of the compose post workload

9   Container Coalescing

In microservice environments, as a result of loose coupling between different modules, huge amounts of data are exchanged between different microservices. The communication overhead induced by Docker can negatively impact performance while huge amounts of data are being exchanged over the network. TRACPAD scheduler improves performance because it tries to minimize the communication overhead. Container coalescing further reduces the impact of communication overhead by eliminating all communication overhead by merging frequently communicating containers. This section outlines the factors to consider before merging containers and shows that strategic coalescing of containers can improve application performance.

9.1   Design Considerations

Containers that functioned as storage backends were not coalesced to ensure business continuity and prevent loss of data on failure. A greedy method was used to coalesce the containers, i.e. the two containers that communicated the most during the course of a workload were coalesced if they were compatible. Determining whether a pair of containers were compatible, comprised of checking whether there were any dependency conflicts and if the two containers were using the same set of internal ports to expose their functionality. In either case, the pair of containers cannot be coalesced.

Algorithm 2: Coalescer

Result: One New Coalesced Image.
Require: ContainerCommunicationTuples
  // Tuple - (SrcContainer, DstContainer, PayloadSize)
  Initialize CCTuples ← ContainerCommunicationTuples();

  sort(CCTuples) *// Descending order of payload size*
  IsCoalesced ← False

  for all T ∈ CCTuples **do**
    SrcBase ← getBaseImage(T.SrcContainer)
    DstBase ← getBaseImage(T.DstContainer)
    if !IsCoalesced ∧ Coalescable(SrcBase, DstBase) **then**
      CoalescedImage ← CreateNewImage(SrcBase, DstBase)
      CreateNewEntryPoint(CoalescedImage)
      IsCoalesced ← True
    end if
  end for
  / Edit the Docker-compose files and any other*
  *application files to support the new image */*

9.2 Methodology

Algorithm 2 outlines the method we have used to coalesce a pair of containers. The 'Coalescable' function in the algorithm checks if the two containers can be coalesced and whether they violate the design considerations outlined in the previous section. While creating a new base image, a new Docker entry point is required. The new entry point should execute the entry point commands of the images being combined in the appropriate order.

9.3 Experimental Setup

To evaluate the impact of the container coalescing methodology, we used two single-socket AMD EPYC 7301 16-Core processors with 64 GB of NUMA RAM on each server. Each server consists of 8 CCXs with each CCX consisting of 2 cores (with 2-way SMT providing 4 logical CPUs) sharing an 8 MB L3 cache. Each physical core has a private 64 KB L1 instruction cache, 32 KB L1 data cache, and a 512 KB L2 cache. The client and the application were deployed on different servers.

9.4 Results

The impact of coalescing was evaluated using three simple workloads from Table 1. The most heavily communicating containers were coalesced in the case of each of these workloads as listed in Table 2.

Table 2. Workloads and coalesced containers

Workload	Containers coalesced
Read home timeline	Home timeline service
	Post storage service
Read user timeline	User timeline service
	Post storage service
Add to cart	Web UI service
	Persistence service

On coalescing, the amount of data transmitted over the network reduced by over 10%. Figure 10 illustrates the improvement in performance for the 'Get Products' workload. After the containers were coalesced, the TRACPAD scheduler was applied to further improve performance. Figure 11 illustrates the combined performance gain of coalescing and scheduling for the workloads. TRAC-PAD schedules the new set of containers, both original and coalesced, to reduce resource contentions and further reduce the impact of the network communication overhead.

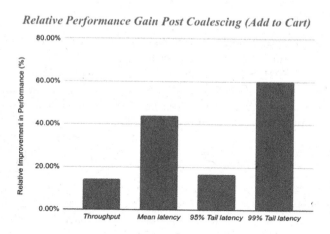

Fig. 10. Relative gain in performance after coalescing.

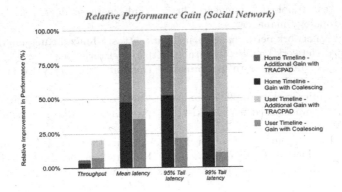

Fig. 11. Combined performance gain of coalescing and TRACPAD

10   Conclusion and Further Work

This paper presents a local container scheduler that creates placement schemes based on the underlying server architecture. The scheduler is evaluated using 4 representative microservice applications and using the scheduler improves the application performance. A detailed analysis of improvement in application performance is also studied. The scheduler tries to minimize resource contentions as well as minimize the communication overhead induced by Docker. To eliminate this overhead between a pair of communicating containers, a container coalescing methodology is outlined in the latter sections of this paper. This method also improves performance and combined with the TRACPAD scheduler, can offer significant reductions in user-perceived latencies.

As part of future work, we plan to implement NUMA node based memory scheduling by factoring in the memory utilization of each container. This will help reduce the memory contentions between the containers scheduled on the same NUMA node and as a result, improve application performance. We also plan to investigate the security implications of coalescing containers and develop a coalescing strategy that does to impact the security provided by containers adversely. Our final goal is to automate the process of container coalescing and integrate it with the TRACPAD scheduler so that their combined performance gains can benefit application performance.

Acknowledgement. We would like to thank AMD India Private Limited for their funding of this project.

References

1. Amd μprof. https://developer.amd.com/amd-uprof
2. Docker swarm overview. https://docs.docker.com/engine/swarm/
3. Facebook social networks. http://networkrepository.com/socfb
4. Kubernetes: Production-grade container orchestration. https://kubernetes.io

5. Kubernetes topology manager. https://kubernetes.io/docs/tasks/administer-cluster/topology-manager/

6. Netperf: A network performance benchmark. https://linux.die.net/man/1/netperf

7. Networkx: Network analysis in python. https://networkx.org

8. perf: Linux profiling with performance counters. https://perf.wiki.kernel.org/index.php/Main_Page

9. Sock shop microservice application. https://microservices-demo.github.io

10. Tshark: Terminal based wireshark. https://www.wireshark.org/docs/man-pages/tshark.html

11. Alles, G.R., Carissimi, A., Schnorr, L.M.: Assessing the computation and communication overhead of Linux containers for HPC applications. In: 2018 Symposium on High Performance Computing Systems (WSCAD), pp. 116–123. IEEE (2018)

12. Athlur, S., Sondhi, N., Batra, S., Kalambur, S., Sitaram, D.: Cache characterization of workloads in a microservice environment. In: 2019 IEEE International Conference on Cloud Computing in Emerging Markets (CCEM), pp. 45–50. IEEE (2019)

13. Buzato, F.H., Goldman, A., Batista, D.: Efficient resources utilization by different microservices deployment models. In: 2018 IEEE 17th International Symposium on Network Computing and Applications (NCA), pp. 1–4. IEEE (2018)

14. Caculo, S., Lahiri, K., Kalambur, S.: Characterizing the scale-up performance of microservices using teastore. In: 2020 IEEE International Symposium on Workload Characterization (IISWC), pp. 48–59. IEEE (2020)

15. Chen, J., Chiew, K., Ye, D., Zhu, L., Chen, W.: AAGA: affinity-aware grouping for allocation of virtual machines. In: 2013 IEEE 27th International Conference on Advanced Information Networking and Applications (AINA), pp. 235–242. IEEE (2013)

16. Chen, S., Delimitrou, C., Martínez, J.F.: Parties: QoS-aware resource partitioning for multiple interactive services. In: Proceedings of the Twenty-Fourth International Conference on Architectural Support for Programming Languages and Operating Systems, pp. 107–120 (2019)

17. Daoud, M.I., Kharma, N.: A high performance algorithm for static task scheduling in heterogeneous distributed computing systems. J. Parallel Distrib. Comput. **68**(4), 399–409 (2008)

18. Dean, J., Barroso, L.A.: The tail at scale. Commun. ACM **56**(2), 74–80 (2013)

19. Delimitrou, C., Kozyrakis, C.: Paragon: QoS-aware scheduling for heterogeneous datacenters. ACM SIGPLAN Not. **48**, 77–88 (2013)

20. Dragoni, N., et al.: Microservices: yesterday, today, and tomorrow. In: Dragoni, M., Meyer, B. (eds.) Present and Ulterior Software Engineering, pp. 195–216. Springer, Cham (2017). https://doi.org/10.1007/978-3-319-67425-4_12

21. Felter, W., Ferreira, A., Rajamony, R., Rubio, J.: An updated performance comparison of virtual machines and Linux containers. In: 2015 IEEE International Symposium on Performance Analysis of Systems and Software (ISPASS), pp. 171–172. IEEE (2015)

22. Gan, Y., et al.: An open-source benchmark suite for microservices and their hardware-software implications for cloud & edge systems. In: Proceedings of the Twenty-Fourth International Conference on Architectural Support for Programming Languages and Operating Systems, pp. 3–18. ACM (2019)

23. Georgiou, Y., Jeannot, E., Mercier, G., Villiermet, A.: Topology-aware job mapping. Int. J. High Perform. Comput. Appl. **32**(1), 14–27 (2018)

24. Glozer, W.: WRK - a http benchmarking tool. https://github.com/wg/wrk

25. Goutham, K.S., Ujjaini Kempaiah, B., John Mampilli, R., Kalambur, S.: Performance sensitivity of operating system parameters in microservice environments (in press)
26. Guo, Y., Yao, W.: A container scheduling strategy based on neighborhood division in micro service. In: NOMS 2018–2018 IEEE/IFIP Network Operations and Management Symposium, pp. 1–6. IEEE (2018)
27. Hu, Y., De Laat, C., Zhao, Z.: Multi-objective container deployment on heterogeneous clusters. In: 2019 19th IEEE/ACM International Symposium on Cluster, Cloud and Grid Computing (CCGRID), pp. 592–599. IEEE (2019)
28. Hu, Y., Zhou, H., de Laat, C., Zhao, Z.: ECSched: efficient container scheduling on heterogeneous clusters. In: Aldinucci, M., Padovani, L., Torquati, M. (eds.) Euro-Par 2018. LNCS, vol. 11014, pp. 365–377. Springer, Cham (2018). https://doi.org/10.1007/978-3-319-96983-1_26
29. Hu, Y., Zhou, H., de Laat, C., Zhao, Z.: Concurrent container scheduling on heterogeneous clusters with multi-resource constraints. Futur. Gener. Comput. Syst. **102**, 562–573 (2020)
30. Kaewkasi, C., Chuenmuneewong, K.: Improvement of container scheduling for docker using ant colony optimization. In: 2017 9th International Conference on Knowledge and Smart Technology (KST), pp. 254–259. IEEE (2017)
31. Kaffes, K., Yadwadkar, N.J., Kozyrakis, C.: Centralized core-granular scheduling for serverless functions. In: Proceedings of the ACM Symposium on Cloud Computing, pp. 158–164 (2019)
32. Karypis, G., Schloegel, K., Kumar, V.: Parmetis. Parallel graph partitioning and sparse matrix ordering library. Version 2 (2003)
33. von Kistowski, J., Eismann, S., Schmitt, N., Bauer, A., Grohmann, J., Kounev, S.: TeaStore: a micro-service reference application for benchmarking, modeling and resource management research. In: 2018 IEEE 26th International Symposium on Modeling, Analysis, and Simulation of Computer and Telecommunication Systems (MASCOTS), pp. 223–236. IEEE (2018)
34. Kramer, S.: Gigaom–the biggest thing amazon got right: the platform (2011)
35. Liu, B., Li, P., Lin, W., Shu, N., Li, Y., Chang, V.: A new container scheduling algorithm based on multi-objective optimization. Soft. Comput. **22**(23), 7741–7752 (2018). https://doi.org/10.1007/s00500-018-3403-7
36. Mao, Y., Oak, J., Pompili, A., Beer, D., Han, T., Hu, P.: DRAPS: dynamic and resource-aware placement scheme for docker containers in a heterogeneous cluster. In: 2017 IEEE 36th International Performance Computing and Communications Conference (IPCCC), pp. 1–8. IEEE (2017)
37. Mars, J., Tang, L., Hundt, R., Skadron, K., Soffa, M.L.: Bubble-up: increasing utilization in modern warehouse scale computers via sensible co-locations. In: Proceedings of the 44th Annual IEEE/ACM International Symposium on Microarchitecture, pp. 248–259 (2011)
38. Mars, J., Vachharajani, N., Hundt, R., Soffa, M.L.: Contention aware execution: online contention detection and response. In: Proceedings of the 8th annual IEEE/ACM International Symposium on Code Generation and Optimization, pp. 257–265 (2010)
39. Mauro, T.: Adopting microservices at Netflix: lessons for architectural design (2015). https://www.nginx.com/blog/microservices-at-netflix-architectural-best-practices
40. Nathuji, R., Kansal, A., Ghaffarkhah, A.: Q-clouds: managing performance interference effects for QoS-aware clouds. In: Proceedings of the 5th European Conference on Computer Systems, pp. 237–250 (2010)

41. Novaković, D., Vasić, N., Novaković, S., Kostić, D., Bianchini, R.: DeepDive: transparently identifying and managing performance interference in virtualized environments. In: Presented as Part of the 2013 USENIX Annual Technical Conference ATC 2013), pp. 219–230 (2013)

42. Patel, T., Tiwari, D.: CLITE: efficient and QoS-aware co-location of multiple latency-critical jobs for warehouse scale computers. In: 2020 IEEE International Symposium on High Performance Computer Architecture (HPCA), pp. 193–206. IEEE (2020)

43. Petrucci, V., et al.: Octopus-man: QoS-driven task management for heterogeneous multicores in warehouse-scale computers. In: 2015 IEEE 21st International Symposium on High Performance Computer Architecture (HPCA), pp. 246–258. IEEE (2015)

44. Rahman, J., Lama, P.: Predicting the end-to-end tail latency of containerized microservices in the cloud. In: 2019 IEEE International Conference on Cloud Engineering (IC2E), pp. 200–210. IEEE (2019)

45. Sampaio, A.R., Rubin, J., Beschastnikh, I., Rosa, N.S.: Improving microservice-based applications with runtime placement adaptation. J. Internet Serv. Appl. **10**(1), 1–30 (2019). https://doi.org/10.1186/s13174-019-0104-0

46. Sonnek, J., Greensky, J., Reutiman, R., Chandra, A.: Starling: minimizing communication overhead in virtualized computing platforms using decentralized affinity-aware migration. In: 2010 39th International Conference on Parallel Processing, pp. 228–237. IEEE (2010)

47. Sriraman, A., Wenisch, T.F.: μtune: auto-tuned threading for {OLDI} microservices. In: 13th {USENIX} Symposium on Operating Systems Design and Implementation ({OSDI} 2018), pp. 177–194 (2018)

48. Tang, L., Mars, J., Zhang, X., Hagmann, R., Hundt, R., Tune, E.: Optimizing Google's warehouse scale computers: the NUMA experience. In: 2013 IEEE 19th International Symposium on High Performance Computer Architecture (HPCA), pp. 188–197. IEEE (2013)

49. Tene, G.: WRK2 - a constant throughput, correct latency recording variant of wrk. https://github.com/giltene/wrk2

50. Thiyyakat, M., Kalambur, S., Sitaram, D.: Improving resource isolation of critical tasks in a workload. In: Klusáček, D., Cirne, W., Desai, N. (eds.) JSSPP 2020. LNCS, vol. 12326, pp. 45–67. Springer, Cham (2020). https://doi.org/10.1007/978-3-030-63171-0_3

51. Ueda, T., Nakaike, T., Ohara, M.: Workload characterization for microservices. In: 2016 IEEE International Symposium on Workload Characterization (IISWC), pp. 1–10. IEEE (2016)

52. Xu, X., Yu, H., Pei, X.: A novel resource scheduling approach in container based clouds. In: 2014 IEEE 17th International Conference on Computational Science and Engineering, pp. 257–264. IEEE (2014)

53. Zhang, D., Yan, B.H., Feng, Z., Zhang, C., Wang, Y.X.: Container oriented job scheduling using linear programming model. In: 2017 3rd International Conference on Information Management (ICIM), pp. 174–180. IEEE (2017)

Learning-Based Approaches to Estimate Job Wait Time in HTC Datacenters

Luc Gombert and Frédéric Suter[✉]

IN2P3 Computing Center/CNRS, Lyon-Villeurbanne, France
{luc.gombert,frederic.suter}@cc.in2p3.fr

Abstract. High Throughput Computing datacenters are a cornerstone of scientific discoveries in the fields of High Energy Physics and Astroparticles Physics. These datacenters provide thousands of users from dozens of scientific collaborations with tens of thousands computing cores and Petabytes of storage.

The scheduling algorithm used in such datacenters to handle the millions of (mostly single-core) jobs submitted every month ensures a *fair sharing* of the computing resources among user groups, but may also cause unpredictably long job wait times for some users. The time a job will wait can be caused by many entangled factors and configuration parameters and is thus very hard to predict. Moreover, batch systems implementing a fair-share scheduling algorithm cannot provide users with any estimation of the job wait time at submission time.

Therefore, we investigate in this paper how learning-based techniques applied to the logs of the batch scheduling system of a large HTC datacenter can be used to get an estimation of job wait time. First, we illustrate the need for users for such an estimation. Then, we identify some intuitive causes of this wait time from the information found in the batch system logs. We also formally analyze the correlation between job and system features and job wait time. Finally, we study several Machine Learning algorithms to implement learning-based estimators of both job wait time and job wait time ranges. Our experimental results show that a regression-based estimator can predict job wait time with a median absolute percentage error of about 54%, while a classifier that combines regression and classification assigns nearly 77% of the jobs in the right wait time range or in an immediately adjacent one.

1 Introduction

High Energy Physics and Astroparticles Physics experiments are heavy consumers of computing resources. Numerical simulations of physical processes generate massive amounts of data that are compared to data produced by detectors, satellites, or telescopes. The analysis and comparison of these experimental and simulated data allow physicists to validate or disprove theories and led to major scientific discoveries over the last decade. In 2012, two experiments running on the Large Hadron Collider (LHC) at CERN, both observed a new particle which is consistent with the Higgs boson predicted by the Standard Model. In 2016, the

© Springer Nature Switzerland AG 2021
D. Klusáček et al. (Eds.): JSSPP 2021, LNCS 12985, pp. 101–125, 2021.
https://doi.org/10.1007/978-3-030-88224-2_6

LIGO and VIRGO scientific collaborations announced the first observation of gravitational waves which confirmed the last remaining unproven prediction of general relativity. In both cases, these observations were awarded a Nobel Prize.

A characteristic shared by many physics experiments is that their computing models rely on single-core but numerous, and sometimes very long lasting, jobs, e.g., Monte-Carlo simulations and data analyses, to obtain scientific results. Then, this scientific community benefits more of High Throughput Computing (HTC) than High Performance Computing (HPC).

The Computing Center of the National Institute of Nuclear Physics and Particle Physics (CC-IN2P3) [21] is one of the thirteen Tier-1 centers in the *Worldwide LHC Computing Grid* (WLCG) engaged in the primary processing of the data produced by the LHC. About 2,500 users from more than 80 scientific collaborations share nearly 35,000 cores to execute a large HTC workload of about 3 million jobs per month. These resources are managed by Univa Grid Engine [23] which implements the *Fair Share Scheduler* [10] and thus assigns priorities to all the unscheduled jobs to determine their order of execution. HTC jobs being in a vast majority single-core jobs, scheduling is much easier than with parallel jobs in HPC systems. The main operational objectives are to maximize resource utilization and ensure that every group is served according to its expressed resource request for the year.

In a previous study we showed that two distinct sub-workloads are executed at CC-IN2P3 [2]. Some jobs are submitted by a small number of large user groups through a *Grid* middleware, at a nearly constant rate and with an important upstream control of the submissions while *Local* users from about 60 different groups directly submit their jobs to the batch system. We also showed that the jobs submitted by Local users suffer from larger wait times than Grid jobs. Job wait time can even become unpredictably long for some users and is caused by many entangled factors and configuration parameters. It is thus very hard to predict and may lead to a poor Quality of Service. Moreover, the Fair-Share scheduling algorithm cannot provide users with any estimation of job wait time at submission time as other scheduling algorithms, e.g., Conservative Backfilling [15], can do.

In this work we investigate how learning-based techniques applied to the logs of the batch scheduling system of a large HTC datacenter can be used to provide users with an estimation of the time their jobs will wait when they submit them. While this study focuses on the specific configuration and workload of the CC-IN2P3, we believe that our findings can be straightforwardly applied to other large HTC datacenters involved in the WLCG that show common characteristics. To this end, we make the following contributions:

- Motivate the need for a job wait time estimator.
- Identify some intuitive causes of the job wait time.
- Formally analyze the correlation between job and system features and job wait time.
- Propose a learning-based estimator of job wait time and a classifier in wait time ranges.

The remaining of this paper is organized as follows. Section 2 presents the related work. We analyze in Sect. 3 the distribution of the job wait time and detail some of its intuitive causes. In Sect. 4 we confront these intuitive causes to the correlation of job wait time with job and system features. Section 5 details the proposed learning-based approaches and presents our experimental results. We discuss the applicability of the proposed work to other workloads in Sect. 6. Finally, Sect. 7 summarizes our findings and outlines future work directions.

2   Related Work

Knowing when a job will start when it is submitted, and thus for how long it will wait in a queue, is a long-time concern, and a well-studied problem, for batch-managed datacenters. This is even more important when users have access to more than one datacenter. Then, job wait time becomes an important component of a *meta-scheduling* process to decide where to submit a job. The Karnak service [18] was for instance deployed on TeraGrid to predict job wait time within a certain confidence interval for the different sites composing the infrastructure, before or once a job is submitted. Karnak maintains a database of job features, system state, and experienced wait time and then derives a prediction for a new job by finding similar entries in this database. This approach is referred as *Instance Based Learning* [12,13]. Another technique is to predict job wait time as a range (e.g., between 1 and 3 h), for instance by using a k-Nearest Neighbors algorithm to select similar instances and then refine the prediction using Support Vector Machines [11]. In addition to these similarity-based approaches, some works directly use job and/or system features to predict upper bounds [4], by matching distributions, or ranges [9], using a Naive Bayes classifier, for job wait time. Another approach consists in defining job templates, leveraging the similarity of a new job with historical information to estimate its runtime, and then simulate the behavior of the batch scheduling algorithm to derive the wait time of each job [19,20]. However, such a simulation-based approach is too compute-intensive to build an online estimator.

In this work, we apply Machine Learning (ML) techniques to both job and system features to determine into which of the predefined time ranges the wait time of a new job will fall. Moreover, all the aforementioned works consider HPC workloads where the size of a job, in terms of both number of cores/nodes and requested runtime, play an important role in job wait time. Indeed, the more cores a job requests, the harder it is to fit in a schedule, hence the longer it may wait. Moreover, long jobs are bad candidates for backfill. Here, we consider a HTC workload made of a vast majority of single-core jobs scheduled with no backfill. Then, the causes of job wait time are completely different in our case.

3   Wait Time Distribution and Intuitive Causes

To understand the causes of job wait time, we analyze the workload executed on the resources of the CC-IN2P3 over 23 weeks from Jun. 25, 2018 to Dec. 2,

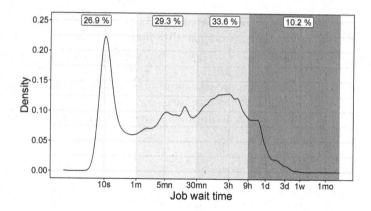

Fig. 1. Probability density function of local job wait time.

2018. This corresponds to a stable period during which nearly 35,000 cores were made available to the users. This workload is composed of 7,749,500 *Grid* jobs and 5,748,922 *Local* jobs, for a total of 13,498,422 jobs. Hereafter we focus only on the Local jobs, as they experience larger wait times than Grid jobs [2].

Figure 1 shows the Probability Density Function (PDF) of Local job wait time. For the sake of readability, we used a logarithmic scale on the x-axis and highlighted four regions. The labels at the top of the graph show the respective percentage of jobs in each region.

The leftmost region corresponds to jobs that start almost right after their submission, i.e., within a minute. It represents more than one fourth of the total workload. For these jobs, and the users who submitted them, the Quality of Service is very good. Jobs in the second to left region experience a wait time between 1 and 30 min, which can be seen as reasonable. Indeed, users are asked to submit jobs whose requested runtime is at least of one hour. These two regions combined amount for 56.2% of the submitted Local jobs.

What really motivates this work are the remaining two regions. We can see on Fig. 1 that the job wait time of about one third of the workload spans from 30 min to 9 h following a lognormal distribution. Then, it is hardly possible for users whose jobs fall into this category to guess when they will start. However, having an estimation of this delay may have a direct impact on their working behavior [17]. If a user knows that their job will start within the next hour, and also knows for how long this job will last, they may want to wait for the job completion before submitting other jobs. Conversely, if the user knows the job will not start before several hours, they can proceed with other activities and come back the next day to get the results. For the jobs in the last category, which amount for 10% of the workload, a wait time of more than nine hours corresponds to a poor Quality of Service experienced by the users.

The Quality of Service experienced by the users, i.e., the job *response time*, does not only depend on how much time the job waits but also on its execution time. For instance, a wait time of two hours does not have the same impact whether the job lasts for one hour or one day. The *bounded slowdown* metric [5] captures this impact of job wait time on the response time. Using a bound on job execution time of 10 min, this metric indicates that 25% of the jobs in the third (resp. fourth) region wait between 3.2 and 8.5 (resp. 10.6 and 58.6) times their execution times. By further analyzing the distribution of job execution time, we observed that more than half of the jobs in these two regions run for less than 3 h, and nearly 75% complete in less than 6 h. Job wait time is thus not only unpredictable but can also be highly detrimental to users.

To understand which of the many different and entangled factors and configurations parameters can cause large job wait times, we propose to answer to the four following basic questions:

Who Submits the Job? Each entry in the logs of the batch system corresponds to a job and comprises two fields that allow us to identify which *user* from which *user group* is submitting a job: `owner` and `group`. According to the resource allocation policy of the CC-IN2P3 and the pledges made by the scientific collaborations for the year [1], each user group is allocated a *share* of the total available computing power proportional to its needs. This defines a consumption objective used by the job scheduler to compute its fair-share schedule.

What is the Job Requesting? A job is mainly characterized by the *time* the user estimates it will run and the *memory* it will need. These quantities are expressed at submission time by setting *hard* or *soft* limits through flags provided by the batch system. If a job hits a hard limit, it is killed and its results are lost. Using a soft limit allows the job to catch a signal before being killed, and thus to react accordingly. Time can be expressed as an expected runtime (i.e., `s_rt` and `h_rt` flags) or CPU time (i.e., `s_cpu` and `h_cpu` flags), both expressed in seconds. Memory can be expressed as a resident set size (i.e., `s_rss` and `h_rss` flags) or virtual memory size (i.e., `s_vmem` and `h_vmem` flags), both in bytes. If no value is given for these flags, default values depending on the submission queues are applied. Users can also specify the number of cores, or *slots* in the UGE terminology, and whether the job requires a specific resource, e.g., access to a given storage subsystem, database, or licensed software. To prevent the saturation of these critical resources or the violation of licenses, the batch administrators set up several limits as *Resource Quota Sets* (RQSs). These limits can be applied globally or on a per group basis and change over time.

When is the Job Submitted? The batch system logs submission times as timestamps from which the *hour* and *day* of submission can easily be derived.

Where is the Job Submitted? During the considered time period, jobs could be submitted to 6 different scheduling queues that mainly differ by maximum allowed duration, both in terms of runtime and CPU time, available memory and scratch disk space per job, and the type of jobs allowed to enter the queue, i.e., single- or multi-core. The bulk of the Local jobs is directed to the generic `long` queue while the others can accommodate jobs with special needs. This queue can access to almost all the available cores but has a rather low priority. By analyzing all this information we identify some *intuitive causes* of why a job

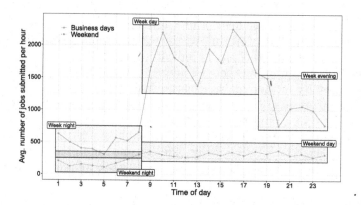

Fig. 2. Daily submission rate for local jobs on business days or during the weekend.

would wait more than another that we detail hereafter. The first two identified causes come from when a job is submitted.

3.1 Submission Period

Figure 2 shows the daily submission rate for Local jobs. We distinguish five different periods in this graph. First, there are much less submissions during the weekend than over the rest of the week, with a slight day/night difference. Then, on business days, e.g., Monday to Friday, we clearly see more submissions during the working hours than over night. We also distinguish a "*Week evening*" period whose submission rate is between those of the working hours and the night. Such a submission pattern is classical and representative of most HTC and HPC centers. As more concurrent job submissions obviously lead to more competition for resources, we can suppose that a job submitted during a week day is likely to wait more than a job submitted in around midnight or on a Sunday morning.

3.2 Number of Pending Jobs in Queue

The number of jobs already waiting in queues can also influence job wait time. To illustrate this, we focus in Fig. 3 on a typical 5-day period. The top graph shows the evolution of the total number of pending slot requests while the bottom graph displays how many jobs are waiting for a certain amount of time in each period. For the sake of readability, we sampled the logs using a 3-hour range, but a more detailed sampling confirmed our observations.

We can see two consequences of an increase of the number of pending jobs on job wait time. First, when a burst of submission occurs in the long queue, e.g., on Monday between 8 and 9 AM or on Wednesday around noon, we observe a dramatic increase of job wait time with many jobs waiting for more than twelve hours. Second, when a burst of submission occurs in another queue, e.g., on Tuesday around noon, we also observe an increase of the number of jobs waiting

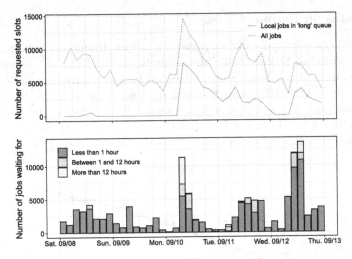

Fig. 3. Evolution of the number of requested slots by jobs waiting in queue (top). Distribution of wait time for local jobs in each 3-h period (bottom).

between one and twelve hours. This can be explained by the fact that the burst happens in a queue of higher priority which causes delays for a large fraction of the jobs submitted to the less priority long queue. This focus outlines the importance of taking the *system state* into account at the queue and global levels when estimating job wait time.

3.3   Share Consumption

The concept of *shares* is at the core of the scheduling algorithm ran by UGE. First, it allows the batch system to give higher priorities to jobs submitted by user groups with bigger needs. With nearly 80 user groups to serve, whose size and needs are very heterogeneous, the allocated shares cover a wide range of values with differences up to two orders of magnitude between some groups. Then, a job submitted by a user from a small group with a small share is likely to wait more than a similar job from another larger group with a bigger share.

The scheduling algorithm also takes into account the recent resource consumption, over a sliding time window, of the different groups. If a user group starts to submit jobs after a period of inactivity, these jobs will get a priority boost. Conversely, a group that consumed a lot of resources over a short period of time will get some priority penalty. Finally, if a group consumed all its allocated share, its jobs will be executed if and only if there are still some resources available once jobs from the other groups are scheduled. Our job wait time estimator thus has to consider the initial share allocated to a group, which fraction of it has already been consumed, and the recent resource consumption of the group to estimate whether a job will be delayed or not.

3.4   Quotas on Resource Usage

A job can also see its wait time increase, sometimes dramatically, because of the different quotas, or RQSs, set by the administrators of the batch system. If a RQS is violated, at any level, jobs are blocked in queue until the quota violation is solved. We illustrate the impact of such quotas on job wait time in Fig. 4 with the extreme case of a single user who submitted more than 2,000 jobs in one minute on Nov. 14, 2018 at 6:20PM. The vertical line shows the submission burst while each black segment represents the execution of a single job.

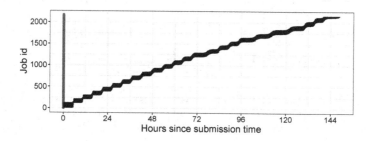

Fig. 4. Execution span of jobs submitted by a single user limited by a stringent RQS. The verticle line shows the submission burst and each black segment represents the execution of a job.

We can see that all the submitted jobs cannot start at once, but are executed by batches of 90 jobs, which corresponds to the limit applied to the group of this user on how many jobs requesting access to a specific storage subsystem can run concurrently. The direct consequence of this stringent quota (which was later increased and eventually removed) is that the last jobs wait for nearly six days before starting their execution. We can conclude from this example that quota violations must be taken into account by our estimator.

3.5   Resource Requests

Finally, the study of the related work presented in Sect. 2 showed that the resource requests made by a job, in terms of runtime, number of cores, or memory, can have a great impact on job wait time. However, this observation is valid for HPC systems where jobs can have different shapes and backfill mechanisms are implemented by the batch system. In the specific context of HTC datacenters such as CC-IN2P3, the vast majority of the jobs are single-core. Then, the produced schedule is almost free of idle times which makes backfilling meaningless. Moreover, the queue configuration neither reflects nor leverages the fact that 14% of the jobs express a runtime of less than 6 h and 41% of less than 24 h. Time and memory requests should nevertheless be taken into account but their impact is expected to be smaller than for traditional HPC workloads.

4 Job Features Correlation Analysis

In the previous section we identified a set of intuitive causes of job wait time. To confirm them, we extracted a set of job and system features related to these causes from the information available in the logs and conducted a detailed pairwise correlation analysis of these features. This allowed us to merge the eight metrics related to the requested time and memory into only two features. We also replaced the day and hour of submission features by the five categories from Fig. 2 (i.e., week day, week evening, week night, weekend day, and weekend night). Finally, we made a Primary Component Analysis (PCA) on eleven features describing the system state. This analysis allows us to keep 99.98% of the observed variance with only four generated features. We verified that these modifications did not imply an important loss of information or accuracy. The obtained reduced set of features that directly derive of our analysis of the intuitive causes of job wait time is summarized in Table 1. We will use them to design the learning-based job wait time estimators detailed in the next section.

4.1 Spearman's Rank Correlation of Numerical Features

To determine the influence of each of our numerical job and systems features, we compute their respective correlation with job wait time. As the distribution of several of these features is heavy-tailed or comprises outliers, we favor the Spearman's rank correlation over the traditional Pearson correlation. Moreover, this allows us to detect monotonic relationships beyond simple linear relationships. In our case, the values of each pair of features X and Y are converted to ranks r_X and r_y and the Spearman correlation coefficient ρ is computed as the covariance of the rank variables divided by the product of their standard deviations. Figure 5 shows the obtained coefficients for the nine numerical job and system features.

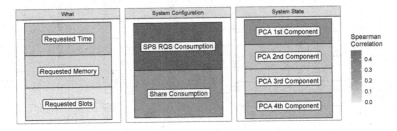

Fig. 5. Spearman correlation of numerical features with job wait time.

As expected, the job resource requests have almost no influence on job wait time in HTC datacenters. Conversely, the most impacting features are the system state and the current RQS and share consumption of the job owner's group. The other features have only a moderate impact.

Table 1. List of job and system features derived from the batch system logs and the analysis of intuitive causes.

	Name	Description	Transformation	Type
Who	Job owner	Name of the user who submitted the job	Anonymization	Categorical
	User group	Group to which the job owner belongs	Anonymization	Categorical
What	Requested number of slots	Number of cores/slots needed by the job	None	Numerical
	Requested storage subsystem	Job needs access to SPS, HPSS, or iRODS	None	Boolean
	Requested time	Maximum CPU time ([s, h]_cpu+) or runtime ([s, h]_rt) Default to the queue limits when no value is specified	Fusion	Numerical
	Requested memory	Maximum resident ([s, h]_rss) or virtual ([s, h]_vmem) memory. Default to the queue limits when no value is specified.	Fusion	Numerical
When	Submission Period	Period when the job is submitted (i.e., week {day, evening, night} and weekend {day, night})	Computed	Categorical
Where	Queue name	Name of the submission queue	None	Categorical
System configuration	Share consumption	Current relative resource consumption of the user group at the submission time of the job	Computation	Numerical
	RQS Consumption	Current consumption of the Resource Quota Set of the user group at the submission time of the job	Computation	Numerical
System State	PCA components	Number of jobs currently waiting to be executed or running at *group*, *queue*, and *global* levels	PCA	Numerical

4.2   Regression-Based Correlation for All Features

We propose to determine the impact of the additional categorical and boolean features (i.e., job owner, user group, requested storage, submission period, and queue name), by computing their correlations with job wait time with a regression tree. Indeed, Pearson and Spearman correlation computation methods are respectively based on linear and isotonic regressions. The regression method consists in splitting our data set and trying to maximize the variance between the subsets. It is particularly suited for categorical variables and can also handle the other numerical features. Figure 6 presents the obtained correlation values with a regression tree of depth eight.

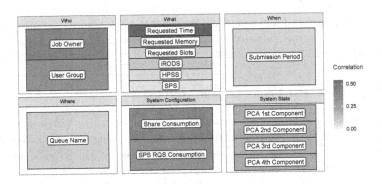

Fig. 6. Correlations of all features with job wait time.

Among the categorical features, the most influential category is related to who submitted the job. This is rather logical as the numerical feature with the highest Spearman's rank correlation is the RQS consumption that defines the most stringent constraints at group level.

A more surprising result is that *Requested Time* becomes the most influential feature according to this second correlation computation method, while its Spearman's rank correlation was pretty low. This can be explained by the limited number of requested time values that are provided by users. Indeed, each value corresponds to a small set of well-defined jobs always submitted by the same users with the same submission habits. Therefore, these are more likely to wait for similar amounts of time. A known drawback of this correlation computation method is that the algorithm learns on the same data it tries to predict. This causes an over-fitting of the regression which in turn leads to a good correlation factor for this feature. This is even amplified by users who do not indicate any particular requested time. In that case, the queue limits are used as default value and this information thus also includes knowledge about the submission queue and its relative priority. The observed high correlation between *Requested Time* and *Job Wait Time* may thus be artificial. However, cautiously using it in the training of our estimators can still be beneficial. While it could cause similar biases for estimators based on a decision tree, this can also allow us to detect recurring behaviors related to certain users and leverage this knowledge to improve the prediction accuracy. This can be seen as a bad practice from a Machine Learning theory point of view but the practical interest cannot be neglected.

5   Learning-Based Job Wait Time Estimators

This section presents how we apply Machine Learning techniques to pre-processed batch system logs to provide users with an estimation of the time their jobs will wait when they submit them. We first introduce the form taken by this estimation and the performance metrics used to estimate its quality in Sect. 5.1. Then we detail and discuss in Sect. 5.2 the ML algorithms considered to produce this estimation, while the obtained experimental results are presented in Sect. 5.3.

5.1   Objectives and Performance Metrics

Our first objective is to predict the time a job will wait as a single value based on the features of the newly submitted job and a training on a set of previously executed jobs for whom the wait time is known. However, this kind of estimation can quickly become inaccurate for several reasons. As shown in Fig. 1, about 56% of the jobs in the considered workload start less than 30 min after their submission and nearly 30% wait only for a few seconds. For such *quick starter* jobs [11] an estimation can easily be largely off without giving a useful information to the user. Moreover, the large number of features describing a job and the diversity of experienced wait times for jobs with similar features make it difficult to obtain a very accurate estimation. However, most users do not need an exact estimation of job wait time but would rather be interested in knowing a time range in which they can expect to see their job start. Then, we define in Table 2 eight wait time ranges. We also show the percentage of Local jobs belonging to each of these ranges in the original workload.

Table 2. Target wait time ranges.

Class	Wait Time Range	Workload fraction
1	Less than 30 minutes	56.21%
2	30 minutes to 2 hours	15.96%
3	2 hours to 4 hours	8.88%
4	4 hours to 6 hours	4.85%
5	6 hours to 9 hours	3.90%
6	9 hours to 12 hours	2.44%
7	12 hours to 24 hours	5.14%
8	more than 24 hours	2.61%

The first and dominant range corresponds to the fusion of the two leftmost regions of Fig. 1. Ranges 2 to 5 allow us to provide users whose jobs fall in the third region (30 min to 9 h) with a more accurate estimation of the job wait time. Ranges 6 to 8 have the same purpose for jobs in the rightmost region that wait for more than nine hours.

To select the candidate ML algorithms to build our job wait time estimator, we rely on two complementary performance metrics. The *learning time* measures the time taken by an algorithm to process the entire set of historical data and build its prediction model. It mainly depends on the complexity of the algorithm itself and the size of the input data set. As the learning phase has to be done periodically to ensure keeping a good predictive power, this learning time has to remain reasonable. Then, we arbitrarily decided to set an upper limit to twenty four hours and discard candidate algorithms that need more time to learn. The *prediction time* is the time needed by an algorithm to infer the wait time of a newly submitted job. As we aim at returning the produced estimation to the user right after the submission of a job, we will favor the fastest algorithms and discard those taking more than two minutes to return an estimation.

To evaluate how close the predictions of the job wait time are to the observed values and be able to compare the accuracy of the considered ML algorithms we rely on the classical *Absolute Percentage Error* (APE) metric defined as $100 \times \frac{|y_i - \hat{y}_i|}{y_i}$ for $i \in 1, \ldots, n$ jobs, where y_i and $\hat{y}_i$ are the logged and predicted wait time of job i. However, this metric is known to be very sensitive to small logged data and to produce many outliers, so we will focus on the median and inter-quartile range of the distribution of this metric.

To evaluate the accuracy of the classification in wait time ranges, we analyze the confusion matrices produced by the different ML algorithms. A confusion matrix C is defined such that $C_{i,j}$ is the number of jobs whose wait time is known to be in range i and predicted to be in range j. We not only measure the percentage of jobs classified in the right range or in an adjacent range, but also the capacity of the algorithm to class jobs in every available ranges.

5.2   Job Wait Time Estimators

Our two objectives correspond to two classical applications of *Supervised Learning*. Estimating the exact time a newly submitted job will wait is a *regression* problem while determining to which wait time range it will belong is a typical *classification* problem. Multiple ML algorithms can be used to solve each of these two problems. They mainly differ from the tradeoff made between the time to produce a result and the accuracy of that result. In addition to the constraints on the learning and prediction times expressed in the previous section, the size of our data set raises another constraint on the amount of memory needed to perform the regression. This discards some methods such as the Logistic and Multivariate regression methods or the Least Absolute Shrinkage and Selection Operator (LASSO) [22] that would require several Terabytes of memory.

We selected four regression-based algorithms among the implementations made available by the Scikit-learn toolkit [16] to estimate the wait time of a newly submitted job. The *linear regression* method is very fast to train and to return an estimation. However, it can be inaccurate when the relationship between features is not linear, which is the case for our data set. The *Decision Tree regression* [14] is a recursive partitioning method which is also fast but better handles data variability and categorical features. However, the depth of the tree has to be carefully chosen: if too shallow, the estimation will be inaccurate, while if too deep, there is a risk of data over-fitting. We also consider two ensemble learning methods which consist in combining several weak learners to achieve a better predictive performance. *AdaBoost* [7] starts by assigning an equal weight to the training data and computes a first probability distribution. It then iteratively boosts the weight of the mis-predicted instances to improve the accuracy of the final estimation. However, this method is known to be sensitive to noisy data and outliers. The *Bagging* [3] method consists in generating multiple training sets by uniform sampling with replacement of the initial data. Then, a weak learner is fitted for each of these sets and their results are aggregated to produce the final estimation. For both ensemble methods, we use a decision tree of variable depth as weak learner and split the training set into 50 subsets.

To solve our classification problem in wait time ranges, we follow two different approaches. The former consists in simply applying a classical classification algorithm to directly assign jobs in the different ranges from Table 2, while in the latter we first solve the regression problem of estimating the exact wait time of a job and then straightforwardly derive the wait time range for the job. We rely on the same families of algorithms as for solving the regression problem, i.e., Decision Tree, AdaBoost, and Bagging, but replace the basic Linear Regression method by a simple probabilistic classifier, i.e., Naive Bayes. For the Ensemble methods we use a Decision Tree classifier of variable depth as base estimator.

5.3 Experimental Evaluation

To evaluate the quality of a ML algorithm, the common approach is to split the initial data set into two parts. First, the algorithm has to be *trained* on a large fraction of the data set, typically 80%. Second, the *evaluation* of the performance of the algorithm is done on the remaining 20%. As our data are time-ordered, we cannot randomly pick jobs to build these two subsets. Indeed, when a new job enters the system, information is available only for jobs that have been *completed before* its submission. Consequently, our training set corresponds to the first 80% of the logs and the evaluation is done on the last 20%.

Leaning and Prediction Time. We start by comparing in Fig. 7 the learning and prediction times of the candidate ML algorithms. For the Decision Tree and Ensemble methods, we consider different tree depths, while we have a single value for the Linear Regression and Naive Bayes approaches. We also distinguish the use of these algorithms to solve our regression and direct classification problems. These timings were obtained on one of the servers of the CC-IN2P3 equipped with a 40-cores Intel Xeon Silver 4114 CPU running at 2.20 GHz.

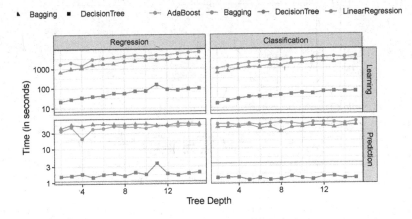

Fig. 7. Learning and prediction times of the different ML algorithms.

We can see that the Ensemble methods require much more time to be trained and produce an estimation than the basic regression and classification methods. The use of a deep Decision Tree is a good compromise with a training time of less than two minutes and only a few seconds to return a prediction.

Accuracy of Algorithms for the Regression Problem. To evaluate the accuracy of the four ML algorithms used to solve the regression problem, we first have to determine what is the best tree depth for three of them. Figure 8 shows the evolution of the median Absolute Percentage Error with the depth of the tree. The dashed line corresponds to the accuracy of the Linear Regression. As APE leads to very large values for very short waiting times, the presented

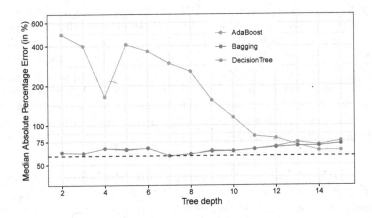

Fig. 8. Evolution of the Median Absolute Percentage Error with tree depth for jobs waiting for more than 30 min. The dashed line corresponds to the Median APE of the Linear Regression method.

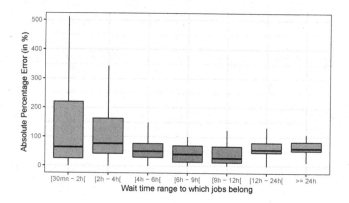

Fig. 9. Distribution of the Absolute Percentage Error achieved by a Decision Tree Regressor of depth 7 for jobs in different wait time ranges.

medians have been computed only for the jobs that waited for more than 30 min, i.e., about half of the initial workload.

The accuracy achieved by the AdaBoost algorithm is much worse than those of the others, because of its sensitivity to variable and noisy data. The Bagging and Decision Tree algorithms have very close accuracy and evolution along with the tree depth, but Decision Tree is much faster. We also see that the basic Linear Regression is on par with the more complex algorithms. However, we also measured the Absolute Error (in seconds) for the short-waiting jobs. We observed similar trends as in Fig. 8 for all algorithms but also a clear advantage of Decision Tree (median of 1h12 at depth 7) over Linear Regression (median of 2h20). Based on these results, we select a *Decision Tree Regressor of depth 7* as our regression-based job wait time estimator.

We complete this evaluation of the accuracy of the regression-based approach by analyzing the distribution of the APE in the different wait time ranges we target for the classification problem. Figure 9 shows this distribution for the selected Decision Tree Regressor of depth 7. We can see that the median APE is consistent across the different ranges and remains in the reasonable range of [26.8%; 76.6%]. We also see that the values of the third quartile and top whisker (i.e., 1.5 the inter-quartile range from the third quartile) tend to decrease as the job wait time grows. This means that the quality of the prediction becomes slightly better for long job wait times, i.e., where users need to know the most that they have to expect long delays.

Accuracy of Algorithms for the Classification Problem. Table 3 evaluates the accuracy of the four direct classification methods we consider and that of the alternate approach that first solves a regression problem and then classifies the obtained predictions in wait time ranges. The accuracy is measured as the percentage of jobs that are classified either in the correct time range or in a directly adjacent one and the sum of these two values.

Table 3. Accuracy of the different classification algorithms.

Method	Correct	Adjacent	Combined
Naive Bayes	44.57%	19.55%	64.12%
Ada Boost (Depth 11)	44.81%	29.59%	74.40%
Decision Tree (Depth 9)	49.73%	19.55%	75.19%
Bagging (Depth 9)	47.08%	28.28%	75,36%
Reg. + Clas. (Depth 8)	22.26%	54.65%	76.92%

There is no clear winner among the four direct classifiers, with a difference of 5.16% of jobs classified in the right time range between the best (Decision Tree) and worst (Naive Bayes) algorithms. If we add the jobs classified in a directly adjacent time range, the Bagging algorithm becomes slightly better than the Decision Tree. The alternate approach (Reg. + Clas.) leads to more mixed results. It classes much less jobs in the correct time range but achieves the best percentage overall when including the adjacent ranges. However, these coarse grain results hide some important characteristics of the produced classifications. To better assess the respective quality of each algorithm, we study the confusion matrices for the different algorithms.

Figures 10 shows the confusion matrix for the Naive Bayes classifier and reads as follows. The tile on the sixth column of the third row indicates the percentage of jobs whose *measured* wait time was between 2 and 4 h (third range) that have been classified in the [9 h–12 h[time range (sixth range). Then, the sum of the tiles on each row is 100%. The panel on the right of the confusion matrix indicates for each row the percentage of jobs that have been classified in the correct range or in an immediately adjacent one.

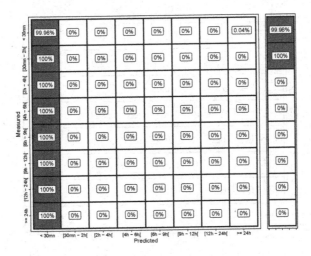

Fig. 10. Confusion matrix of the Naive Bayes classifier.

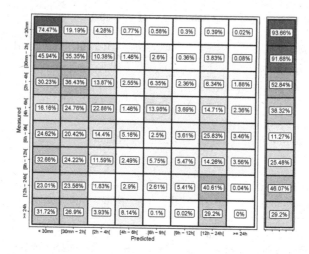

Fig. 11. Confusion matrix of the AdaBoost classifier.

We can see that almost all the jobs are classified in the first time range (i.e., less than 30 mn). Then, the apparent good results of this method in Table 3 actually mean that Naive Bayes correctly classifies only jobs in that first range, which are dominant in our test set, but fails for all the jobs in other time ranges.

Figure 11 shows that while not being as binary as Naive Bayes, the AdaBoost classifier suffers from a similar bias and tends to classify too many jobs in one of the first two ranges (i.e., less than 30 mn and from 30 mn to 2 h). In other words, this methods largely underestimates the wait time for most of the jobs. Then, the percentage of jobs classified in the right time range or an adjacent one clearly drops as soon as jobs wait for more than two hours.

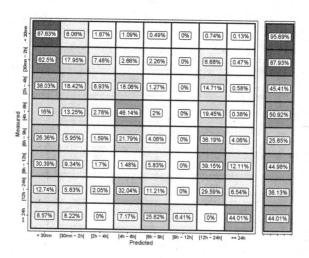

Fig. 12. Confusion matrix of the Decision Tree classifier at depth 9.

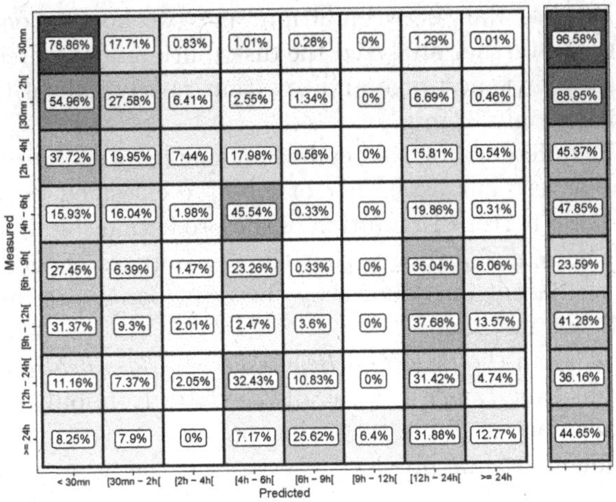

Measured \ Predicted	<30mn	[30mn–2h[	[2h–4h[	[4h–6h[	[6h–9h[	[9h–12h[	[12h–24h[	>=24h	
<30mn	78.86%	17.71%	0.83%	1.01%	0.28%	0%	1.29%	0.01%	96.58%
[30mn–2h[	54.96%	27.58%	6.41%	2.55%	1.34%	0%	6.69%	0.46%	88.95%
[2h–4h[	37.72%	19.95%	7.44%	17.98%	0.56%	0%	15.81%	0.54%	45.37%
[4h–6h[	15.93%	16.04%	1.98%	45.54%	0.33%	0%	19.86%	0.31%	47.85%
[6h–9h[	27.45%	6.39%	1.47%	23.26%	0.33%	0%	35.04%	6.06%	23.59%
[9h–12h[	31.37%	9.3%	2.01%	2.47%	3.6%	0%	37.68%	13.57%	41.28%
[12h–24h[	11.16%	7.37%	2.05%	32.43%	10.83%	0%	31.42%	4.74%	36.16%
>=24h	8.25%	7.9%	0%	7.17%	25.62%	6.4%	31.88%	12.77%	44.65%

Fig. 13. Confusion matrix of the Bagging classifier at depth 9.

The first two columns of the confusion matrices for the Decision Tree (Fig. 12) and Bagging (Fig. 13) classifiers also show that they greatly underestimate the wait time of many jobs. However, they lead to slightly better predictions than AdaBoost as they both able to correctly classify more jobs in the fourth (4 to 6 h) and eighth (more than 24 h) ranges.

The last confusion matrix shown in Fig. 14 is that obtained for when we classify the predictions made by a Decision Tree Regressor of depth 8. First, it explains why this approach leads to only 22.26% of correct predictions overall, while the direct classifiers are above 44%. This is mainly caused by the results for the shortest time range. Most of the jobs that actually waited for less than

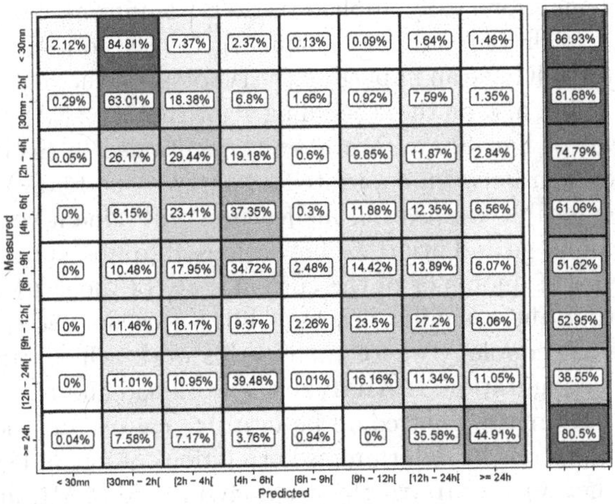

Measured \ Predicted	<30mn	[30mn–2h[	[2h–4h[	[4h–6h[	[6h–9h[	[9h–12h[	[12h–24h[	>=24h	
<30mn	2.12%	84.81%	7.37%	2.37%	0.13%	0.09%	1.64%	1.46%	86.93%
[30mn–2h[	0.29%	63.01%	18.38%	6.8%	1.66%	0.92%	7.59%	1.35%	81.68%
[2h–4h[	0.05%	26.17%	29.44%	19.18%	0.6%	9.85%	11.87%	2.84%	74.79%
[4h–6h[	0%	8.15%	23.41%	37.35%	0.3%	11.88%	12.35%	6.56%	61.06%
[6h–9h[	0%	10.48%	17.95%	34.72%	2.48%	14.42%	13.89%	6.07%	51.62%
[9h–12h[	0%	11.46%	18.17%	9.37%	2.26%	23.5%	27.2%	8.06%	52.95%
[12h–24h[	0%	11.01%	10.95%	39.48%	0.01%	16.16%	11.34%	11.05%	38.55%
>=24h	0.04%	7.58%	7.17%	3.76%	0.94%	0%	35.58%	44.91%	80.5%

Fig. 14. Confusion matrix of the Regression + Classification approach.

30 min are predicted to wait between 30 min and two hours, hence classified in the second range. We further analyzed the distribution of the predicted job wait time in that particular time range and saw that nearly half of these jobs were predicted to wait for only 38 min.

Another main difference of this confusion matrix with those of the direct classifiers is that a very small number of jobs are classified in the first range. Instead, we observe a better distribution of the predictions along the diagonal of the matrix. A direct consequence is that the percentages of jobs in the correct time range or an adjacent one, shown by the right panel, are much better and more stable with this method.

To summarize, when the proposed *Regression + Classification* approach fails to predict the right time range, it generally deviates from only one class, hence the best overall accuracy in Table 3. We thus propose to use this original method to implement a job wait time prediction service for the users of the CC-IN2P3.

6   Applicability to Other Workloads

The present work is tightly coupled to a specific workload processed at a specific computing center. In this section we discuss the legitimate question of whether the proposed methodology can be transposed to another computing center.

The IN2P3 Computing Center is a large scale *High Throughput Computing Center* implementing a *Fair-share* scheduling algorithm configured with *scheduling queues, resource quotas,* and *priorities* that processes a workload composed of a vast majority of *single-core* jobs with a *utilization* close to 100%. Note that such a settings is at least representative of the twelve other large computing centers worldwide involved in the processing of the data produced by the LHC and the rest of the associated computing grid. This represents hundreds of smaller scale computing centers dealing with similar workloads and sharing similar configurations of their infrastructures and working habits. The proposed study can thus be rather straightforwardly applied to these computing centers.

Going from a High Throughput Computing Center to a High Performance Computing Center will have an impact on the typology of the submitted jobs, i.e., more parallel jobs, but also on the scheduling algorithm, i.e., EASY/Conservative backfilling instead of Fair-Share. We already mentioned in Sect. 4 that it will change the correlation between associated resource requests and job wait time, hence impact the results. However, some features will remain very similar, such as the difference of usage and priorities between user groups, submission patterns [6], or the influence of quotas or of the current state of the system.

We believe that these similarities and differences do not compromise the soundness of the methodology we followed in this work, which can be applied to any workload or configuration: i) **Analyze** the workload and **review** the system configuration; ii) **Identify** what could be intuitive causes for a job to wait; iii) **Confirm** these intuitions by determining correlations of job and system features with job wait time; iv) **Compare** the accuracy of several ML algorithms; and v) **Question** the obtained results by looking at them from different angles.

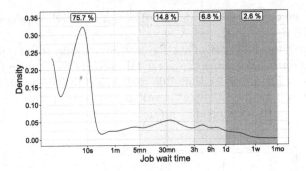

Fig. 15. Probability Density Function of job wait time in the KIT FH2 workload.

To illustrate this, we applied our methodology to one of the workloads in the Parallel Workloads Archive [6]. We selected the KIT FH2 workload that is composed of 114,355 jobs submitted by 166 distinct users on 24,048 cores over a two-year period. This workload is described in the Standard Workload Format (SWF), which means that several features in Table 1, i.e., requested storage subsystem and memory and share and RQS consumption, are not available.

The absence of these features, some of them being among the most impacting on job wait time in our study, is not the only difference between our workload and the KIT FH2 data. If we look at the distribution of the job wait time shown in Fig. 15, we see that the fraction of jobs that start their execution less than five minutes after their submission is much greater (75%). This is easily easily explained by the lower average resource utilization of the resources in the KIT FH2 workload (60.34% vs. 93.68%). The rest of the distribution is also different, which led us to redefine the first target wait time ranges for the resolution of the classification problem (less than 5 min, 5 to 30 min, 30 min to one hour, 1 to 2 h, 2 to 3 h, and 3 to 6 h).

Then, the job submission pattern is also different as illustrated by Fig. 16. First, there are more than a hundred times less (parallel) jobs submitted per

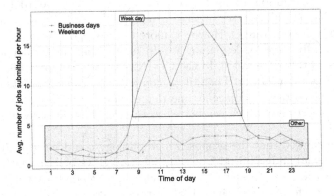

Fig. 16. Daily submission rate for the KIT FH2 workload.

hour. Second, we cannot clearly identify different submission periods except for the "Business days" period.

We prepared the KIT FH2 data for learning taking these differences into account but following the same experimental protocol to produce the confusion matrix shown in Fig. 17. Note that this matrix has one more time range than the ones generated for the CC-IN2P3 workload to better reflect the distribution of job wait time in this workload.

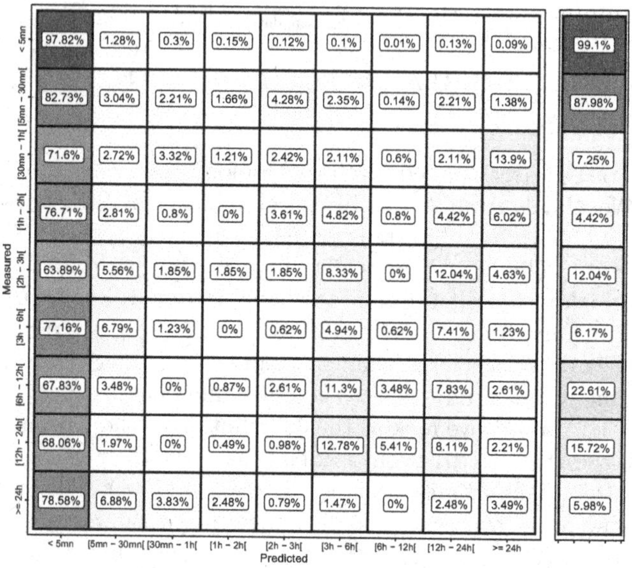

Measured \ Predicted	<5mn	[5mn–30mn]	[30mn–1h]	[1h–2h]	[2h–3h]	[3h–6h]	[6h–12h]	[12h–24h]	>=24h	
<5mn	97.82%	1.28%	0.3%	0.15%	0.12%	0.1%	0.01%	0.13%	0.09%	99.1%
[5mn–30mn]	82.73%	3.04%	2.21%	1.66%	4.28%	2.35%	0.14%	2.21%	1.38%	87.98%
[30mn–1h]	71.6%	2.72%	3.32%	1.21%	2.42%	2.11%	0.6%	2.11%	13.9%	7.25%
[1h–2h]	76.71%	2.81%	0.8%	0%	3.61%	4.82%	0.8%	4.42%	6.02%	4.42%
[2h–3h]	63.89%	5.56%	1.85%	1.85%	1.85%	8.33%	0%	12.04%	4.63%	12.04%
[3h–6h]	77.16%	6.79%	1.23%	0%	0.62%	4.94%	0.62%	7.41%	1.23%	6.17%
[6h–12h]	67.83%	3.48%	0%	0.87%	2.61%	11.3%	3.48%	7.83%	2.61%	22.61%
[12h–24h]	68.06%	1.97%	0%	0.49%	0.98%	12.78%	5.41%	8.11%	2.21%	15.72%
>=24h	78.58%	6.88%	3.83%	2.48%	0.79%	1.47%	0%	2.48%	3.49%	5.98%

Fig. 17. Confusion matrix of the Regression + Classification approach applied to the KIT FH2 workload.

At first glance, the results shown by this confusion matrix do not seem as convincing as those in Fig. 14 but closer to those achieved by the AdaBoost direct classifier in Fig. 11. Indeed, we observe a tendency to classify to many jobs in the first two wait time ranges. However, more than 80% of the jobs in KIT FH2 workload actually wait for less than 30 min before their execution starts, and thus belongs to this time range. In the CC-IN2P3 workload, only 56.21% of the jobs waited less than 30 min. Then, if we compute the same percentages of jobs classified in the correct or adjacent time ranges as in Table 3, we obtain 85.29% and 4.36% respectively, which is a better score than the best obtained result for the CC-IN2P3.

While we showed that the proposed methodology could be applied to a very different workload and still lead to promising results, we believe that the lack of important information about both the workload and the infrastructure severely impacted the performance of the ML algorithm. However, the missing information is usually available to batch system operator even though it is not exported when giving access to the job scheduling community to a workload. Then, to ensure the reproduction and further investigation of the presented results, as well as the adaptation of the proposed methodology to another context, we prepared an experimental artifact that comprises the anonymized batch logs and metadata, and all the data preparation scripts, calls to ML algorithms, and obtained results in a companion document [8].

7   Conclusions and Future Work

The Quality of Service experienced by users of a batch system mainly depends on the time submitted jobs wait before being executed. However, in High Throughput Computing datacenters whose batch system implements the Fair-Share scheduling algorithm, this job wait time can quickly become unpredictable and range from a few seconds to several hours, or even days in some pathological cases. Therefore, we proposed in this article to leverage Machine Learning techniques to provide users with an estimation of job wait time. To this end, we analyzed 23 weeks of logs of the batch system of the IN2P3 Computing Center, the main French academic HTC datacenter. First, we identified some intuitive causes of the job wait time and determined its formal correlation with sixteen job and system features. Then, we compared four Machine Learning algorithms to either determine an estimation of the wait time or a wait time range for each newly submitted job.

We found out that the best tradeoff between learning and prediction times and accuracy to solve the regression problem of estimating the job wait time was achieved by a *Decision Tree Regressor of depth seven*. It allows us to obtain consistent and relatively good estimations in only a few seconds, hence enabling a direct return to users at submission time. We also observed that the direct classification of jobs in wait time ranges led to imperfect results, with a severe underestimation of the wait time for a majority of jobs. The imbalance of the workload with more than 50% of *quick starter* jobs may be the main cause of the observed results by creating a bias in the training of the algorithm. However, we also showed that classifying the jobs thanks to a regression-based estimation of their wait time led to more promising results with nearly 77% of the jobs assigned in the right wait time range or in an immediately adjacent one.

As future work, we plan to refine our classification algorithms to account for the heterogeneity of the distribution of training jobs in the different time ranges. Thanks to an initial fast clustering of the training set, we should be able to derive a weighting scheme for the target classes and thus improve the quality of predictions. We also plan to design an original learning-based estimator that would leverage the expertise of both the batch system operators and members of user groups. The idea is to build on the set of intuitive causes identified in Sect. 3 to derive a new set of features on which to train the algorithms. For instance we could include more information about the facility internal policies (e.g., job boost after maintenance, or penalties for bad usage) or annual/seasonal patterns (e.g., paper or experiment deadlines). Finally, we will investigate the use of Deep Learning methods to solve this job wait time prediction problem.

On a more practical side, we plan to transfer the tools developed during this study to the team in charge of user support at CC-IN2P3. The objective is to integrate a new service letting users know how much time their jobs are likely to wait once submitted to the recently deployed user portal of the computing center. As part of this effort, we also aim at determining the minimal size of the training set that would allow us to obtain accurate enough results. Indeed, the training of the ML algorithms has to be done again periodically to account for variations in the workload or changes of the infrastructure. Reducing the size of the training set will reduce the onus on the support team and allow for better reactivity. Finally, we aim at providing users with some feedback on their submission habits in order to help them reduce the wait time of their jobs.

Acknowledgments. The authors would like to thank Wataru Takase and his colleagues from the Japanese High Energy Accelerator Research Organization (KEK) for providing the initial motivation for this work.

References

1. Azevedo, F., Gombert, L., Suter, F.: Reducing the human-in-the-loop component of the scheduling of large HTC workloads. In: Klusáček, D., Cirne, W., Desai, N. (eds.) JSSPP 2018. LNCS, vol. 11332, pp. 39–60. Springer, Cham (2018). https://doi.org/10.1007/978-3-030-10632-4_3
2. Azevedo, F., Klusáček, D., Suter, F.: Improving fairness in a large scale HTC system through workload analysis and simulation. In: Yahyapour, R. (ed.) Euro-Par 2019. LNCS, vol. 11725, pp. 129–141. Springer, Cham (2019). https://doi.org/10.1007/978-3-030-29400-7_10
3. Breiman, L.: Stacked regressions. Mach. Learn. **24**(1), 49–64 (1996). https://doi.org/10.1007/BF00117832
4. Brevik, J., Nurmi, D., Wolski, R.: Predicting bounds on queuing delay for batch-scheduled parallel machines. In: Proceedings of the ACM SIGPLAN Symposium on Principles and Practice of Parallel Programming (PPOPP), New York, NY, pp. 110–118, March 2006. https://doi.org/10.1145/1122971.1122989
5. Feitelson, D.G.: Metrics for parallel job scheduling and their convergence. In: Feitelson, D.G., Rudolph, L. (eds.) JSSPP 2001. LNCS, vol. 2221, pp. 188–205. Springer, Heidelberg (2001). https://doi.org/10.1007/3-540-45540-X_11
6. Feitelson, D., Tsafrir, D., Krakov, D.: Experience with using the parallel workloads archive. J. Parallel Distri. Comput. **74**(10), 2967–2982 (2014)
7. Freund, Y., Schapire, R.: A Decision-Theoretic Generalization of On-Line Learning and an Application to Boosting. J. Comput. Syst. Sci. **55**(1), 119–139 (1997). https://doi.org/10.1006/jcss.1997.1504
8. Gombert, L., Suter, F.: Companion of the "learning-based approaches to estimate job wait time in HTC datacenters" article (2021). https://doi.org/10.6084/m9.figshare.13913912
9. Jancauskas, V., Piontek, T., Kopta, P., Bosak, B.: Predicting queue wait time probabilities for multi-scale computing. Philos. Trans. Roy. Soc. A **377**(2142) (2019). https://doi.org/10.1098/rsta.2018.0151
10. Kay, J., Lauder, P.: A fair share scheduler. Commun. ACM **31**(1), 44–55 (1988)

11. Kumar, R., Vadhiyar, S.: Prediction of queue waiting times for metascheduling on parallel batch systems. In: Cirne, W., Desai, N. (eds.) JSSPP 2014. LNCS, vol. 8828, pp. 108–128. Springer, Cham (2015). https://doi.org/10.1007/978-3-319-15789-4_7

12. Li, H., Chen, J., Tao, Y., Groep, D., Wolters, L.: Improving a local learning technique for QueueWait time predictions. In: Proceedings of the Sixth IEEE International Symposium on Cluster Computing and the Grid (CCGrid), Singapore, pp. 335–342, May 2006.https://doi.org/10.1109/CCGRID.2006.57

13. Li, H., Groep, D., Wolters, L.: Efficient response time predictions by exploiting application and resource state similarities. In: Proceedings of of the 6th IEEE/ACM International Conference on Grid Computing (GRID), Seattle, WA, pp. 234–241, November 2005. https://doi.org/10.1109/GRID.2005.1542747

14. Loh, W.Y.: Classification and regression trees. Wiley Interdisc. Rev.: Data Min. Knowl. Discov. 1, 14–23 (2011). https://doi.org/10.1002/widm.8

15. Mu'alem, A., Feitelson, D.: Utilization, predictability, workloads, and user runtime estimates in scheduling the IBM SP2 with backfilling. IEEE TPDS 12(6), 529–543 (2001)

16. Pedregosa, F., et al.: Scikit-learn: machine learning in Python. J. Mach. Learn. Res. 12, 2825–2830 (2011)

17. Schlagkamp, S., Ferreira da Silva, R., Allcock, W., Deelman, E., Schwiegelshohn, U.: Consecutive job submission behavior at mira supercomputer. In: Proceedings of the 25th ACM International Symposium on High-Performance Parallel and Distributed Computing (HPDC), Kyoto, Japan, pp. 93–96, May 2016. https://doi.org/10.1145/2907294.2907314

18. Smith, W.: A service for queue prediction and job statistics. In: Proceedings of the 2010 Gateway Computing Environments Workshop, Los Alamitos, CA, pp. 1–8, November 2010. https://doi.org/10.1109/GCE.2010.5676119

19. Smith, W., Foster, I., Taylor, V.: Predicting application run times with historical information. JPDC 64(9), 1007–1016 (2004). https://doi.org/10.1016/j.jpdc.2004.06.008

20. Smith, W., Taylor, V., Foster, I.: Using run-time predictions to estimate queue wait times and improve scheduler performance. In: Feitelson, D.G., Rudolph, L. (eds.) JSSPP 1999. LNCS, vol. 1659, pp. 202–219. Springer, Heidelberg (1999). https://doi.org/10.1007/3-540-47954-6_11

21. The IN2P3/CNRS Computing Center. http://cc.in2p3.fr/en/

22. Tibshirani, R.: Regression shrinkage and selection via the lasso. J. Roy. Stat. Soc. Ser. B (Methodol.) 58(1), 267–288 (1996). https://doi.org/10.2307/2346178

23. Univa Corporation: Grid Engine. http://www.univa.com/products/

A HPC Co-scheduler with Reinforcement Learning

Abel Souza[1]([✉]) , Kristiaan Pelckmans[2] , and Johan Tordsson[3]

[1] University of Massachusetts Amherst, Amherst, USA
asouza@cs.umass.edu
[2] Uppsala University, Uppsala, Sweden
kristiaan.pelckmans@it.uu.se
[3] Umeå University, Umeå, Sweden
tordsson@cs.umu.se

Abstract. Although High Performance Computing (HPC) users understand basic resource requirements such as the number of CPUs and memory limits, internal infrastructural utilization data is exclusively leveraged by cluster operators, who use it to configure batch schedulers. This task is challenging and increasingly complex due to ever larger cluster scales and heterogeneity of modern scientific workflows. As a result, HPC systems achieve low utilization with long job completion times (makespans). To tackle these challenges, we propose a co-scheduling algorithm based on an adaptive reinforcement learning algorithm, where application profiling is combined with cluster monitoring. The resulting cluster scheduler matches resource utilization to application performance in a fine-grained manner (i.e., operating system level). As opposed to nominal allocations, we apply decision trees to model applications' actual resource usage, which are used to estimate how much resource capacity from one allocation can be co-allocated to additional applications. Our algorithm learns from incorrect co-scheduling decisions and adapts from changing environment conditions, and evaluates when such changes cause resource contention that impacts quality of service metrics such as jobs slowdowns. We integrate our algorithm in an HPC resource manager that combines Slurm and Mesos for job scheduling and co-allocation, respectively. Our experimental evaluation performed in a dedicated cluster executing a mix of four real different scientific workflows demonstrates improvements on cluster utilization of up to 51% even in high load scenarios, with 55% average queue makespan reductions under low loads.

Keywords: Datacenters · Co-scheduling · High performance computing · Adaptive reinforcement learning

---

A. Souza—Research performed while working at Umeå University.

D. Klusáček et al. (Eds.): JSSPP 2021, LNCS 12985, pp. 126–148, 2021.
https://doi.org/10.1007/978-3-030-88224-2_7

1   Introduction

High Performance Computing (HPC) datacenters process thousands of applications supporting scientific and business endeavours across all sectors of society. Modern applications are commonly characterized as data-intensive, demanding processing power and scheduling capabilities that are not well supported by large HPC systems [34]. Data-intensive workflows can quickly change computational patterns, e.g., amount of input data at runtime. Unfortunately, traditional HPC schedulers like Slurm [19] do not offer Application Programming Interfaces (APIs) that allow users and operators to express these requirements. Current resource provisioning capabilities barely satisfy today's traditional non-malleable workloads, and as a result, most HPC centers report long queue waiting times [1], and low utilization [5]. These problems delay scientific outputs, besides triggering concerns related to HPC infrastructure usage, particularly in energy efficiency and in the gap between resource capacity and utilization [38].

In contrast to HPC infrastructures that use batch systems and prioritize the overall job throughput at the expense of latency, cloud datacenters favor response time. On the one hand, cloud resource managers such as Kubernetes/Borg [7] and Mesos [17] assume workloads that change resource usage over time and that can scale up, down, or be migrated at runtime as needed [26]. This model allows cloud operators to reduce datacenter fragmentation and enable low latency scheduling while improving cluster capacity utilization. On the other hand, HPC resource managers such as Slurm and Torque [37], assume workloads with fixed makespan and constant resource demands throughout applications' lifespan, which must be acquired before jobs can start execution [13,32]. Consequently, to improve datacenter efficiency and to adapt to quick workload variations, resources should be instantly re-provisioned, pushing for new scheduling techniques.

Thus, this paper proposes an algorithm with strong theoretical guarantees for co-scheduling batch jobs and resource sharing. Considering the problem of a HPC datacenter where jobs need to be scheduled and cluster utilization needs to be optimized, we develop a Reinforcement Learning (RL) algorithm that models a co-scheduling policy that minimizes idle processing capacity and also respects jobs' Quality of Service (QoS) constraints, such as total runtimes and deadlines (Sect. 3.1). Our co-scheduling algorithm is implemented by combining the Slurm batch scheduler and the Mesos dynamic job management framework. The potential benefit of more assertive co-allocation schemes is substantial, considering that – in terms of actual resource utilization, as opposed to nominal allocations – the current HPC practice often leaves computational units idling for about 40% [31,40].

We evaluate our solution by experiments in a real cluster configured with three different sizes and four real scientific workflows with different compute, memory, and I/O patterns. We compare our co-scheduling strategy with traditional space-sharing strategies that do not allow workload consolidation and with a static time-sharing strategy that equally multiplexes the access to resources. Our RL co-scheduler matches applications QoS guarantees by using a practical algorithm that improves cluster utilization by up to 51%, with 55% reductions in queue makespans and low performance degradation (Sect. 4).

2   Background and Challenges

The emergence of cloud computing and data-intensive processing created a new class of complex and dynamic applications that require low-latency scheduling and which are increasingly being deployed in HPC datacenters. Low latency scheduling requires a different environment than batch processing that is dominant in HPC environments. HPC systems are usually managed by centralized batch schedulers that require users to describe allocations by the total run time (makespan) and amounts of resources, such as the number of CPUs, memory, and accelerators, e.g., GPUs [14,19,32]. As depicted in Fig. 1(a), in the traditional HPC resource reservation model, known as space sharing, each job arrives and waits to be scheduled in a queue until enough resources that match the job's needs are available for use. In this scenario, the batch system uses backfilling [24] to keep resources allocated and maximize throughput, and users benefit from having jobs buffered up (queued) and scheduled together, a technique known as gang scheduling [12].

The main scheduling objectives in traditional HPC is performance predictability for parallel jobs, achieved at the expense of potential high cluster fragmentation, scalability and support for low latency jobs. In addition, this model assumes that the capacity of allocated computing resources is fully used, which is rarely the case [40], especially at early stages of development. This static configuration can be enhanced through consolidation, where jobs that require complementary resources share the same (or parts of) physical servers, which ultimately increases cluster utilization. In HPC, consolidation happens mostly in non-dedicated resource components, such as the shared file systems and the network. Resource managers, such as Slurm, allow nodes to be shared among multiple jobs, but do not dynamically adjust the preemption time slices.

2.1   Resource Management with Reinforcement Learning

Reinforcement learning (RL) is a mathematical optimization problem with states, actions, and rewards, where the objective is to maximize rewards [28]. In HPC, this can be formulated as a set of cluster resources (i.e., the environment) to where jobs need to be assigned by following an objective function (i.e., the rewards). Three common objective functions in HPC are minimizing expected queue waiting times, guaranteeing fairness among users, and increasing the cluster utilization and density. The scheduler's role is to model the cluster – i.e., to map applications behaviour to provisioned resources – through actionable interactions with the runtime system, such as adjusting cgroup limits [27]. Finally, to evaluate actions, the scheduler can observe state transitions in the cluster and subsequently calculate their outcomes to obtain the environment's reward. One example of action used extensively in this work is to co-schedule two applications

A and B onto the same server and measure the reward (or loss) in terms of runtime performance. The latter compared to a scenario with exclusive node access for A and B. In this RL framework, the scheduler is the learner and interactions allow it to model the environment, i.e., the quantitative learning of the mapping of actions to outcomes observed by co-scheduling applications. A reward (or objective) function describes how an agent (i.e., a scheduler) should behave, and works as a normative evaluation of what it has to accomplish. There are no strong restrictions regarding the characteristics of the reward function, but if it quantifies observed behaviors well, the agent learns fast and accurately.

2.2   Challenges

Common HPC resource managers do not profile jobs nor consider job performance models during scheduling decisions. Initiatives to use more flexible policies are commonly motivated by highly dynamic future exascale applications, where runtime systems need to handle orchestration due to the large number of application tasks spawned at execution time [9,43]. Currently, dynamic scheduling in HPC is hindered as jobs come with several constraints due to their tight coupling, including the need for periodic message passing for synchronization and checkpointing for fault-tolerance [15]. Characteristics such as low capacity utilization [5] show a potential to improve cluster efficiency, where idle resources – ineffectively used otherwise – can be allocated to other applications with opposite profile characteristics.

Thus, different extensions to the main scheduling scheme are of direct relevance in practical scenarios. Server *capacity* can be viewed as a single-dimensional variable, though in practice it is multivariate and includes CPU, memory, network, I/O, etc. As such, a practical and natural extension to this problem is to formulate it as a multi-dimensional metric [23]. However, co-scheduling one or more jobs affects their performance as a whole [18], meaning that the actual capacity utilization of a job depends on how collocated jobs behave, making this capacity problem even more complex.

2.3   The Adaptive Scheduling Architecture

ASA – The Adaptive Scheduling Architecture is an architecture and RL algorithm that reduces the user-perceived waiting times by accurately estimating queue waiting times, as well as optimizes scientific workflows resource and cluster usage [36]. ASA encapsulates application processes into containers and enable fine-grained control of resources through and across job allocations. From userspace, ASA enables novel workflow scheduling strategies, with support for placement, resource isolation and control, fault tolerance, and elasticity. As a scheduling algorithm, ASA performs best in settings where similar jobs are queued repeatedly as is common setting in HPC. However, ASA's inability to handle states limits its use in broader scheduling settings. As this paper shows, embedding states such as application performance, users' fair-share priorities, and the

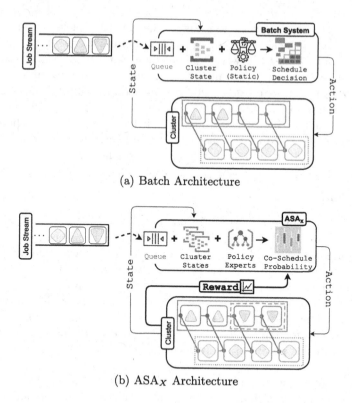

(a) Batch Architecture

(b) ASA_X Architecture

Fig. 1. (a) Batch and (b) ASA_X Architectures: (a) A traditional batch system such as Slurm. The Upside down triangle (green) job waits for resources although the cluster is not fully utilized; (b) ASA_X, where rewards follow co-scheduling decision actions, steered through *Policy Experts*. In this example, the upside down triangle job (green) is co-allocated with the triangle job (blue). (Color figure online)

cluster capacity directly into the model enables more accurate scheduling decisions.

3   A Co-scheduler Architecture and Algorithm

In this section we introduce ASA_X: the HPC co-scheduler architecture and its algorithm. The goals of ASA_X are higher cluster throughput and utilization, while also controlling performance degradation as measured by application completion time. Additionally, ASA_X introduces the concept of cluster and application states (Sect. 3.1). When measured, these concepts influence how each co-scheduling action is taken. Handling states is the main difference to ASA and enables the creation of scheduling strategies that achieve an intelligent exploitation (finding the Pareto frontier) of the space spanned by the application QoS requirements and the available compute capacity. As such, evaluating ASA_X's performance depends on how time-sharing strategies compare to space-sharing strategies, the default policy of most HPC clusters that guarantees predictable performance. We handle the problem of growing number of actions by incorporating expert decision tree structures that can be computed efficiently. Together with the loss functions, decision trees can be used efficiently, and easily be updated to modify the probabilities that affect how co-scheduling actions are chosen and how resources are used.

3.1 Architecture and Algorithm Overview

Figure 1(b) shows ASA_X's architecture, where jobs are queued as in regular HPC environments, but allocated resources are shared with other jobs. The main differences from regular batch scheduling (illustrated in Fig. 1(a)) is that a single deterministic cluster policy is replaced with a probabilistic policy that evolves as co-scheduling decision outcomes are evaluated. The job co-scheduling is implemented by an algorithm (see Sect. 3.2) that creates a collocation probability distribution by combining the cluster and application states, the cluster policy, and the accumulated rewards. Note that the cluster 'Policy' is analytically evaluated through decision trees (DTs) (Fig. 2), which correspond to the (human) *experts* role in RL. Experts map the applications and system online features, represented by internal cluster metrics such as CPU and memory utilization, into collocation decisions. Combined through multiple DTs, these metrics form the cluster *state*. Each leaf in the DT outputs a multi-variate distribution $p_{i,j}$ that represents the likelihood of taking a specific action, and combined they affect how co-scheduling decisions are made. In here, actions are defined by how much CPU cgroup [27] quota each job receives from the resources allocated to them, which influence how the operating system scheduler schedules application processes at runtime. Another difference with traditional HPC architectures is the addition of a feedback mechanism, where *rewards* are accumulated after each co-scheduling action. This mechanism allows the architecture to asses the outcome of a co-scheduling decision to improve future decisions. To enable a job-aware scheduler, decisions are implemented in a per-job basis (see Sect. 3.2). Thus, ASA_X aims at discovering which expert is the best to minimize the performance degradation faced by a job due to co-scheduling decisions.

There can be an arbitrary number of experts, and they can be described by anything that is reasonably lean to compute, from functions to decision trees. However, the combination of all experts needs to approximate the current cluster state as precisely as possible. To define and compute experts, in this paper we use metrics such as CPU (CPU%) and memory utilization (Mem%), workflow stage type (i.e. *sequential*, where only one core is utilized, or *parallel*, where all cores are utilized), time interval since the job started execution related to its duration (e.g. 25%, 50%, 75%). In addition to these metrics, we also define Hp(t), a happiness metric that is defined at time t for a given job as

$$Hp(t) = \frac{|t_{Walltime} - t| * \#RemainingTasks}{\#Tasks/s}. \tag{1}$$

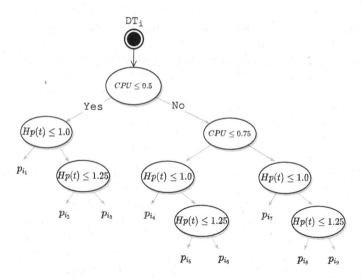

Fig. 2. A Decision tree (DT) expert structure illustrating the evaluation of the 'CPU' state in an allocation. For each DT 'Metric' (CPU%, Mem%, type, and interval), an action strategy is devised by combining four different distributions p_i. Then, depending on the state for each 'Metric', one distribution among nine $(p_{i_1}, ..., p_{i_9})$ is returned.

Devised from a similar concept [21], the happiness metric relates the job's remaining execution time with its remaining amount of work. It enables the analytical evaluation of a running job in regards to the allocated resource capacity and its overall throughput. Given the remaining time $(|t_{Walltime} - t|)$ and performance $(\#Tasks/s)$, if Hp(t) is near to, or greater than 1.0, then it can be inferred that the job is likely to complete execution within the wall-time limit; else (if Hp(t) < 1.0), the job is likely to not complete by the wall-time. It is important to note that the Hp(t) metric best describes jobs that encapsulate one application process. This is achieved by encapsulating each workflow stage into a single job, as is common in scientific workflows (see Sect. 4).

Cluster Policy. We combine states through DTs for each metric with the happiness metric. Figure 2 illustrates one possible expert for the CPU state. It evaluates if the CPU% is high (e.g. >0.75), and if so, and if Hp(t) is near to 1.0, the policy expects high performance degradation due to job collocation. Conversely, if the CPU% is low, and the Hp(t) is greater than 1.1, the performance degradation is likely to be small, and the expert increases the probability for jobs to be collocated. Rather than describing these relations explicitly, we work with a mixture of different decision trees. Hence, $\mathbf{p}_{i,j}(\mathbf{x})$ represents how likely an action a_j is to be taken given the evaluated state x_t, according to the i-th expert in DT_i. For instance, if there are four CPU quota co-allocations e.g. (0%, 25%, 50%, 75%), each degrading Hp(t) differently, DT1 may evaluate how state x_t is mapped into a distribution of performance degradation $\mathbf{p}_{i,j}(\mathbf{x})$ for a situation where `CPU%` > 0.75, and `Hp(t)` ≈ 1.0. This scenario could return $\mathbf{p}_1(\mathbf{x}) = (0.6, 0.3, 0.05, 0.05)$, meaning action a_0 ($=0\%$), i.e. no co-allocation, is likely the best co-schedule decision. Another DT2 could evaluate another state, e.g. related to memory or to how a given special resource behaves, etc., returning a different $\mathbf{p}_{i,j}(\mathbf{x})$, with a different co-allocation action, impacting the final $\mathbf{p}$ accordingly (line 6 in Algorithm 1). In general, we design our decision trees to suggest more collocation when $Hp(t) \geq 1.0$, and ASA$_X$ looks for other ongoing allocations whenever a 0% co-allocation is the best decision for a certain running job.

3.2   Algorithm Details

Table 1. Algorithm variables and their descriptions.

Feature	Name	Description
$\{a\}$	Action set	Actions that users or operators can take while scheduling or allocating resources to applications
DT_i	Decision tree	Used to assess the weight a given application or resource metric value ought to influence actions
$\mathbf{R}_i$	Risk	Risk for using DT_i
r_i	Accumulated risk	Accumulation of all risks incurred by DT_i
$\ell(a)$	Loss function	The performance degradation due to collocation

In here we describe the internal details of how ASA$_X$ is implemented, with variable and details presented in Table 1. A co-scheduling action depends on the associated state $\mathbf{x} \in \mathbb{R}^d$, where d depends on the number of selected cluster metrics as shown in Fig. 2. A state $\mathbf{x}$ is a vector that combines the assessment of all distributions output by the DTs. At any time t that a co-scheduling decision is to be made, one action a out of the m possible actions $a = \{a_0, a_1, \ldots, a_{m-1}\}$ is taken with the system in state $\mathbf{x}$. However, while in state $\mathbf{x}$, co-allocating resources from a running Job$_a$ to a Job$_b$ may degrade Job$_a$'s performance, and this incurs in an associated loss $\ell(a)$. This overall idea is represented in Algorithm 1, where we have a nested loop. The outer loop (starting in line 1) initiates and updates the parameters for each scheduling decision that can be made. Once an ongoing job allocation candidate is presented, the inner loop (line 3) co-allocates resources to other jobs until the cumulative loss exceeds a threshold, in which case learning needs to be updated. In mathematical terms, let $\mathbf{p} : \mathbb{R}^d \to \mathbb{R}^m$ be a function of states $\mathbf{x} \in \mathbb{R}^d$ to co-allocation actions, and the goal of learning is to optimally approximate this mathematical relationship. The central quantity steering $\mathbf{p}$ is the *risk* $\mathbf{R}$, here defined for each DT$_i$ as a vector in $\mathbb{R}^n$ where

$$\mathbf{R}_i = \ell(a)\mathbf{p}_i(a). \tag{2}$$

To quantify the performance degradation due to co-scheduling at iteration t, we maintain a vector $\mathbf{r}_t$ of the total accumulated risk (line 10). At each co-scheduling decision at time t, we let $\mathbf{r}_{t,i}$ denote the accumulated risk of the ith expert. ASA_X then creates a strategy to minimize $\mathbf{r}_i$:

$$\min_* \sum_{s=1}^{t} \sum_{j=1}^{n_s} \mathbf{p}_*(\mathbf{x}_{sj}) \ell(a_{sj}). \tag{3}$$

Note that the strategy minimising $\mathbf{r}_t$ corresponds to the maximum likelihood estimate, meaning we want to follow the expert that assigns the highest probability to the actions with the lowest loss. In here m actions $a = \{a_0, a_1, \ldots, a_{m-1}\}$ correspond to a discretization of resource allocations, and are expressed in terms of CPU% quota allocation ratios of m intervals, e.g. if $m = 10$ then $a = \{a_0 = 0\%, a_1 = 10\%, \ldots, a_9 = 90\%\}$. This means a fraction a_m of an ongoing Job_a allocation is re-allocated to a Job_b. When co-scheduling a_m from an allocation to other job, we calculate the performance degradation loss $\ell(a)$, limiting it to 1.0 and proportionally to the actual job submission execution time, normalized by its wall-time. For example, if an user requests a wall-time of 100s, and the submission finishes in 140s, the loss would be proportional to $min(1.0, |140 - 100|/100)$. On the other hand, if the submission finishes in 70s, then the loss is 0, because it successfully completed within its wall-time limits. ASA_X then optimizes $\mathbf{p}$ over the m quota allocations (actions) according to the loss $\ell(a)$ and the accumulated risks $\mathbf{r}_{ti}$ for Job_a. Accumulated risks help in cases where the co-scheduling strategy incurs in high performance degradation. Therefore, in Algorithm 1 we set a threshold $\mathbf{r}_t$ (line 3) bounding the accumulated risk for a given Job_a, and reset it in the situation when the co-location actions resulted in large performance degradation losses (line 12). This allows Algorithm 1 to update its knowledge about Job_a and bound the accumulated mistakes. Notably, we prove that the *excess risk* E_t after t co-scheduling decisions is bound, meaning the algorithm converges to an optimal point in a finite time after a few iterations (see Appendix A).

Finally, rigid jobs can only start execution when all requested resource are provisioned (see Sect. 2). To simultaneously achieve this and to improve cluster utilization, HPC infrastructures use *gang scheduling* [12]. By running on top of Mesos [17] (see Sect. 2.3), ASA_X can scale to manage thousands of distributed resources. These features include fine-grained resource isolation and control (through cgroup quotas), fault tolerance, elasticity, and support for new scheduling strategies. However, although Mesos supports resource negotiation, it does not support gang scheduling, nor timely reservation scheduling. Therefore, ASA_X also works as a framework to negotiate resource offers from Mesos in a way that satisfies queued jobs' requirements and constraints. ASA_X withholds offers, allocating them when enough resources fulfill the job's requirements, and releasing the remaining ones for use by other allocations. This is a basic version of the *First fit* capacity based algorithm [12]. Our focus is towards improving cluster throughput and utilization, which may have direct impacts on reducing queue waiting times and jobs response times. Although in general many other

---

Algorithm 1. ASA$_x$

Require:
    Queued Job_b
    Job_a allocation satisfying Job_b `#In terms of resource`
    m co-allocation actions a, e.g. $m = 10$ and $a = \{a_0 = 0\%, ..., a_{m-1} = 90\%\}$
    Initialise $\alpha_{0i} = \frac{1}{n}$ for $i = 1, ..., n$ `#metrics in state x, e.g. CPU, Mem.`

1: **for** $t = 1, 2, ...$ **do**
2:     Initialise co-allocation risk $r_{ti} = 0$ for each i-th metric
    `#Co-allocation assessment:`
3:     **while** $\max_i r_{ti} \leq 1$ **do**
4:         Evaluate Job_a's state $\mathbf{x}$:
5:         Compute each ith-DT metric expert $\mathbf{p}_i(\mathbf{x}) \in \mathbb{R}^m$
6:         Aggregate Job_a's co-schedule probability as $\mathbf{p} = \sum_{i=1}^n \alpha_{t-1,i} \mathbf{p}_i(\mathbf{x}) \in \mathbb{R}^m$
7:         j = sample one action from a according to $\mathbf{p}$
8:         Allocate a_j from Job_a's to co-schedule Job_b
9:         Compute Job_a's performance loss $|\ell(a_j)| \leq 1$ due to co-allocation
10:       For all i, update Job_a's risk $r_{ti} = r_{ti} + \mathbf{p}_i(a_j)\ell(a_j)$
11:     **end while**
12:     For Job_a and for all i, update $\alpha_{t,i}$ as

$$\alpha_{t,i} = \frac{\alpha_{t-1,i}}{N_t} \times e^{-\gamma_t r_{ti}}$$

    where N_t is a normalising factor such that $\sum_{i=1}^n \alpha_{t,i} = 1$.
13: **end for**

---

aspects such as data movement and locality also influence parallel job scheduling, we do not (explicitly) address them.

4 Evaluation

In this section we evaluate ASA$_X$ with respect to workloads' total makespan, cluster resource usage, and workflows total runtime. We compare ASA$_X$ against a default backfilling setting of Slurm and a static co-allocation setting.

4.1 Computing System

The experimental evaluation is performed on a system with high performance networks, namely a NumaScale system [35] with 6 nodes, each having two AMD Opteron Processor (6380) 24-cores and 185 GB memory. The NumaConnect hardware interconnects these nodes and appears to users as one large *single* server, with a total of 288 cores and 1.11 TB of memory. Memory coherence is guaranteed at the hardware level and totally transparent to users, applications, and the OS itself. Servers are interconnected through a switch fabric 2D Torus network which supports sub microsecond latency accesses. The NumaScale storage uses a XFS file system, providing 512 GB of storage. The system runs a CentOS 7 (Kernel 4.18) and jobs are managed by Slurm (18.08) with its default backfilling setting enabled. When managing resources in the static and ASA_X settings, jobs are managed by Mesos 1.9 that uses our own framework/co-scheduler on top of it (see Fig. 1(b) and Sect. 3.1).

4.2 Applications

Four scientific workflows with different characteristics were selected for our evaluation Montage, BLAST, Statistics, and Synthetic.

Montage [6] is an I/O intensive application that constructs the mosaic of a sky survey. The workflow has nine stages, grouped into two parallel and two sequential stages. All runs of Montage construct an image survey from the 2mass Atlas images.

BLAST [4] is a compute intensive applications comparing DNA strips against a database larger than 6 GB. It maps an input file into many smaller files and then reduces the tasks to compare the input against the large sequence database. BLAST is composed of two main stages: one parallel followed by one sequential.

Statistics is an I/O and network intensive application which calculates various statistical metrics from a dataset with measurements of electric power consumption in a household with an one-minute sampling rate over a period of almost four years [20]. The statistics workflow is composed mainly of two stages composed of two sequential and two parallel sub-stages. The majority of its execution time is spent exchanging and processing messages among parallel tasks.

Synthetic is a two stages workflow composed of a sequential and a parallel task. This workflow is both data and compute intensive. It first loads the memory with over one billion floating point numbers (sequential stage), and then performs additions and multiplications on them (parallel stage).

4.3 Metrics

The following metrics are used in the evaluation. The *total runtime* is measured by summing up the execution times for each workflow stage, submitted as separate jobs. Equally important, *the response time* (also known as makespan, or flow time) is defined as the time elapsed between the submission and the time when the job finishes execution. A related metric is the waiting time, which is the time one job waits in the queue before starting execution. Additional metrics are CPU and memory utilization as measured by the Linux kernel. These latter two capture the overall resource utilization, and aids understanding of how well co-schedulers such as ASA_X model application performance.

4.4 Workloads

To evaluate ASA_X co-scheduling we compare it against a Static CPU quota configuration and a default (space-sharing) Slurm setting with backfilling enabled.

We execute the same set of 15 workflow jobs (4 Montage, 4 BLAST and 4 Statistics [8, 16, 32, 64 cores], and 3 Synthetic [16, 32, 64 cores]) three times, each with three size configurations: namely 64 (x2), 128 (x4), and 256 (x8) cores. The workflows have different job geometry scaling requests ranging from 8 cores to up to 64 cores (smallest cluster size, x2), totalling 512 cores and 45 job submissions for each cluster size. This workload selection demonstrates how the different scheduling strategies handle high (cluster size x8 = 256 cores), medium (x4 = 128 cores), and low loads (x2 = 64 cores), respectively. When comparing the Static setting and ASA_X against Slurm, neither of them get access to more resources (i.e. cores) than the cluster size for each experimental run. In all experiments, Slurm statically allocates resources for the whole job duration. Moreover, when scheduling jobs in the Static configuration, collocations of two jobs in a same server are allowed and the time-sharing CPU quota ratio is set to 50% for each job (through cgroups [27]). Collocation is also done for ASA_X, but the CPU quotas are dynamically set and updated once the rewards are collected according to Algorithm 1. Notably, to reduce scheduling complexity, our First Fit algorithm does not use Mesos resource offers coming from multiple job allocations. Finally, as mentioned in the previous section, the loss function $\ell(a)$ to optimize the co-schedule actions is calculated proportionally to the user requested wall-time and to the actual workflow runtime, similarly to the Hp(t) metric. The $\ell(a)$ values span 0.0 and 1.0, where 1.0 means performance degraded by at least 50%, and 0.0 means no performance degradation.

4.5   Results

Figures 3(a) and 3(b), and Tables 2 and 3 summarize all experimental evaluation, which is discussed below.

Makespan and Runtimes. Figures 3(a) and 3(b) show respectively queue workload makespans and workflow runtimes, both in hours. We note that the total makespan reduces as the cluster size is increased. As expected, Slurm experiments have small standard deviations as they use the space-sharing policy and isolate jobs with exclusive resource access throughout their lifespan. Static allocation yields longer makespans as this method does not consider actual resource usage by applications, but rather takes deterministic decisions about co-scheduling decisions, i.e. allocates half the CPU capacity to each collocated application. In contrast, ASA_X, reduces the overall workload makespan by up to 12% (64 cores) as it learns overtime which jobs do not compete for resources when co-allocated. For this reason, some initial ASA_X scheduling decisions are incorrect, which explains the higher standard deviations shown in Fig. 3(a).

Table 2 and Fig. 3(b) show the aggregated average runtimes for each workflow, with their respective standard deviations. Notably, the high standard deviations illustrate the scalability of each workflow, i.e. the higher standard deviation, the more scalable the workflow is (given the same input, as it is the case in the experiments). Figure 3(b) shows different runs for the same application with different number of cores. If an application is scalable, the more cores the allocation gets, the faster the application completes execution, and the larger the standard deviation. Conversely, when the application is not scalable, performance is not improved when more cores are added to the allocation. The application cannot take advantage of extra resources, resulting in more idle resources, thus reducing the standard deviation between the runs. Finally, BLAST and Synthetic are two very scalable, CPU intensive workloads, which do not depend on I/O and network as Montage and Statistics do. The Static strategy has the highest standard deviations overall because its workload experiences more performance degradation when compared to both Slurm and ASA_X, which this is due to its static capacity allocation.

Table 2 shows workflows runtime as well as CPU and memory resource utilization, all normalized against Slurm. It can be seen that ASA_X is close to Slurm regarding average total runtimes, with low overall overheads up to 10%, reaching as low as 3% increase for Montage. A predictable, but notable achievement for both the Static setting and ASA_X is the improved CPU utilization. As only a specific fraction of resources are actually allocated in both strategies, the utilization ratio increases considerably. For instance, when a job requests 1 CPU, the Static setting allocates 50% of one CPU to one job and the other 50% is co-allocated to other job. For non CPU intensive workloads (Montage and Statistics), this strategy results in higher utilization ratios because such workloads consume less than the upper bound capacity, which is noticeable when comparing to Slurm. For CPU intensive workloads such as BLAST, this strategy hurts performance, extending the workflow total runtime, most noticeably in the Static results. In contrast, as ASA_X learns overtime that co-scheduling jobs with either BLAST or Synthetic results in poor performance, its scheduling decisions become biased towards co-allocating Montage and Statistics workflows, but not BLAST or Synthetic. Also notable is the increased CPU utilization for the Statistics workflow, a non CPU intensive workload. The only workload capable of utilizing most of the memory available in the system is the Synthetic workflow, which is both memory and CPU intensive. This property makes ASA_X avoid co-placing any other workload with Synthetic jobs, as memory is one of the key metrics in our decision trees (see previous section).

Aggregated Queue and Cluster Metrics. Whereas total runtime results are important for the individual users, aggregated cluster metrics such as queue waiting times matter for cluster operators. The latter metrics are summarized in Table 3 that shows average waiting times (h), cluster CPU utilization (%), and response times (h). The key point in Table 3 relates to both average response time and queue waiting time. Queue waiting times are reduced by as much as 50% in both Static and ASA_X compared to Slurm. ASA_X has 55% lower response time (256 cores) than Slurm or Static, which shows that it makes co-scheduling decisions that – for the proposed workload – result in fast executions. Similarly to the Static setting, ASA_X also increases cluster (CPU) utilization by up to

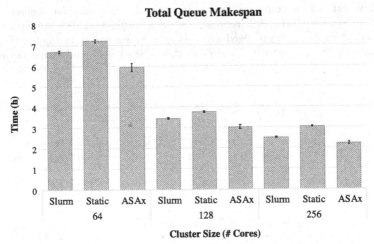

(a) Total workload queue makespan per strategy and cluster size

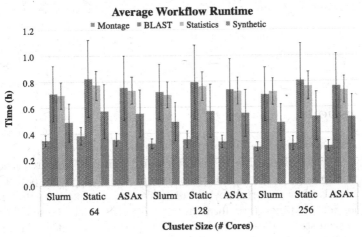

(b) Average total runtime per strategy and cluster size

Fig. 3. Slurm, Static, and ASA$_X$ strategy results - Total (a) Queue makespan and (b) runtime of each cluster size (64, 128, and 256 cores) and scheduling strategy.

59%, but with the advantage of low performance degradation while also reducing queue waiting times considerably. This also happens for low cluster loads, as can be seen in the x2 workload case, with 51% average waiting time reductions. Conversely, Slurm decreases CPU utilization as the load decreases, and it is thus not able to improve response time.

Table 2. Workflows summary for Slurm, Static, and ASA$_X$ in three different cluster sizes. CPU Util. and Mem Util. represent resource utilization (%) proportionally to total allocated capacity. Normalized averages over Slurm are shown below results for each cluster size. Acronyms: WF (Workflow), Stats (Statistics), and Synth. (Synthetic).

Cluster size	WF	Slurm			Static			ASA$_X$		
		Runtime (h)	CPU util. (%)	Mem util. (%)	Runtime (h)	CPU util. (%)	Mem util. (%)	Runtime (h)	CPU util. (%)	Mem util. (%)
64	Montage	0.35 ± 4%	45 ± 5	10 ± 5	0.38 ± 7%	94 ± 5	10 ± 5	0.35 ± 5%	95 ± 4	10 ± 4
	BLAST	0.71 ± 21%	96 ± 4	44 ± 5	0.82 +30%	99 ± 1	44 ± 5	0.75 ± 25%	99 ± 1	44 ± 5
	Stats	0.69 ± 10%	26 ± 2	5 ± 1	0.77 ± 30%	51 ± 3	6 ± 1	0.73 ± 11%	61 ± 4	5 ± 1
	Synth.	0.49 ± 15%	99 ± 1	95 ± 3	0.57 ± 21%	99 ± 1	95 ± 1	0.56 ± 18%	99 ± 1	95 ± 1
Normalized average		*–*	*–*	*–*	*+10%*	*+230%*	*0%*	*+3%*	*+227%*	*0%*
128	Montage	0.32 ± 4%	33 ± 5	7 ± 3	0.35 ± 6%	73 ± 5	7 ± 3	0.33 ± 5%	75 ± 5	7 ± 3
	BLAST	0.72 ± 22%	95 ± 3	45 ± 5	0.79 ± 29%	99 ± 1	44 ± 5	0.73 ± 24%	99 ± 1	44 ± 5
	Stats	0.70 ± 10%	16 ± 2	1 ± 1	0.76 ± 11%	36 ± 6	2 ± 1	0.72 ± 11%	43 ± 7	1 ± 1
	Synth.	0.50 ± 15%	99 ± 1	93 ± 4	0.57 ± 21%	99 ± 1	93 ± 3	0.55 ± 18%	99 ± 1	93 ± 4
Normalized average		*–*	*–*	*–*	*+19%*	*+5%*	*0%*	*+9%*	*+5%*	*0%*
256	Montage	0.29 ± 4%	21 ± 5	5 ± 3	0.32 ± 6%	55 ± 5	5 ± 3	0.30 ± 4%	51 ± 5	5 ± 3
	BLAST	0.70 ± 21%	91 ± 3	42 ± 6	0.80 ± 29%	99 ± 1	43 ± 6	0.76 ± 25%	99 ± 1	43 ± 6
	Stats	0.72 ± 10%	10 ± 2	1 ± 1	0.76 ± 11%	26 ± 2	1 ± 1	0.73 ± 11%	86 ± 6	1 ± 1
	Synth.	0.48 ± 14%	99 ± 1	92 ± 2	0.53 ± 19%	99 ± 1	91 ± 2	0.52 ± 17%	99 ± 1	93 ± 1
Normalized average		*–*	*–*	*–*	*+10%*	*+36%*	*0%*	*+5%*	*+50%*	*+1%*

5   Discussion

The evaluation demonstrates how ASA$_X$ combines application profiling with an assertive learning algorithm to simultaneously improve resource usage and cluster throughput, with direct reductions on the workload makespan. By combining an intuitive but powerful abstraction (decision tree experts) and an application agnostic (happiness) performance, ASA$_X$ efficiently co-schedules jobs and improves cluster throughput. The overall performance degradation experienced by ASA$_X$ (10% average runtime slowdown) is negligible when compared to its benefits, in particular as HPC users are known to overestimate walltimes [10,33,41]. When compared to Slurm, a very common batch system used in HPC infrastructures, ASA$_X$ reduces average job response times by up to 10%, enabling HPC users to achieve faster time to results. Notably, these improvements are achieved also for lightly loaded clusters, where the co-scheduling actions optimize cluster resources and allows them to be shared with other jobs.

It is important to note that current HPC scheduling strategies, specially those based on backfilling, aim to maximize resource allocation at a coarse granularity level. It is generally assumed this is good policy, as it guarantees high allocation ratios without interfering with users' workflows and thus achieves predictable job performance. However, such strategies do not take advantage of the characteristics of modern dynamic workflows, namely adaptability to changed

Table 3. Slurm, Static, and ASA_X - Average results for three strategies in each cluster size.

	Cluster size	Cluster load	Waiting time (h)	CPU util. (%)	Response time (h)
Slurm	64	8×	3.5 ± 1%	53 ± 5	4.4 ± 1%
	128	4×	1.5 ± 1%	45 ± 5	2.4 ± 1%
	256	2×	0.5 ± 1%	32 ± 6	1.4 ± 1%
Static	64	8×	1.7 ± 1%	90 ± 5	4.8 ± 1%
	128	4×	0.8 ± 1%	92 ± 3	2.8 ± 1%
	256	2×	0.3 ± 1%	89 ± 5	2.0 ± 1%
ASA_X	64	8×	1.8 ± 5%	82 ± 7	3.5 ± 3%
	128	4×	1.0 ± 8%	84 ± 5	2.0 ± 2%
	256	2×	0.3 ± 7%	83 ± 4	0.9 ± 2%

resource allocation, faults, and even on input accuracy. Nor does backfilling strategies take advantage of modern operating system capabilities such as fine-grained processes scheduling and access control such as Linux [27], available in userspace. Notably in HPC, even classical rigid jobs may suffer from traditional space-sharing policies, as the reservation based model does not take into consideration how resources are utilized in runtime. This is due to historical reasons, mostly related to CPU scarcity and the need for application performance consistency and SLO guarantees. In contrast, by leveraging the dynamic nature of modern workflows, and by using well fine-grained resource control mechanisms such as cgroups, ASA_X is able to improve the cluster utilization without hurting jobs performance. Although applicable across a wide range of HPC environments, such scheduling features are particularly suitable for rackscale systems like Numascale that offers close to infinite vertical scaling of applications. In such systems, scheduling mechanisms like ASA_X are key as the default Linux Completely Fair Scheduler (CFS) – beyond cache-locality – does not understand fine-grained job requirements, such as walltimes limits and data locality.

Given one cluster workload, the goals of ASA_X are higher cluster throughput and increased resource utilization. A constraint for these goals is the performance degradation caused by resource sharing and collocation, as measured by applications' completion time. In our experiments, the same queue workload is submitted to three resource capacity scenarios and cluster sizes that creates low, medium, and high demand, respectively. This captures the main characteristics that many HPC clusters face as the cluster size and workload directly affect how resources should be scheduled, in particular given the goal to maximize resource utilization without affecting application runtime. As shown in Table 2 (Response Time), and due to collocation and sharing of resources, ASA_X impacts all application's completion time. This is mitigated by decisions the algorithm takes at runtime, which uses the applications state to evaluate the impacts of each collocation. However, it must also be noted that no hard deadlines are set for jobs' wall-clock times. This allows comparison of ASA_X to worst case scenarios, and enables evaluation of the overhead caused by resource sharing due to collocation. Collocation has neglectable total runtime impacts (up to 5% in our experiments) and users are known to request more time than needed when submitting their jobs. Some predictable noisy interference is bound to happen at runtime, and ASA_X's goal is simply to model this expected behavior. By learning from mistakes, ASAx avoids collocating two applications that may negatively impact the scheduler's loss function as described by the decision trees, evaluated at each time that the scheduler has to make a collocation decision.

Finally, the proposed *happiness* metric (Eq. 1) can enable ASA_X to mitigate and control the possible performance degradation due to bad collocation decisions. Together with the decision trees, this characteristic is specially useful for queues that share nodes among two or more jobs, e.g. debugging queues used during scientific applications development stages. It is important to note though, that the happiness metric assumes all tasks in a single job are sufficiently homogeneous, i.e., need approximately the same amount of time to complete execution. This is however the common case in most stages of a scientific workflow, as in-stage heterogeneity leads to inefficient parallelization and poor performance. As such, monitoring $Hp(t)$ before and after the co-scheduling of a job can also be useful to understand if such a decision actually is likely to succeed. However, this is outside the scope of this paper but can be seen as an natural extension to our co-scheduling algorithm as such feature can enable ASA_X to foresee performance degradation in running applications. This can ultimately enable ASA_X to optimize its co-scheduling actions already before collocation, which further protects performance of collocated jobs. Another possible extensions is to generalize the ASA_X allocation capacity to accommodate more than two jobs in the same node simultaneously as long as they all impose limited performance degradation on one other.

6   Related Work

The scale and processing capacities of modern multi-core and heterogeneous servers create new HPC resource management opportunities. With increasing concerns in datacenter density, idle capacity should be utilized as efficiently as possible [38]. However, the low effective utilization of computing resources in datacenters is explained through certain important requirements. For instance, to guarantee user Quality-of-Services (QoS), datacenter operators adopt a worst-case policy in resource allocations [42], while in HPC, users expect stable performance guarantees. To reach QoS guarantees, users often overestimate resource requests and total execution times (wall-clock), further degrading datacenter throughput. Runtime Service Level Objectives (SLOs) are achieved through more efficient job scheduling, but this is rarely deployed in modern HPC infrastructures due to fear of performance degradation when sharing resources. Most of HPC batch systems use resource reservation with backfilling strategies, and rely on users to provide application resource and walltime requirements [19,37].

This model is based on the assumption that jobs fully utilize the allocated capacity constantly throughout their lifespan. This is needed for some purposes such as cache optimizations, debugging, and is thus important during application development and testing. However, more often than not, jobs utilize less than this upper capacity [40], which is rarely the case, specially at early stages of development. Some proposals [3,11] aim to extend this traditional model, with impacts need to be studied in more depth. Public cloud datacenters, on the other hand, offer alternatives for running HPC workloads, such as Kubernetes [7], and Mesos [17]. Their resource management policies are centered around low latency scheduling, offering fairness and resource negotiation [16]. However, these systems lack main capabilities such as resource reservation, gang scheduling, and also assume that applications fully utilize allocated resources [12,40].

Tackling the utilization problem from a different angle, stochastic schedulers have been proposed as solutions to overcome user resource overestimates [15]. ASA_X can be used as an extension to this class of schedulers, because it offers a new scheduling abstraction through its experts, which can model stochastic applications as well. Similarly to ASA_X, Deep RL schedulers have been proposed [11,22,25,43], though they focus either on dynamic applications, or on rigid-jobs. As previously discussed, an increasingly diverse set of applications are flooding new HPC infrastructure realizations. [30] uses Bayesian optimization to capture performance models between low latency and batch jobs. It differs from our experts approach in that ASA_X uses decision trees to assess such relationship, and [30] targets only two types of applications. Machine Learning (ML) models have been proposed to take advantage of the large datasets already available in current datacenters [8]. For instance, [29] repeatedly runs micro-benchmarks in order to build a predictive model for the relationship between an application and resource contention. In contrast to that type of ML, RL algorithms such as the one used in ASA_X and in [43] do not require historical training data to optimize scheduling. As mentioned in previous sections, ASA_X is a stateful extension of [36], where the main difference is that ASA_X can incorporate previous decisions in a RL approach. In [39], the authors combine offline job classification with online RL to improve collocations. This approach can accelerate convergence, although it might have complex consequences when new unknown jobs do not fit into the initial classification. Similarly to ASA_X, the Cognitive ScHeduler (CuSH) [11] decouples job selection from the policy selection problem and also handles heterogeneity. Finally, as an example of scheduling policy optimization, [43] selects among several policies to adapt the scheduling decisions. This approach is similar to our concept of a forest of decision trees (experts), although their work do not consider co-scheduling to target queue waiting time minimization combined with improved cluster utilization.

7   Conclusion

Since mainframes, batch scheduling has been an area of research, and even more since time-sharing schedulers were first proposed. However, today's HPC schedulers face a diverse set of workloads and highly dynamic requirements, such as low latency and streaming workflows generated by data-intensive applications. These workflows are characterized by supporting many different features, such as system faults, approximate output, and resource adaptability. However, current HPC jobs do not fully utilize the capacity provided by these high-end infrastructures, impacting datacenter operational costs, besides hurting user experience due to long waiting times. To mitigate these, in this paper we propose a HPC co-scheduler (ASA$_X$) that uses a novel and convergence proven reinforcement learning algorithm. By analytically describing a cluster's policy through efficient decision trees, our co-scheduler is able to optimize job collocation by profiling applications and understanding how much of ongoing allocations can be safely reallocated to other jobs. Through real cluster experiments, we show that ASA$_X$ is able to improve cluster CPU utilization by as much as 51% while also reducing response time and queue waiting times, hence improving overall datacenter throughput, with little impacts on job runtime (up to 10%, but 5% slower on average). Together with the architecture, our algorithm forms the basis for efficient resource sharing and an application-aware co-scheduler for improved HPC scheduling with minimal performance degradation.

A Convergence of ASA$_X$

In here we explain how we can statistically bound the accumulated loss and create a strategy to take the best available actions in a given environment. For doing so, we define the *excess risk*, which estimates how "risky" taking an action can be. It is defined here as

$$E_t = \sum_{s=1}^{t} \sum_{j=1}^{n_s} \left(\sum_{i=1}^{n} \alpha_{s-1,i} \mathbf{p}_i(\mathbf{x}_{sj}) \ell\left(a_{sj}\right) \right) - \atop \min_{*} \sum_{s=1}^{t} \sum_{j=1}^{n_s} \mathbf{p}_*(\mathbf{x}_{sj}) \ell\left(a_{sj}\right), \tag{4}$$

where $\mathbf{x}_{sj}$ denotes the decision tree states of the j-th case in the s-th round, and where a_{sj} is the action taken at this case.

Theorem 1 shows that the excess risk for Algorithm 1 is bound as follows.

Theorem 1. *Let $\{\gamma_t > 0\}_t$ be a non-increasing sequence. The excess risk E_t after t rounds is then bound by*

$$E_t \leq \gamma_t^{-1} \left(\ln n + \frac{1}{2} \sum_{s=1}^{t} \gamma_s^2 \right). \tag{5}$$

Proof. Let a_{tj} denote the action taken in round t at the jth case, and let n_t denote the number of cases in round t. Similarly, let $\mathbf{x}_{tj}$ denote the state for this case, and let $\mathbf{p}_i(\mathbf{x}_{tj})$ denote the distribution over the a actions as proposed by the ith expert. Let $\ell_{tj}(a)$ denote the (not necessarily observed) loss of action a as achieved on the tjth case.

Define the variable Z_t as

$$Z_t = \sum_{i=1}^{n} \exp\left(-\sum_{s=1}^{t} \gamma_s \sum_{j=1}^{n_s} \mathbf{p}_i(\mathbf{x}_{sj})\ell_{sj}\left(a_{sj}\right) \right). \tag{6}$$

Then

$$\sum_{s=1}^{t} \ln \frac{Z_s}{Z_{s-1}} = \ln Z_t - \ln Z_0. \tag{7}$$

Moreover

$$\ln Z_t = \ln \sum_{i=1}^{n} \exp\left(-\sum_{s=1}^{t} \gamma_s \sum_{j=1}^{n_s} \mathbf{p}_i(\mathbf{x}_{sj})\ell_{sj}\left(a_{sj}\right) \right) \geq$$

$$-\sum_{s=1}^{t} \gamma_s \sum_{j=1}^{n_s} \mathbf{p}_*(\mathbf{x}_{sj})\ell_{sj}\left(a_{sj}\right), \tag{8}$$

for any expert $* \in \{1,\ldots,n\}$. Conversely, we have

$$\ln \frac{Z_t}{Z_{t-1}} = \ln \frac{\sum_{i=1}^{n} \exp\left(-\sum_{s=1}^{t} \gamma_s \sum_{j=1}^{n_s} \mathbf{p}_i(\mathbf{x}_{sj})\ell_{sj}\left(a_{sj}\right) \right)}{\sum_{i=1}^{n} \exp\left(-\sum_{s=1}^{t-1} \gamma_s \sum_{j=1}^{n_s} \mathbf{p}_i(\mathbf{x}_{sj})\ell_{sj}\left(a_{sj}\right) \right)}$$

$$= \ln \sum_{i=1}^{n} \alpha_{t-1,i} \exp\left(-\gamma_t \sum_{j=1}^{n_t} \mathbf{p}_i(\mathbf{x}_{tj})\ell_{tj}\left(a_{tj}\right) \right). \tag{9}$$

Application of Hoeffding's lemma gives then

$$\ln \frac{Z_s}{Z_{s-1}} \leq -\gamma_s \sum_{j=1}^{n_s} \left(\sum_{i=1}^{n} \alpha_{s-1,i}\mathbf{p}_i(\mathbf{x}_{sj})\ell_{sj}\left(a_{sj}\right) \right) + \frac{4\gamma_s^2}{8}, \tag{10}$$

using the construction that $\max_i \sum_{j=1}^{n_t} \mathbf{p}_i(\mathbf{x}_{sj})\ell_{sj}\left(a_{sj}\right) \leq 1$. Reshuffling terms gives then

$$\sum_{s=1}^{t} \gamma_s \sum_{j=1}^{n_s} \left(\sum_{i=1}^{n} \alpha_{s-1,i}\mathbf{p}_i(\mathbf{x}_{sj})\ell_{sj}\left(a_{sj}\right) \right) -$$

$$\sum_{s=1}^{t} \gamma_s \sum_{j=1}^{n_s} \mathbf{p}_*(\mathbf{x}_{sj})\ell_{sj}\left(a_{sj}\right) \leq \ln n + \frac{1}{2} \sum_{s=1}^{t} \gamma_s^2. \tag{11}$$

Application of Abel's second inequality [2] gives the result.

References

1. ARCHER User Survey (2019). https://www.archer.ac.uk/about-archer/reports/annual/2019/ARCHER_UserSurvey2019_Report.pdf
2. Abel, N.H.: Abel inequality - encyclopedia of mathematics (2021). https://encyclopediaofmath.org/index.php?title=Abel_inequality&oldid=18342
3. Ahn, D.H., Garlick, J., Grondona, M., Lipari, D., Springmeyer, B., Schulz, M.: Flux: a next-generation resource management framework for large HPC centers. In: 43rd International Conference on Parallel Processing Workshops. IEEE (2014)
4. Altschul, S.F., et al.: Gapped BLAST and PSI-BLAST: a new generation of protein database search programs. Nucleic Acids Res. **25**, 3389–3402 (1997)
5. Ambati, P., Bashir, N., Irwin, D., Shenoy, P.: Waiting game: optimally provisioning fixed resources for cloud-enabled schedulers. In: International Conference for High Performance Computing, Networking, Storage and Analysis (2020)
6. Berriman, G., et al.: Montage: a grid enabled image mosaic service for the national virtual observatory. In: Astronomical Data Analysis Software and Systems (ADASS) XIII (2004)
7. Burns, B., Grant, B., Oppenheimer, D., Brewer, E., Wilkes, J.: Borg, Omega, and Kubernetes. Queue (2016)
8. Carastan-Santos, D., De Camargo, R.Y.: Obtaining dynamic scheduling policies with simulation and machine learning. In: Proceedings of the International Conference for High Performance Computing, Networking, Storage and Analysis (2017)
9. Castain, R.H., Hursey, J., Bouteiller, A., Solt, D.: PMIx: process management for exascale environments. Parallel Comput. **79**, 9–29 (2018)
10. Cirne, W., Berman, F.: A comprehensive model of the supercomputer workload. In: Proceedings of the Fourth Annual IEEE International Workshop on Workload Characterization. WWC-4 (Cat. No. 01EX538), pp. 140–148. IEEE (2001)
11. Domeniconi, G., Lee, E.K., Venkataswamy, V., Dola, S.: Cush: cognitive scheduler for heterogeneous high performance computing system. In: Workshop on Deep Reinforcement Learning for Knowledge Discover, DRL4KDD 2019 (2019)
12. Feitelson, D.G.: Packing schemes for gang scheduling. In: Feitelson, D.G., Rudolph, L. (eds.) JSSPP 1996. LNCS, vol. 1162, pp. 89–110. Springer, Heidelberg (1996). https://doi.org/10.1007/BFb0022289
13. Feitelson, D.G., Rudolph, L.: Toward convergence in job schedulers for parallel supercomputers. In: Feitelson, D.G., Rudolph, L. (eds.) JSSPP 1996. LNCS, vol. 1162, pp. 1–26. Springer, Heidelberg (1996). https://doi.org/10.1007/BFb0022284
14. Feitelson, D.G., Tsafrir, D., Krakov, D.: Experience with using the parallel workloads archive. J. Parallel Distrib. Comput. **74**, 2967–2982 (2014)
15. Gainaru, A., Aupy, G.P., Sun, H., Raghavan, P.: Speculative scheduling for stochastic HPC applications. In: Proceedings of the 48th International Conference on Parallel Processing, ICPP 2019, pp. 32:1–32:10. ACM (2019). https://doi.org/10.1145/3337821.3337890
16. Ghodsi, A., Zaharia, M., Hindman, B., Konwinski, A., Shenker, S., Stoica, I.: Dominant resource fairness: fair allocation of multiple resource types. In: USENIX Symposium on Networked Systems Design and Implementation (2011)
17. Hindman, B., et al.: Mesos: a platform for fine-grained resource sharing in the data center (2011)
18. Janus, P., Rzadca, K.: SLO-aware colocation of data center tasks based on instantaneous processor requirements. arXiv preprint arXiv:1709.01384 (2017)

19. Yoo, A.B., Jette, M.A., Grondona, M.: SLURM: simple Linux utility for resource management. In: Feitelson, D., Rudolph, L., Schwiegelshohn, U. (eds.) JSSPP 2003. LNCS, vol. 2862, pp. 44–60. Springer, Heidelberg (2003). https://doi.org/10.1007/10968987_3

20. Kolter, J.Z., Johnson, M.J.: REDD: a public data set for energy disaggregation research. In: Workshop on Data Mining Applications in Sustainability (SIGKDD), San Diego, CA (2011)

21. Lakew, E.B., Klein, C., Hernandez-Rodriguez, F., Elmroth, E.: Performance-based service differentiation in clouds. In: 2015 15th IEEE/ACM International Symposium on Cluster, Cloud and Grid Computing. IEEE (2015)

22. Li, Y., Sun, D., Lee, B.C.: Dynamic colocation policies with reinforcement learning. ACM Trans. Architect. Code Optim. (TACO) **17**, 1–25 (2020)

23. Li, Y., Tang, X., Cai, W.: On dynamic bin packing for resource allocation in the cloud. In: Proceedings of the 26th ACM Symposium on Parallelism in Algorithms and Architectures. ACM (2014)

24. Lifka, D.: The ANL/IBM SP scheduling system. In: Job Scheduling Strategies for Parallel Processing. IEEE (1995)

25. Mao, H., Schwarzkopf, M., Venkatakrishnan, S.B., Meng, Z., Alizadeh, M.: Learning scheduling algorithms for data processing clusters. In: ACM Special Interest Group on Data Communication (2019)

26. Mell, P., Grance, T., et al.: The NIST definition of cloud computing (2011)

27. Menage, P.B.: Adding generic process containers to the Linux kernel. In: Proceedings of the Linux Symposium. Citeseer (2007)

28. Monahan, G.E.: State of the art - a survey of partially observable Markov decision processes: theory, models, and algorithms. Manag. Sci. **28**, 1–16 (1982)

29. Moradi, H., Wang, W., Fernandez, A., Zhu, D.: uPredict: a user-level profiler-based predictive framework in multi-tenant clouds. In: 2020 IEEE International Conference on Cloud Engineering (IC2E). IEEE (2020)

30. Patel, T., Tiwari, D.: CLITE: efficient and QoS-aware co-location of multiple latency-critical jobs for warehouse scale computers. In: 2020 IEEE International Symposium on High Performance Computer Architecture (HPCA). IEEE (2020)

31. Reiss, C., Tumanov, A., Ganger, G.R., Katz, R.H., Kozuch, M.A.: Heterogeneity and dynamicity of clouds at scale: Google trace analysis. In: Proceedings of the Third ACM Symposium on Cloud Computing (2012)

32. Reuther, A., et al.: Scalable system scheduling for HPC and big data. J. Parallel Distrib. Comput. **111**, 76–92 (2018)

33. Rocchetti, N., Da Silva, M., Nesmachnow, S., Tchernykh, A.: Penalty scheduling policy applying user estimates and aging for supercomputing centers. In: Barrios Hernández, C.J., Gitler, I., Klapp, J. (eds.) CARLA 2016. CCIS, vol. 697, pp. 49–60. Springer, Cham (2017). https://doi.org/10.1007/978-3-319-57972-6_4

34. Rodrigo Álvarez, G.P., Östberg, P.O., Elmroth, E., Ramakrishnan, L.: A2L2: an application aware flexible HPC scheduling model for low-latency allocation. In: Proceedings of the 8th International Workshop on Virtualization Technologies in Distributed Computing. ACM (2015)

35. Rustad, E.: Numascale: Numaconnect (2013). https://www.numascale.com/index.php/numascale-whitepapers/

36. Souza, A., Pelckmans, K., Ghoshal, D., Ramakrishnan, L., Tordsson, J.: Asa - the adaptive scheduling architecture. In: The 29th International Symposium on High-Performance Parallel and Distributed Computing. ACM (2020)

37. Staples, G.: Torque resource manager. In: Proceedings of the 2006 ACM/IEEE Conference on Supercomputing, SC 2006. ACM (2006)

38. Stevens, R., Taylor, V., Nichols, J., Maccabe, A.B., Yelick, K., Brown, D.: AI for science. Technical report, Argonne National Lab. (ANL), Argonne, IL (United States) (2020)
39. Thamsen, L., et al.: Hugo: a cluster scheduler that efficiently learns to select complementary data-parallel jobs. In: Schwardmann, U., et al. (eds.) Euro-Par 2019. LNCS, vol. 11997, pp. 519–530. Springer, Cham (2020). https://doi.org/10.1007/978-3-030-48340-1_40
40. Tirmazi, M., et al.: Borg: the next generation. In: SIGOPS European Conference on Computer Systems (EuroSys 2020) (2020)
41. Uchroński, M., Bożejko, W., Krajewski, Z., Tykierko, M., Wodecki, M.: User estimates inaccuracy study in HPC scheduler. In: Zamojski, W., Mazurkiewicz, J., Sugier, J., Walkowiak, T., Kacprzyk, J. (eds.) DepCoS-RELCOMEX 2018. AISC, vol. 761, pp. 504–514. Springer, Cham (2019). https://doi.org/10.1007/978-3-319-91446-6_47
42. Yang, H., Breslow, A., Mars, J., Tang, L.: Bubble-flux: precise online QoS management for increased utilization in warehouse scale computers. In: ACM SIGARCH Computer Architecture News. ACM (2013)
43. Zhang, D., Dai, D., He, Y., Bao, F.S.: RLScheduler: learn to schedule HPC batch jobs using deep reinforcement learning. arXiv preprint arXiv:1910.08925 (2019)

Performance-Cost Optimization of Moldable Scientific Workflows

Marta Jaros$^{(\boxtimes)}$ and Jiri Jaros

Faculty of Information Technology, Centre of Excellence IT4Innovations,
Brno University of Technology, Brno, Czech Republic
{martajaros,jarosjir}@fit.vutbr.cz

Abstract. Moldable scientific workflows represent a special class of scientific workflows where the tasks are written as distributed programs being able to exploit various amounts of computer resources. However, current cluster job schedulers require the user to specify the amount of resources per task manually. This often leads to suboptimal execution time and related cost of the whole workflow execution since many users have only limited experience and knowledge of the parallel efficiency and scaling. This paper proposes several mechanisms to automatically optimize the execution parameters of moldable workflows using genetic algorithms. The paper introduces a local optimization of workflow tasks, a global optimization of the workflow on systems with on-demand resource allocation, and a global optimization for systems with static resource allocation. Several objectives including the workflow makespan, computational cost and the percentage of idling nodes are investigated together with a trade-off parameter putting stress on one objective or another. The paper also discusses the structure and quality of several evolved workflow schedules and the possible reduction in makespan or cost. Finally, the computational requirements of evolutionary process together with the recommended genetic algorithm settings are investigated. The most complex workflows may be evolved in less than two minutes using the global optimization while in only 14 s using the local optimization.

Keywords: Task graph scheduling · Workflow · Genetic algorithm · Moldable tasks · Makespan estimation

1 Introduction

All fields of science and engineering use computers to reach new findings, while the most compute power demanding problems require High Performance Computing (HPC) or Cloud systems to give answers to their questions. The problems being solved nowadays are often very complex and comprise of a lot of various tasks describing different aspects of the investigated problem and their mutual dependencies. These tasks compose a scientific processing workflow [3]. There are immense of such scientific workflows in various fields [22], yet they have one

© Springer Nature Switzerland AG 2021
D. Klusáček et al. (Eds.): JSSPP 2021, LNCS 12985, pp. 149–167, 2021.
https://doi.org/10.1007/978-3-030-88224-2_8

thing in common. They all demand to be computed in the minimum possible time, and more often, for the lowest possible cost.

The execution of a scientific workflow on an HPC system is performed via communication with the HPC front-end, also referred to as job scheduler [13]. After the workflow data has been uploaded to the cluster, the workflow tasks are submitted to the computational queues to wait until the system has enough free resources, and all task dependencies have been resolved (predecessor tasks have been finished).

Modern HPC schedulers control multiple processing queues and implement various techniques for efficient task allocation and resource management [15]. However, the workflow queuing time, computation time and related cost are strongly dependent on the execution parameters of particular tasks provided by the user during submission. These parameters usually include temporal parameters such as requested allocation length, as well as spatial parameters including the number and type of compute nodes, the number of processes and threads, the amount of memory and storage space, and more frequently, the frequency and power cup of various hardware components. These parameters, unfortunately, have to be specified by the end users based on their previous experience with the task implementation and knowledge on the input data nature.

In everyday practice, the estimations of task allocation lengths are quite inaccurate, which disturbs the scheduling process. Most users deliberately overestimate the computational time in order to provide some reserve to mitigate performance fluctuation and prevent premature termination of the task execution [23]. Moreover, many complex tasks are written as moldable distributed parallel programs being able to exploit various amounts and types of computing resources. Nonetheless, it is again the user responsibility to choose appropriate values of these parameters according to the input data.

The task moldability is often limited by many factors, the most important of which being the domain decomposition [6], parallel efficiency [2], and scalability [14]. While the domain decomposition may limit the numbers of processing units (nodes, processes, threads) to rather a sparse list of acceptable values, the parallel efficiency determines the execution time and cost for a given task and a chosen amount of resources. Naturally, the lower the parallel efficiency, the lower the speed-up, and consequently, the longer the computation time and the higher the computational cost. Finally, the scalability upper-bounds the amount of exploitable resources by the overall available memory.

While the field of rigid workflow optimization, where the amount of resources per task cannot be tuned, has been thoroughly studied and is part of common job schedulers such as PBSPro [13] or Slurm [30], the automatic optimization and scheduling of moldable workflows has still been an outstanding problem, although firstly solved two decades ago in [10].

For the last decade, many papers have focused on the estimation of rigid workflow execution time in HPC systems and enhancing the resource management. For example, Chirkin et al. [7] introduces a makespan estimation algorithm that may be integrated into schedulers. Robert et al. [25] gives an overview of task graph scheduling algorithms. The usage of genetic algorithms addressing the task scheduling problems has also been introduced, e.g., a task graph scheduling on homogeneous processors using genetic algorithm and local search strategies [17] and a performance improvement of the used genetic algorithm [24]. However, handful works have taken into the consideration the moldability and scaling behaviour of particular tasks, their dependencies and the current cluster utilization [4,9,29].

This paper focuses on the automation optimization of the moldable scientific workflow execution using genetic algorithms [28]. The optimization of execution parameters is based on collected historical performance data (i.e., strong scaling) for supported tasks in the workflow. The paper presents several objective functions and trade-off coefficients that allow to customize the pressure either on the overall execution time, or the computational cost, or both.

The rest of the paper is structured as follows. Section 2 describes the optimization algorithm, the solution encoding specifying the amount of resources per task, the objective and fitness functions evaluating the quality of the candidate workflow schedule and the details of the applications use cases. Section 3 elaborates on the quality of the genetic algorithm and its best set-up, presents the time complexity of the search process and compares several workflow execution schedules by the optic of particular objective functions. The last section concludes the paper and draws potential future improvements of this technique.

2   Proposed Algorithm

The assignment of optimal amount of compute resources to particular tasks along with the scheduling of the workflow as a whole is known to be an NP-hard problem [9]. There have been several attempts to use heuristics to solve this problem [4,16,18,26], however, they are either tightly connected to an existing HPC cluster and its scheduler, use idealized models of strong scaling and parallel efficiency, or optimize only one criterion such as makespan, cluster throughput, or execution cost. The user tunability of these approaches are thus limited.

Therefore, we decided to use genetic algorithms, which are highly flexible in combinatorial optimization and scheduling [8]. From the vast number of existing implementations, PyGAD [11], an open-source Python library for building the genetic algorithm, was chosen. PyGAD supports various types of genetic operators and selection strategies, and offers a simple interface for objective function definition.

The overall concept of the moldable workflow scheduling optimization using PyGAD is shown in Fig. 1. The structure of the task graph is converted into a 1D array where each element corresponds to a single task and holds its execution parameters. The genetic algorithm traverses the search space and seeks for good solutions by applying genetic manipulations and selection strategies on the population of candidate solutions. The quality of these candidate solutions is evaluated by the fitness function. Although the paper presents three different methods to evaluate the schedule quality, the concept is similar in all cases. First,

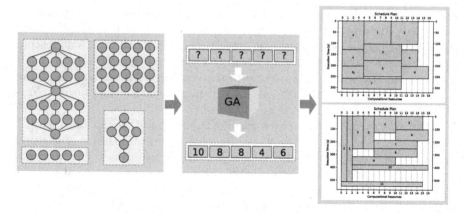

Fig. 1. A workflow is transformed to a vector of integer elements specifying assigned amount of resources to particular tasks. This vector represents a candidate solution of the GA search space. The final output of the optimization can be visualized as a workflow schedule.

the execution time for every task is calculated based on the task type, execution parameters set by the GA, input data size, and known parallel efficiency/strong scaling behavior. Next, the tasks are submitted to the cluster simulator that draws up an execution schedule and calculates the makespan (the critical path through the workflow including queuing times) and execution cost. The output of the optimization is a set of best execution parameters for individual tasks minimizing given criteria implemented by the fitness function.

2.1   Solution Encoding

In order to optimize workflow execution schedules using GA, it is necessary to transform the workflow into a template for candidate solutions (chromosomes) I. The workflow's DAG is traversed in a breath-first manner producing a vector of N tasks (genes). Every gene i corresponds to a single task and holds the execution parameters (resources) R_i assigned to the task i, see Eq. (1).

$$I = (R_1, R_2, \ldots, R_N) \tag{1}$$

The execution parameters being investigated in this study only consider the number of computing nodes assigned to a given task. This set can be simply extended in the future to support, e.g., node cpu frequency and power cup or the number of processes/threads per node.

The number of nodes assignable to a given task is naturally constrained by 1 from the bottom, and by the size of the computing system from the top. Moreover, it is also limited by the type of the task, its scalability, and the size of input data. The strong scaling, parallel efficiency and scalability were measured for each task type and input data size in advance using short benchmark runs and stored in the performance database. These constraints are imposed at the beginning of the fitness function evaluation.

2.2   Fitness Function

This paper considers three different types of the fitness function looking at the optimization problem from different angles: (1) Independent local optimization of the execution time for particular tasks useful when running small tasks on large HPC systems, (2) Global optimization of the whole workflow minimizing the execution time and related computational cost under on-demand resource allocations, (3) Global optimization of the whole workflow time and cost on statically allocated cluster parts, i.e., the idling nodes also contribute to the computational cost.

Local Optimization of Workflow Tasks. This fitness functions optimizes each task independently considering only the execution time while neglecting the computational cost, see Eq. (2). This fitness function does not use the cluster simulator but only sums the execution time of all tasks. Let us note that the highest possible number of computing nodes may not lead to the fastest execution time due to unbalanced local decomposition, high overhead of parallel computation, etc.

This fitness function relies on the cluster scheduler to assemble a good execution schedule of the whole workflow when provided optimal setup for particular tasks. This statement is likely to be valid for large HPC clusters with hundreds of nodes and tasks employing low tens of nodes. From the scheduling point of view, this fitness function is the fastest one.

$$fitness = t = \sum_{i=1}^{N} t_i(R_i) \tag{2}$$

where t is the aggregated net execution time of N tasks in the workflow, each of which running on R_i nodes for time t_i.

Global Optimization with On-Demand Allocation. This fitness function minimizes the overall execution time t of the workflow given by the sum of the execution time of the tasks along the critical path in the workflow graph (makespan [12]), together with the computational cost c given by a sum of computational cost of all tasks in the workflow, see Eq. (5).

As we know from the problem definition, those two requirements usually go against each other. Therefore, an α parameter to prioritize either makespan or cost is introduced. In order to balance between proportionally very different criteria, a kind of normalization is introduced. The makespan is normalized by the maximum total execution time of the workflow t_{max}, which is considered to be the sum of the execution times of all N tasks executed by only a single computation node in a sequential manner. The cost is normalized by the minimum execution cost which is the cost of the workflow computed by a single node in a sequential manner, see Eq. (3). This presumption is valid for typical parallel algorithms with sub-linear scaling, i.e., parallel efficiency as a function of the number of nodes is always smaller than 1, $E(P) < 1$.

$$c_{min} = t_{max} = \sum_{i=1}^{N} t_i(1) \tag{3}$$

$$c_i = t_i(R_i) \cdot R_i \tag{4}$$

$$fitness = \alpha \cdot \sum_{j \in M} (\frac{t_j(R_j)}{t_{max}}) + (1 - \alpha) \cdot \sum_{i=1}^{N} (\frac{c_i(R_i)}{c_{min}}), \tag{5}$$

where $M = \{i | i \in \text{CriticalPath}\}$

This fitness function suits best the workflow being executed in environments with shared resources where only truly consumed resources are paid for, e.g., shared HPC systems.

Global Optimization with Static Allocation. The last fitness function described by Eq. (8) also minimizes the workflow makespan, but the computational cost now takes into the consideration also idling nodes. Let us imagine we have a dedicated portion of the cluster consisting of 64 nodes statically allocated before the workflow has started. The computational cost, the user will be accounted for, equals to the size of the allocation multiplied by the makespan, no matter some nodes are not being used for the whole duration of the workflow execution. The fitness function thus attempts to shake down the tasks to minimize the amount of idling resources while still minimizing the makespan. The execution cost is then normalized by the highest possible cost in the dedicated system where only one node works.

$$c_{max} = t_{max} \cdot P \tag{6}$$

$$c = \sum_{i=1}^{N} t_i(R_i) \cdot R_i \tag{7}$$

$$fitness = \alpha \sum_{j \in M} (\frac{t_j(R_j)}{t_{max}}) + (1 - \alpha) \frac{c_{max} - c}{c_{max}}, \tag{8}$$

where $M = \{i | i \in \text{CriticalPath}\}$

Similarly to the previous case, t is the overall execution time of the workflow, and t_{max} is the maximum overall execution time obtained for a serial scheduling of sequential tasks. The number of nodes statically allocated to the workflow is denoted by P. The number of nodes assigned per tasks i is R_i. The maximum possible cost is represented by c_{max} while the actual cost based on the current execution parameters and the workflow structure is denoted by c.

2.3 Cluster Simulator

In order to create a workflow execution schedule and calculate the makespan, we developed a simple cluster simulator called *Tetrisator*. The name of this component is inspired by the Tetris game [5] since there is a strong analogy in arranging the blocks of different sizes and shapes with the optimization of the execution schedule to minimize execution time and cost. The blocks can be seen as tasks and their sizes are given by required amount of resources and corresponding execution time. The blocks a.k.a tasks may be molded to be "wider" or "longer" by changing the number of resources, however, their surface does not have to stay constant due to varying parallel efficiency.

Tetrisator simulates the operation of an artificial HPC system with a predefined number of computing nodes P. The tasks are submitted to the simulator in the same order as defined in the chromosome (a breadth-first top down traversal). During the submission, the numbers of nodes assigned to particular tasks are taken from the chromosome and the corresponding execution times are located in the performance database. The breadth-first traversal also allows a simple definition of task dependencies the simulator has to obey. If there are multiple tasks being ready to be executed, the submission order is followed. This is inspired the default behaviour of the PBS job scheduler with the backfilling policy switched off [27].

3 Experimental Results

The experiments presented in this paper have the following goals: (1) confirm the hypothesis that it is possible to find suitable schedules for given workflows using genetic algorithms, (2) investigate the suitability of the α parameter to prefer of one optimization criterion over the other one (overall execution time vs. computational cost), and (3) evaluate the computational requirements of the optimization process on various workflow sizes.

3.1 Investigated Moldable Workflows

The performance and search capabilities of the proposed optimization algorithm were investigated on three scientific workflows inspired by real-world applications of the acoustic toolbox k-Wave [19] for validation of neurostimulation procedures, see Fig. 2. The workflows are composed of two different kinds of tasks, simulation tasks (ST) and data processing tasks (PT). The first workflow shows a barrier behaviour where all simulation tasks at the first level have to finish before the data is processed by a single data processing task. Only after that, the second level of STs can continue. The second workflow uses a reduction tree where the data processing is parallelized in order to reduce the execution time of PT tasks. The last workflow, not shown in the figure, is composed of the set of independent STs executed in embarrassingly parallel manner.

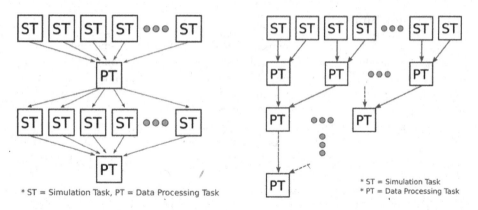

Fig. 2. The structure of two investigated workflows. The simulation tasks are inter-leaved with data processing tasks implying barriers between stages (left), the data produced by the simulation tasks are merged via a reduction tree (right).

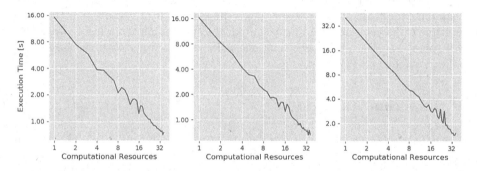

Fig. 3. Strong scaling of the k-Wave toolbox measured for $<1, 36>$ nodes on domain sizes composed of 500^3, 512^3 and 544^3 grid points. k-Wave simulations are the main part of simulations tasks in the examined workflows.

The simulation tasks are heavy computing programs scalable from 1 to 36 nodes, see Fig. 3. Their scaling was measured using the C++/MPI implementation of the k-Wave toolbox on the Barbora supercomputer at IT4Innovations[1]. The scaling behaviour depends on the input data size and shows several local optima for the number of nodes being powers of two. The shortest execution time was seen for 35 nodes. From these three examples, the first one was chosen in our experiments. The data processing tasks are lightweight tasks executable on one or two nodes. Their time complexity grows linearly with the number of input files they have to process.

In real k-Wave applications, the size of the domain for all STs is the same, however, the amount of time steps may vary by up to 25%. This is given by the mutual position of the transducer and the patient's head, which influences

---

[1] https://docs.it4i.cz/barbora/introduction/.

the distance the ultrasound wave has to travel. Moreover, the performance of all processors in the cluster is not equal. According to [1], the fluctuations may cause up to 5% deviations in the execution time. Both factors are considered by adding random perturbations to the task execution time during the workflow generation.

3.2   Local Task Optimization of the Execution Time

First, we investigated the local optimization of the proposed workflows, which is the simplest kind of optimization. This optimization only considers the net execution time of all tasks neglecting the queueing times and simulation cost. Thus no α parameter is used. This technique shows very good capabilities in optimizing particular tasks. From 20 independent runs of the GA, more than 90% of trials always found the best possible solution, the fitness of which can be analytically derived.

Table 1 shows suitable parameters for the genetic algorithm along with the number of generations necessary to find the optimal schedule, the execution time in seconds and the success rate. Since the variability of the results across different workflows was negligible, we collapsed all results into a single table.

The table reveals that the necessary population size linearly grows with the size of the workflow from 25 up to 150 individuals, but still stays quite small. This is natural behaviour since bigger workflows require longer chromosomes which in turn requires larger populations to keep promising building blocks of the solution. The best selection strategy driving the GA through the search spaces appears to be Steady state selection, although the difference to the Rank and Tournament selections was marginal. The number of generations to be evaluated before the GA finds the optimal schedule stays relatively constant close to 200. On the other hand, the execution time appears to grow quadratically. This growth can be attributed to a product of increasing population size which rises the number of fitness function evaluations, and the linearly growing time complexity of the fitness function evaluation. Nevertheless, an execution time of 14s with 95% of success rate for the biggest workflow is an excellent result.

3.3   Global Workflow Optimization of Execution Time and Cost

The global optimization of the workflow considers both criteria and balances between them using the α parameter. In this section we investigate two fitness functions oriented on on-demand and statically allocated resources.

The Influence of the α Parameter. Let us first investigate the influence of the α parameter on both global fitness functions. In practise, the α parameter can be seen as a user-friendly control slider promoting either the execution time or cost. The following values of α were tested: 0.95 and 0.8 prioritizing the minimal makespan, 0.5 balancing the makespan and the cost/usage of resources), and 0.2 and 0.05 prioritizing the minimal execution cost and unused resources, respectively.

Table 1. Computation requirements of the local optimization method together with recommended genetic algorithm (GA) settings that lead to optimal schedules obtained in the shortest time. Other GA settings common for all experiments is uniform crossover of 0.7 probability, random mutation of 0.01 probability, and 5% elitism.

Workflow size	Population size	Selection method	Median number of generations	Average runtime	Success rate
7	25	Steady State, Rank	180	0.27 s	100%
8	25	Steady State, Rank	220–250	0.37–0.42 s	100%
15	50	Steady State, Rank, Tournament, Roulette Wheel	120–200	0.52-0.87s	100%
16	50	Steady State, Rank, Tournament	180–200	0.98–1.08 s	100%
31	100	Steady State, Rank	100	1.40 s	100%
32	100	Steady State, Rank	190	3.41 s	90–95%
63	100	Rank, Steady State	215	5.61 s	100%
64	150	Steady State, Rank	260	13.29 s	90–95%

For each value of α and suitable GA settings, 20 independent runs were carried out. For the sake of brevity, only a few examples of selected workflows with the best GA settings will be shown. For each example, the results from all runs were collected, sorted, and 5% of the best solutions visualized in the form of a Pareto frontier. The color of the data points and lines representing the frontiers correspond to the α parameter used.

Let us start with the quality of solutions produced by the on-demand allocation fitness, see Fig. 4 and 5. Although evolved solutions for various α parameter may slightly overlap, Fig. 4 shows that we managed to drive the genetic algorithm to find desired solutions (forming clusters) that meet given optimization constraints. By adjusting the α parameter, we move along an imaginary curve composed by the combination of all Pareto frontiers. Thus when the importance is attached to the simulation cost, it is possible to get a schedule that reduces the cost by 10%, however, runs for 12% longer time, and vice versa. It can also be seen that each value of α works well only in a relatively short interval (the

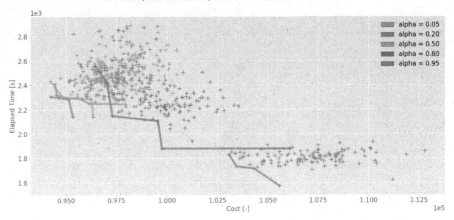

Fig. 4. Pareto frontier and dominated solutions calculated using the fitness function for on-demand allocations for the workflow with two levels of simulation tasks and various values of the α parameter.

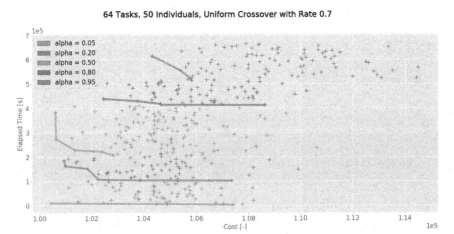

Fig. 5. Pareto frontier and dominated solutions calculated using the fitness function for on-demand allocations for the workflows without dependencies and various values of the α parameter.

middle of the frontier). At the edges it is usually outperformed by a different values of α.

The workflows without dependencies, however, show much worse parametrization, see Fig. 5. The only sensible value of α seems to be 0.05. Other values produce much worse compromises between time and cost. The only exception is the value 0.95 which can offer 15%–20% cost-effective schedules, but many times slower.

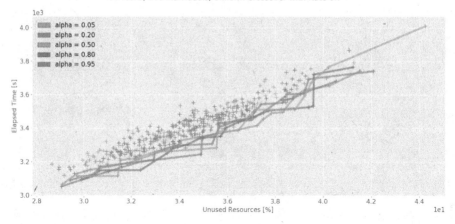

Fig. 6. Pareto frontier and dominated solutions calculated using the fitness function for static allocations for the workflow with two levels of simulation tasks and various values of α balancing between makespan and percentage of unused resources.

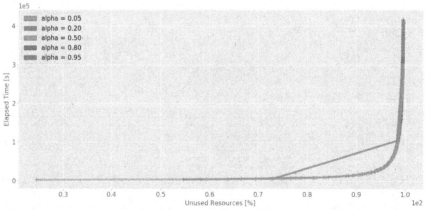

Fig. 7. Pareto frontier and dominated solutions calculated using the fitness function for static allocations for the workflow without dependencies and various values of α balancing between makespan and percentage of unused resources.

For experiments using the fitness function for static cluster allocations, we only show three different α parameters because the solutions highly overlap, see Figs. 6 and 7. The solutions found for workflows containing task dependencies seem to be saturated by the same minimal execution time. Smaller α parameter pushes the genetic algorithm to find solutions with smaller amount of unused resources (up to 44%) but a range of found solutions is quite high. From this point of view, 0.05 for α gives the most reasonable solutions. This is even more

Table 2. Recommended settings for the GA and the on-demand allocation fitness function. Other settings common for all experiments are uniform crossover of 0.7 probability, random mutation and 5% elitism.

Alpha	Workflow size	Population size	Selection method	Mutation probability	Median number of evaluations
0.95	7–16	25	Rank	0.001	2000–19750
	31–64	50	Steady State	0.01	5000–10000
0.80	7–16	25	Steady State	0.01	1250–2500
	31–64	50, 100	Rank	0.001	22000 (50)–45000 (50)
0.50	7–64	50, 100	Rank	0.001	2500 (50)–65000 (100)
0.20	7–64	25, 50	Rank	0.001	8750 (25)–42500 (50)
0.05	7–64	50, 100	Steady State	0.01	5000 (50)–30000 (100)

visible for workflows without task dependencies where 0.05 for the α parameter optimizes both makespan and the amount of unused resources.

The experiments showed that both criteria, the makespan and percentage of idle resources, are highly correlated. Thus, the lower percentage of idle resources the faster execution time. Although this may sound natural, the anomalies in the scaling behaviour of particular tasks has the potential to break this presumption. This experiment, however, shows that the scaling plots in Fig. 3 are very close to the perfect scaling.

Suitable Parameters of the Genetic Algorithm. Table 2 presents recommended settings for the genetic algorithm which produced best results along with the computational requirements expressed as the number of fitness function evaluations (i.e., a product of the number of generations and the population size). When two population sizes are given, the smaller one is used for the smaller workflows, and vice versa. The median number of evaluation is calculated for the actual population size shown in bracket in the last column. The range is bounded by two values, the one for the smallest workflow in the range and the one for the biggest workflow.

Table 3 presents an average execution time for a single generation. In connection with Table 2, the absolute wall clock time of the evolution process can be calculated. As an example, a schedule for a workflow with 64 dependant tasks can be evolved in 2 min and 20 s. We found out that schedules for tasks without dependencies may be evolved in 2 to 3 times shorter time.

The recommended settings of the genetic algorithm covers 0.7 probability of uniform crossover, steady state selection, 1% random mutation and 5% elitism. Workflow with less than 31 tasks could be evolved with 25 individuals in the population whereas bigger workflows (up to 64 tasks) with 50 individuals. It took approximately from 2500 (100 generations for 25 individuals) to 25000 (500 generations for 50 individuals) evaluations to evolve schedules for workflows of 7 to 64 tasks. So, a schedule for the workflow of 64 tasks with dependencies is evolved in a minute.

Table 3. The execution time of the evolution process for various workflows with dependencies and population sizes measured using global fitness functions on the Salomon cluster at IT4Innovations. The evolution runtimes for workflow without dependencies are approximately three times smaller.

Population size	Runtime per a single generation in seconds							
Workflow size	7	8	15	16	31	32	63	64
25	0.004	0.005	0.010	0.010				
50	0.007	0.009	0.019	0.021	0.040	0.043	0.112	0.120
100	0.013	0.018	0.037	0.043	0.077	0.088	0.227	0.220
150					0.110	0.132	0.382	0.335

Investigation of the Workflow Schedules. Here, we show and compare several evolved schedules using different fitness functions. For better visibility, only schedules for workflows of 15 and 16 tasks are shown. Figure 8 shows two execution plans for 15 and 16 tasks, respectively, locally optimized by Eq. (2). Regardless of the number of tasks in the workflow, the genetic algorithm always picks 35 nodes for simulation tasks and 2 nodes for data processing tasks because this selection assures their minimal execution time.

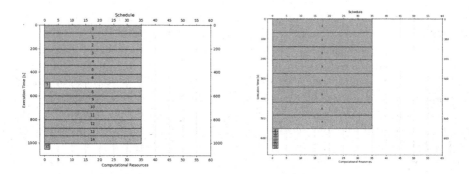

Fig. 8. Evolved schedules for investigated workflows with 16 and 15 dependant tasks using a local optimization.

Figure 9 shows evolved schedules using a global optimization for on-demand allocations balancing the makespan and computational cost with $\alpha = 0.5$. When compared with schedules depicted in Fig. 8, it is evident that the GA preferred much smaller amounts of nodes for simulation tasks which resulted in a cost reduction by 40% and makespan increase by 37% for the workflow of 16 tasks. In the case of the workflow with 15 tasks, we may however observe that the makespan is even better when the global optimization is used. This is given by the way the local optimization works, i.e., the concurrency is not expected. Here,

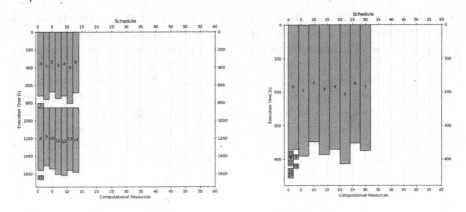

Fig. 9. Evolved schedules for investigated workflows with 16 and 15 dependant tasks using a global optimization for on-demand allocations balancing the makespan and computational cost.

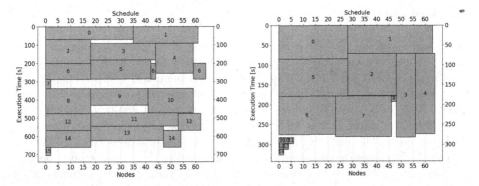

Fig. 10. Evolved schedules for workflows with 16 and 15 dependant tasks using a global optimization balancing the makespan and the amount of unused resources (24.49% for the left workflow, 15.21% for the right workflow).

the global optimization gives better results in both aspects, i.e., the makespan was reduced by 30% and the computational cost by 37%.

Figure 10 shows evolved schedules using a global optimization balancing the makespan and the amount of unused resources with $\alpha = 0.5$. If we compare them with schedules in Fig. 8, we can see that in both cases the makespan is reduced by 51% in case of 15 tasks, and by 35% in case of 16 tasks while the amount of unused resources was reduced from 53.0% and 50.0% to 15.21% and 24.49%, respectively.

Since the global optimization approaches are not comparable, we just emphasize the differences between obtained solutions in Fig. 9 and Fig. 10. It can be seen that the solutions evolved using the global optimization focusing on the amount of unused resources have shorter makespans because there is an effort to use, i.e., pay for, the resources for the shortest time. If we evaluate these solutions using the fitness function for on-demand allocations, it is obvious that we get more expensive solutions than those which were originally evolved using this fitness function. Since we cannot compare the solutions in absolute numbers, we can come out of the premise that computational cost equals to actually used resources. In other words, the solution for 15 tasks found by fitness function for static allocations used 85% of available resources but the solution found by fitness for on-demand allocations used only 42%. The same states for 16 tasks where the solution found by the fitness function for static allocations used 75% of available resources but the solution found by the fitness function for on-demand allocations used only 19%.

The makespans of 15 tasks schedules differ by 29% while there is a 31% difference in obtained computational cost and the amount of unused resources. The schedules of 16 tasks differ by 59% in their makespans and by 14% in the computational cost.

4   Conclusions

This paper investigates the execution optimization of moldable scientific workflows. It uses genetic algorithm to evolve schedules for workflows comprising of two kinds of tasks with and without mutual dependencies. The presented objective functions use collected historical performance data for supported workflow's tasks. Those objective functions implement a trade-off coefficients that allow the schedule customization to either minimize one objective to another or to balance them. The paper introduces three objective functions that provide the (1) local optimization of workflow tasks minimizing their execution times, (2) global optimization with on-demand resource allocation balancing the workflow makespan and its computational cost, and (3) global optimization with static resource allocation balancing the workflow makespan and the cluster's idling nodes.

After performing the experiments, we confirmed our hypothesis that (1) we are able to generate good schedules for various workflows as well as meet different optimization criteria. For local optimization, we got very good results where more than 90% of performed trials found the optimal solution. (2) When performing a multi objective optimization, we introduced an α trade-off parameter and confirmed we can prioritize one objective to another. Here, we got the best results for the global optimization with on-demand resources and workflows with task dependencies where solutions found for the different parameter α form clusters. Let us note, that the trade-off parameter allows to customize the solution parameters only in a limited scale of makespan and cost, e.g., 10%. Much worse parametrization could be seen for workflows without task dependencies for both global optimization methods where the only value 0.05 of α produced sensible solutions. (3) We measured and summarized computational demands of each presented objective function and workflows of different sizes. Using the local optimization, the workflow of 64 tasks could be evolved in 14 s.

Global optimization is more computationally demanding but we managed to get the schedule for the most complex workflow with task dependencies in roughly 2 min. Finally, the paper provides the genetic algorithm settings to reproduce the presented results.

4.1 Future Work

Here we summarize several ideas to be addressed soon. First, we would like to better tune the presented trade-off coefficient α and better define ourselves among other already existing optimization heuristics. Next, we would like to validate our approach against standard task graphs[2] of different sizes.

Furthermore, a couple of the algorithm improvements is to be addressed. Currently used cluster simulator traverses tasks within a workflow in a breadth-first top down order and follows the task submission order when multiple tasks are ready to be executed. A mechanism such as backfilling commonly presented in the PBS job scheduler is not implemented. In practise, we use mainly PBS-based clusters for our workflows, thus, we would like to integrate this functionality to the presented Tetrisator. We will also consider a possibility to integrate an already existing cluster simulator, e.g., ALEA [21].

Next, more real world tasks together with their measured performance data would be incorporated. In reality, we usually cannot measure and hold performance data for all input data sizes and input parameters options. Therefore, we need to implement interpolation based heuristics [20].

Acknowledgments. This project has received funding from the European Union's Horizon 2020 research and innovation programme H2020 ICT 2016–2017 under grant agreement No 732411 and is an initiative of the Photonics Public Private Partnership. This work was supported by the Ministry of Education, Youth and Sports of the Czech Republic through the e-INFRA CZ (ID: 90140). This work was supported by Brno University of Technology under project number FIT/FSI-J-21-7435.

References

1. The shift from processor power consumption to performance variations: fundamental implications at scale. Comput. Sci. - Res. Dev. **31**(4), 197–205 (2016)
2. Amdahl, G.M.: Validity of the single processor approach to achieving large scale computing capabilities. In: Proceedings of the April 1820 1967 Spring Joint Computer Conference, vol. 23, no. 4, pp. 483–485 (1967)
3. Bharathi, S., Chervenak, A., Deelman, E., Mehta, G., Su, M.-H., Vahi, K.: Characterization of scientific workflows. In: 2008 Third Workshop on Workflows in Support of Large-Scale Science, pp. 1–10. IEEE, November 2008
4. Bleuse, R., Hunold, S., Kedad-Sidhoum, S., Monna, F., Mounie, G., Trystram, D.: Scheduling independent moldable tasks on multi-cores with GPUs. IEEE Trans. Parallel Distrib. Syst. **28**(9), 2689–2702 (2017)

---

[2] http://www.kasahara.cs.waseda.ac.jp/schedule/.

5. Breukelaar, R., Demaine, E.D., Hohenberger, S., Hoogeboom, H.J., Kosters, W.A., Liben-Nowell, D.: Tetris is hard, even to approximate. Int. J. Comput. Geomet. Appl. **14**, 41–68 (2004)

6. Chan, T.F., Mathew, T.P.: Domain decomposition algorithms. Acta Numer. **3**, 61–143 (1994)

7. Chirkin, A.M., et al.: Execution time estimation for workflow scheduling. Future Gener. Comput. Syst. **75**, 376–387 (2017)

8. Cotta, C., Fernández, A.J.: Evolutionary Scheduling. Studies in Computational Intelligence, vol. 49. Springer, Heidelberg (2007). https://doi.org/10.1007/978-3-540-48584-1

9. Dutot, P.-F., Netto, M.A.S., Goldman, A., Kon, F.: Scheduling moldable BSP tasks. In: Feitelson, D., Frachtenberg, E., Rudolph, L., Schwiegelshohn, U. (eds.) JSSPP 2005. LNCS (LNAI and LNB), vol. 3834, pp. 157–172. Springer, Heidelberg (2005). https://doi.org/10.1007/11605300_8

10. Feitelson, D.G., Rudolph, L.: Toward convergence in job schedulers for parallel supercomputers. In: Feitelson, D.G., Rudolph, L. (eds.) JSSPP 1996. LNCS (LNAI and LNB), vol. 1162, pp. 1–26. Springer, Heidelberg (1996). https://doi.org/10.1007/BFb0022284

11. Gad, A.F.: Geneticalgorithmpython: Building genetic algorithm in python (2021). https://github.com/ahmedfgad/GeneticAlgorithmPython/tree/05a069abf43146e7f8eb37f37c539523bf62ac9a

12. Hejazi, S.R., Saghafian, S.: Flowshop-scheduling problems with makespan criterion: a review. Int. J. Prod. Res. **43**(14), 2895–2929 (2005)

13. Henderson, R.L.: Job scheduling under the portable batch system. In: Feitelson, D.G., Rudolph, L. (eds.) JSSPP 1995. LNCS (LNAI and LNB), vol. 949, pp. 279–294. Springer, Heidelberg (1995). https://doi.org/10.1007/3-540-60153-8_34

14. Hill, M.D.: What is scalability? ACM SIGARCH Comput. Archit. News **18**(4), 18–21 (1990)

15. Hovestadt, M., Kao, O., Keller, A., Streit, A.: Scheduling in HPC resource management systems: queuing vs. planning. In: Feitelson, D., Rudolph, L., Schwiegelshohn, U. (eds.) JSSPP 2003. LNCS (LNAI and LNB), vol. 2862, pp. 1–20. Springer, Heidelberg (2003). https://doi.org/10.1007/10968987_1

16. Huang, K.-C., Huang, T.-C., Tsai, M.-J., Chang, H.-Y.: Moldable job scheduling for HPC as a service. In: Park, J., Stojmenovic, I., Choi, M., Xhafa, F. (eds.) Future Information Technology. Lecture Notes in Electrical Engineering, vol. 276, pp. 43–48. Springer, Heidelberg (2014). https://doi.org/10.1007/978-3-642-40861-8_7

17. Izadkhah, H.: Learning based genetic algorithm for task graph scheduling. Appl. Comput. Intell. Soft Comput. **2019**, 15 (2019). Article ID 6543957. https://doi.org/10.1155/2019/6543957

18. Jansen, K., Land, F.: Scheduling monotone moldable jobs in linear time. In: 2018 IEEE International Parallel and Distributed Processing Symposium (IPDPS), pp. 172–181. IEEE, May 2018

19. Jaros, J., Rendell, A.P., Treeby, B.E.: Full-wave nonlinear ultrasound simulation on distributed clusters with applications in high-intensity focused ultrasound. Int. J. High Perform. Comput. Appl. **30**(2), 1094342015581024- (2015)

20. Jaros, M., Sasak, T., Treeby, B.E., Jaros, J.: Estimation of execution parameters for k-wave simulations. In: Kozubek, T., Arbenz, P., Jaroš, J., Říha, L., Šístek, J., Tichý, P. (eds.) HPCSE 2019. LNCS, vol. 12456, pp. 116–134. Springer, Cham (2021). https://doi.org/10.1007/978-3-030-67077-1_7

21. Klusacek, D., Podolnikova, G., Toth, S.: Complex job scheduling simulations with Alea 4. In: Tan, G. (ed.) Proceedings of the 9th EAI International Conference on Simulation Tools and Techniques, Belgium, pp. 124–129. ICST (2016)
22. Lamprecht, A.-L., Turner, K.J.: Scientific workflows. Int. J. Softw. Tools Technol. Transf. **18**(6), 575–580 (2016)
23. Mu'alem, A.W., Feitelson, D.G.: Utilization, predictability, workloads, and user runtime estimates in scheduling the IBM SP2 with backfilling. IEEE Trans. Parallel Distrib. Syst. **12**(6), 529–543 (2001)
24. Omara, F.A., Arafa, M.M.: Genetic algorithms for task scheduling problem. J. Parallel Distrib. Comput. **70**(1), 13–22 (2010)
25. Robert, Y., et al.: Task Graph Scheduling. Encyclopedia of Parallel Computing, pp. 2013–2025 (2011)
26. Srinivasan, S., Krishnamoorthy, S., Sadayappan, P.: A robust scheduling technology for moldable scheduling of parallel jobs. In: Proceedings IEEE International Conference on Cluster Computing CLUSTR-03, pp. 92–99. IEEE (2003)
27. Srinivasan, S., Kettimuthu, R., Subramani, V., Sadayappan, P.: Selective reservation strategies for backfill job scheduling. In: Feitelson, D.G., Rudolph, L., Schwiegelshohn, U. (eds.) JSSPP 2002. LNCS (LNAI and LNB), vol. 2537, pp. 55–71. Springer, Heidelberg (2002). https://doi.org/10.1007/3-540-36180-4_4
28. Sudholt, D.: Parallel evolutionary algorithms. In: Kacprzyk, J., Pedrycz, W. (eds.) Springer Handbook of Computational Intelligence, pp. 929–959. Springer, Heidelberg (2015). https://doi.org/10.1007/978-3-662-43505-2_46
29. Ye, D., Chen, D.Z., Zhang, G.: Online scheduling of moldable parallel tasks. J. Sched. **21**(6), 647–654 (2018)
30. Yoo, A.B., Jette, M.A., Grondona, M.: SLURM: simple linux utility for resource management. In: Feitelson, D., Rudolph, L., Schwiegelshohn, U. (eds.) JSSPP 2003. LNCS (LNAI and LNB), vol. 2862, pp. 44–60. Springer, Heidelberg (2003). https://doi.org/10.1007/10968987_3

Temperature-Aware Energy-Optimal Scheduling of Moldable Streaming Tasks onto 2D-Mesh-Based Many-Core CPUs with DVFS

Christoph Kessler[1], Jörg Keller[2(✉)], and Sebastian Litzinger[2]

[1] Linköping University, Linköping, Sweden
christoph.kessler@liu.se
[2] FernUniversität in Hagen, Hagen, Germany
{joerg.keller,sebastian.litzinger}@fernuni-hagen.de

Abstract. We consider the problem of energy-optimally mapping a set of moldable-parallel tasks in the steady-state pattern of a software-pipelined streaming computation onto a generic many-core CPU architecture with a 2D mesh geometry, where the execution voltage and frequency levels of the cores can be selected dynamically from a given set of discrete DVFS levels. We extend the Crown Scheduling technique for parallelizable tasks to temperature-aware scheduling, taking into account the tasks' heat generation, the heat limit for each core, and the heat diffusion along the 2D mesh geometry of typical many-core CPU architectures. Our approach introduces a systematic method for alternating task executions between disjoint "buddy" core groups in subsequent iterations of crown schedules to avoid long-time overheating of cores. We present two integer linear program (ILP) solutions with different degrees of flexibility, and show that these can be solved for realistic problem sizes with today's ILP solver technology. Experiments with several streaming task graphs derived from real-world applications show that the flexibility for the scheduler can be greatly increased by considering buddy-cores, thus finding feasible solutions in scenarios that could not be solved otherwise. We also present a fast heuristic for the same problem.

Keywords: Temperature-aware scheduling · Parallelizable tasks · Many-core CPU · Energy optimization · DVFS

1 Introduction

Modern CMOS CPU chips are increasingly constrained by temperature. Local hot spots such as permanently highly-loaded cores can become problematic because higher temperature affects (static) power consumption negatively and because very high temperatures accelerate the aging process of the hardware (and excessively high temperatures will damage it immediately). Active cooling, even if made adaptive, will thus have to consider the hottest spot (core)

© Springer Nature Switzerland AG 2021
D. Klusáček et al. (Eds.): JSSPP 2021, LNCS 12985, pp. 168–189, 2021.
https://doi.org/10.1007/978-3-030-88224-2_9

on the chip at any time. Dynamic throttling by the operating system's governor is completely unaware of application requirements. Instead, application-level temperature-aware scheduling can help to keep a high and more stable computation throughput across the chip while avoiding overheated cores.

In many cases, the problem of temperature-aware mapping a set of tasks to cores for execution is handled as a dynamic (online) optimization problem. The problem is made more complex by the fact that a high temperature of one core also affects its neighbor cores (with a certain delay) due to heat diffusion on the chip. This property can be used for passive cooling, in addition to local techniques on the hot core itself, such as core DVFS-level downscaling or by pausing running tasks. At the same time, the number of cores per chip continues to grow, also for the foreseeable future. In combination with lower clock frequencies this calls for leveraging parallelism inside tasks, using a parallel algorithm on multiple cores to utilize available resources at limited frequency.

Streaming computations refer to data-parallel computations over large collections of data where input data arrives as a stream of packets and operations are organized as a directed acyclic graph of streaming tasks connected by FIFO-buffered edges. This model, also known as Kahn process networks [13], allows for pipelined execution of dependent operations over subsequent data packets on different execution resources. We consider the steady-state pattern of such software-pipelined computation of streaming tasks. By placing instances of producer and consumer tasks operating on the same data in subsequent schedule iterations, task instances in the same iteration can be considered independent. In many soft-realtime applications, such as video processing, a specific (minimum) data rate is required, translating into a (maximum) makespan for the schedule of one iteration (or round). Hence, even with enough cores available for execution, the heaviest task might be the performance bottleneck in the computation. For such critical tasks, parallelization as well as selecting a high DVFS level (with the negative impact on heat) are options that a static scheduler can exploit to keep the throughput constraint. The schedule for the steady-state pattern should thus be constructed to achieve the throughput goal with minimum power consumption. Nevertheless, a large non-parallelizable task may have to run at the highest DVFS level, which might lead to heat overload of its assigned core.

In this paper, we consider the problem of energy-optimally mapping a set of *moldable* tasks (parallelizable tasks where the degree of parallelism is fixed prior to execution) modeling the steady state pattern of a software-pipelined streaming computation onto a generic many-core CPU architecture with a 2D mesh geometry, where the voltage and frequency levels of the cores can be selected dynamically from a given set of discrete DVFS levels, where a given upper limit for the tolerable temperature on each core must be respected, and where all tasks of one round of the steady state must be executed exactly once within a given common deadline matching e.g. a required frame processing rate.

Our approach builds atop the *Crown Scheduling* technique [17,18] for moldable streaming tasks. Crown scheduling leverages a recursive binary partitioning of the set of p cores into a hierarchy of $2p - 1$ core groups (called the *crown*, cf. Fig. 1) that become the only mapping targets for tasks, and hence restricts

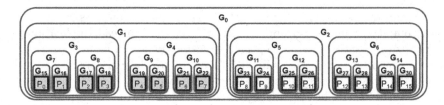

Fig. 1. A binary crown over $p = 16$ cores consists of $2p - 1 = 31$ groups $G_0, ..., G_{30}$.

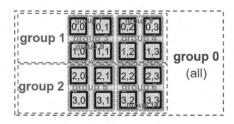

Fig. 2. 4×4 core mesh with 2D core indexing and organized as a 2D balanced binary crown structure by recursive binary space partitioning, where group 0 (root group, G_0) comprises all 16 cores, its child groups indexed 1 to 2 contain 8 cores each, down to the 16 leaf, i.e. single-core, groups.

core allocations of tasks to powers of 2. Also, the independent tasks of one round are ordered by non-increasing core allocation, avoiding idle times between tasks on the same core and decoupling DVFS scaling decisions of any non-overlapping core groups in the crown. Earlier work has shown that restricting core allocation to powers of 2 has only negligible effect on schedule quality in practice [17, 18], but the reduction from $2^p - 1$ to $2p - 1$ mapping targets cuts down problem complexity considerably and makes even exact solutions of this complex optimization problem by integer linear programming (ILP) feasible for relevant problem sizes.

We extend the crown scheduling technique to temperature-aware scheduling, taking into account the tasks' heat generation, the heat limit for each core, and the heat diffusion along the 2D mesh geometry of typical many-core CPU architectures. The 2D layout of the crown and the resulting core index mapping is obtained by a recursive alternating binary space partitioning, as shown in Fig. 2 for a 4×4 core mesh. Hence, all crown subgroups will cover locally contiguous 2D subareas on the chip, and a group's neighbor group to the left and right is physically neighbored also in the 2D mesh network by the embedding.

For scenarios where the power and heat situation can be predicted accurately, the ILPs can compute a static schedule prior to execution, which is then applied for the complete mission time of the streaming application. For scenarios where execution time is too short to warrant static scheduling with long scheduling time, or where the heat situation changes during execution, a heuristic scheduler is presented that also applies the buddy core concept to adapt ILP-based schedules. Here, ILP-based schedules can still serve as a reference to demonstrate how close the heuristic comes to offline solutions.

This work makes the following technical contributions:

- We formalize the problem of energy-optimal, temperature-aware scheduling of multi-variant moldable streaming tasks on a 2D many-core chip geometry with DVFS, given a throughput requirement, and propose an extension of *crown scheduling* [17, 18] for this problem.
- We propose the *buddy-core technique* as a systematic method for alternating tasks between disjoint core groups in subsequent iterations of crown schedules to avoid long-time overheating of cores or core groups.
- We present two ILP-based solutions of the problem that leverage the buddy-core technique with different degrees of flexibility, and show that it can be solved for realistic problem sizes with today's ILP solver technology. Experiments with several streaming task graphs derived from real-world applications show that scheduler flexibility is greatly increased by considering buddy-cores, especially in scenarios with tight deadlines and few/no DVFS levels, thus finding feasible solutions in otherwise unsolvable scenarios.
- We also present a fast heuristic for the same problem and evaluate it with the more flexible ILP solution as a baseline.

The remainder of this paper is organized as follows: Sect. 2 revisits related work. Section 3 introduces our task and architecture models as well as crown scheduling. Section 4 presents the buddy-core technique. Sections 5 and 6 present ILP models with fixed and flexible buddy core selection, resp. Sect. 7 reports on experimental results for ILP and heuristic scheduling, and Sect. 8 concludes and proposes future work.

2   Related Work

Basically all existing literature of temperature-aware mapping and scheduling for multi-core architectures focuses on sequential tasks, thus disregarding the effect of optional parallelization for increasing flexibility and relaxing temperature hot spots. Moreover, a number of approaches rely on dynamic techniques alone, i.e. it is not clear how close they are to offline solutions.

Lu et al. [16] present a reinforcement learning-based approach for allocating sequential tasks at runtime to cores of a network-on-chip manycore CPU depending on current core and router temperatures in an attempt to minimize maximum temperatures in the future. DVFS is not considered in this work. Coskun et al. [6] design and evaluate OS-level dynamic scheduling policies with negligible performance overhead. They do not consider parallel tasks. Rayan and Yu [20] consider OS-level techniques for CPU throughput throttling for data centers to keep CPU temperature below a certain threshold.

Bampis et al. [2] consider approximation algorithms for static and on-line scheduling to minimize for makespan, maximum temperature or weighted average temperature. They consider non-multicore multiprocessors as target, i.e., spatial temperature diffusion between processors is not modeled. They assume unit-sized tasks and use a simplified theoretical temperature model that assumes that a processor's temperature change per unit of time equals half the difference between its previous processor temperature and the steady-state temperature of the task. They do not consider DVFS nor energy optimization.

Chantem et al. [5] present a mixed integer linear program (MILP) for static temperature-aware scheduling and mapping for hard real-time applications on MPSoCs with DVFS. Also their work only considers sequential tasks. Where necessary, idle periods are inserted into the schedule to cool down a core before the next task can be started safely. They also present a heuristic algorithm for the same problem. But they do not consider moldable tasks and do not model a 2D many-core geometry nor spatial heat diffusion.

Jayaseelan and Mitra [12] consider temperature-aware dynamic scheduling of a mix of soft real-time and best-effort tasks for single-core embedded processors. They use an exponential function-based increase/decay model for temperature changes depending on power, with the model parameters calibrated from simulation experiments. Like our approach, they classify tasks into hot and cold tasks, based on the sign of the difference of their steady-state temperature from the maximum safe temperature at which a (hot) task still can be started. Hot and cold tasks are kept in two separate queues, and the scheduler keeps dynamically track of the share of CPU time that can be safely allocated to hot tasks. Voltage scaling is used to control the trade-off between fairness and temperature safety, by promoting down-scaled deadline-critical hot tasks to the cold queue.

The synthesis approach in Alkabani et al. [1] uses a linear programming framework that searches the best N versions of the mapping and schedule, deploys them together on the hardware platform and constructs a thermal-aware rotational schedule that switches between these in order to balance the thermal profile of the processor. Their experiments show a very low overhead and an average 5% decrease in the steady-state peak temperature produced on the benchmark designs compared to using a schedule that balances the amount of usage of different modules.

Bao et al. [3,4] consider temperature-aware dynamic voltage scaling in combination with mapping and scheduling of single-threaded tasks and of idle time intervals on a sequential CPU resp. on a multiprocessor to minimize the temperature-dependent share of energy (i.e., leakage energy). The technique leverages the non-linearity of the temperature impact on leakage energy e.g. by equally spreading out idle time in a schedule between tasks to maximize their cooling effect, instead of closing up idle times to a single idle interval. Parallel tasks or temperature diffusion in multicore architectures are not considered.

Pierson et al. [19] present mixed ILPs for optimizing energy consumption or makespan of sets of jobs in a datacenter with heat constraints, taking into account heat diffusion. Their jobs are only executed once, while we target a long sequence of similar execution rounds for a streaming application.

3   Architecture and Application Model

All symbols and parameters introduced in this and the following sections are summarized in Table 1.

Table 1. Notation summary

Symbol	Meaning
n	Number of tasks
n_j	Number of task j's variants
$w_{j,v}$	Minimum parallelism degree for task j's variant v
$W_{j,v}$	Maximum width of task j's variant v
$\text{eff}_{j,v}(q)$	Parallel efficiency for task j's variant v when run on q cores
p	Number of cores
s	Number of discrete core operating frequency levels
f_k	Core operating frequency on frequency level k
f_{min}	Minimum core operating frequency
f_{max}	Maximum core operating frequency
G_l	Set of groups core l belongs to
M	Length of execution round
$\text{work}(j, v)$	Workload of task j's variant v
$Pow(j, v, k)$	Core power consumption when running task j's variant v at frequency f_k
$\text{time}(q, j, v, k)$	Runtime of task j's variant v on q cores at frequency f_k
$E(q, j, v, k)$	Energy consumption for execution of task j's variant v on q cores at frequency f_k
$x_{i,j,v,k}$	Binary ILP decision variable, $=1$ iff task j's variant v is run in core group i at frequency f_k
$\text{size}(i)$	Number of cores in core group i
$\text{heat}(l) = \text{heat}(u, w)$	Core-local heat load of core l, i.e. core at position u, w in 2D grid
$\text{Heat}(l) = \text{Heat}(u, w)$	Overall heat load of core l, i.e. core at position u, w in 2D grid
α	Weight for net influx/outflux of heat to/from direct neighbor cores
β	Weight for net in-/outflux of heat to/from diagonal neighbor cores
maxHeat	Core heat limit
T_0	Room temperature
$P_{diff}(T)$	Additional power consumption for core at temperature T
hot_l	Binary ILP decision variable, $=1$ iff core l is classified as hot core
$sHeat(l)$	Scaled overall heat load of core l
C_{hot}	Hotness threshold
$MinHeat$	Minimum value of $\text{Heat}(l)$
$MaxHeat$	Maximum value of $\text{Heat}(l)$
γ_j	Reduction of buddy core group idle period, as fraction of buddied task j's duration
$y_{i,j,k}$	Binary ILP decision variable, $=1$ iff task j runs in variant 0 in core group i at frequency f_k with buddying enabled
$\text{heatodd}(l)$	Continuous ILP decision variable, core-local heat load of core l in odd rounds
$\text{heateven}(l)$	Continuous ILP decision variable, core-local heat load of core l in even rounds
$\text{Heatodd}(l)$	Overall heat load of core l in odd rounds
$\text{Heateven}(l)$	Overall heat load of core l in even rounds
$\text{penalty}(i, j)$	Continuous ILP decision variable, penalty for execution of task j's variant 0 in core group i in the first round and subsequent execution of its variant V in a different core group in the second round
$F(i)$	Set of all groups sharing a core with group i
$\text{misscost}(i, i')$	$\text{penalty}(i, j)$ for second-round group i'
ϵ	Weight for penalty term in objective function
LARGECONST	A large constant
d	Deadline tightness factor
λ_j	$\text{work}(j, 0)$, i.e. workload of task j's variant 0

3.1   Generic Multi-/Many-core Architecture with DVFS

We consider a generic multi-/many-core architecture with 2D mesh layout of p cores on the chip as introduced in Sect. 1. Each core can select its DVFS level dynamically (namely, between any two tasks) from a given set of s discrete frequencies $\{f_1 = f_{min}, ..., f_s = f_{max}\}$ in ascending order, applying voltage co-scaling to always use the lowest voltage still applicable for a chosen frequency. We make no assumptions about the power/energy cost function and its dependence on the DVFS level; it could be measured by microbenchmarking on the target system as in [9] or derived from a theoretical model, and becomes a set of constant model parameters to our optimization, with power values indexed by frequency level, temperature, and possibly instruction mix, i.e. task index.

One can simplify the table of power values by partitioning temperatures into a small number of temperature ranges, and classifying instruction mixes into task type categories. We will do especially the former by categorizing a core as hot or cold. Following [3], the difference in power consumption between hot and cold core is mostly due to static power difference and thus can be simplified to a core type-specific constant.

A core that draws power produces heat, which influences its temperature and the temperature of the nearby cores via heat diffusion. Thus, the temperatures of a set of cores with given workloads can be derived by solving differential equations. As a simplification, we will compute the heat flow between cores by a discretized and linearized set of equations, to include this into the ILP.

3.2   Multi-variant Moldable Streaming Tasks

We consider a streaming task graph with n nodes or tasks as introduced in Sect. 1. We assume *multi-variant tasks* where each task j (i.e., a node in the streaming task graph) can have $n_j \geq 1$ different variants $(j, 0), ..., (j, n_j - 1)$ that might internally differ e.g. in the algorithm used, in the compiler options or in settings of tunable parameters such as tile sizes.

Some of the task variants (j, v) of task j might be *inherently sequential* (modeled by setting its maximum parallelism parameter $W_{j,v} = 1$), *fully moldable* ($W_{j,v} = \infty$) or *partially moldable* ($W_{j,v}$ is given as some fixed maximum number of cores). We also allow to define a *minimum parallelism degree* $w_{j,v}$ for each task variant, which will be 1 in most cases but might be > 1 in special scenarios, which we will exploit later. Moldable task variants (j, v) (i.e., $W_{j,v} > 1$) internally use a parallel algorithm that executes simultaneously on all cores assigned to (j, v), and have an efficiency parameter table $\text{eff}_{j,v}(q)$ that models its scalability to q cores, with $1 \leq q \leq W_{j,v}$. The $\text{eff}_{j,v}$ values can either be provided by a performance model of the parallel algorithm within (j, v), or by measuring the execution time of (j, v) for the different applicable values of q on the target[1].

---

[1] We assume that tasks are computation-bound, i.e. that task runtime is inverse to core frequency, so that decisions on resource allocation and frequency scaling can be separated. Extensions to memory-bound or communication-bound tasks are possible.

As an example, consider the binary stream merge tasks in parallel stream mergesort where each task instance works on a pair of sorted input buffers to merge. The binary merge functionality is usually implemented by the well-known sequential merge algorithm, which performs work linear in the size of the input. Also parallel algorithms for merging are known [11], e.g. based on binary search, which performs work $O(N \log N)$ for input buffer size N and also has higher constant factors. As long as the root merger task (which is the performance bottleneck in the merger tree pipeline because it has the highest data throughput) still can be accommodated using DVFS scaling, the sequential merge variant will usually be the most energy-efficient one. However, if the root merger can no longer make the requested throughput rate but enough idle cores are available, even an inefficient parallel variant might (have to) be preferred for it.

Each task variant (j, v) has a certain instruction mix that influences the core power consumption for any given frequency level. To reduce complexity in ILPs, one might combine similar power profiles and thus create task types.

3.3 Scheduling for the Steady State

As introduced in Sect. 1, to run a streaming task graph with a throughput of X packets per second, every $M = 1/X$ seconds one instance of the streaming task graph must complete. Hence, each task must execute once within a round of length M. As the tasks belong to different graph instances, they can be considered independent. The tasks communicate via the on-chip network, but as the communication is from one round to the next, we assume that the on-chip network's delay is low enough and its capacity large enough to achieve this, and leave modelling of the tasks' communications on the on-chip network (and the resulting energy consumption) as a subject of future work.

For each task, we must determine in which variant, with which possible width and which frequency it will be executed. As the tasks are known beforehand, this can be done prior to execution as static scheduling, which also arranges the tasks such that a core never must execute two tasks simultaneously (non-preemptive scheduling) and that all tasks complete before the deadline. Finally, heat constraints have to be obeyed. Among all feasible schedules for such a situation, we are interested in one with minimum energy consumption per round.

Yet, given all these constraints, there might not be any feasible schedule. For such situations, there is the possibility of using a repeating sequence of differing schedules [1], so that the sequence obeys all constraints (in particular the heat constraints), while the sum of the schedules' energy consumptions is minimized. To achieve this, we will build on previous work.

Crown scheduling [17, 18] is a technique for resource allocation, mapping and DVFS selection for a given set of independent moldable tasks, which is based on a recursive partitioning of the set of p cores into up to $2p - 1$ core groups jointly referred to as the *crown* (see Fig. 1), and requests that tasks are allocated and mapped to entire such groups only, thus cutting down the complexity of possible mapping targets of each task from up to $2^p - 1$ in the unrestricted case to $2p - 1$. It also requests that in a schedule, tasks are ordered by decreasing core allocation, so that a parallelized task always starts simultaneously on the different cores it is mapped to. Scheduling decisions are done such that all tasks complete before the deadline and that cores' energy consumption is minimized. Extensions of the crown scheduling technique for architectures with DVFS islands and with multiple core types have been described in [14].

4 Temperature-Aware Crown Scheduling with Buddying

Some tasks may be considered by the scheduler as inherently hot yet they constitute a performance bottleneck for the steady-state schedule, i.e., they might be sequential and cannot be shortened by parallel processing, and they need to run at the highest DVFS level to make the deadline constraint. For these tasks, the only way to avoid thermal runaway on the cores they are mapped to is to spread out execution in consecutive rounds over multiple cores in an alternating fashion so that cores used in the previous round can cool down again during idle periods in the following round. This alternation however requires that we reserve sufficient capacity on a number of spare cores for these tasks. In general, it would be wasteful to do a conservative a-priori reservation, so the decision about such reservations needs to be made together with the other scheduling decisions (i.e., core allocation, mapping, and DVFS level selection). We also refrain from a complex multi-round schedule with a cyclic migration scheme for all tasks because this causes additional cache misses and overhead for many tasks, and it also would increase scheduling complexity considerably. Instead, we use one reserve core per core running a hot task, i.e., hot tasks lead to a duplication of core allocation. This choice is only for simplification of presentation and can be generalized to more than two-way alternation (preferably, by powers of 2).

The set of cores is first organized in pairs of physically neighbored cores ("buddies"); w.l.o.g. let us assume these are pairs of neighbored odd and even-indexed cores, only one of which will be used for a hot task at any time, and the runtime system can toggle between a core and its "buddy core" for the execution of a hot task between any two subsequent (hot) tasks whenever a core gets too warm. Note that the "idle" buddy core is not necessarily idle for a complete round but still runs at least all cool tasks that have been mapped to it, while it will simply skip the instances of hot tasks that will be executed by its buddy core instead. Because the buddies are physically neighbored and thus share most cache levels, the penalty of switching between buddy cores for a hot task due to additional cold misses in core-local cache levels will be relatively low. This buddy-core concept can be generalized towards (non-root) groups in the crown.

Hence, in a crown schedule, any hot task must now be mapped *twice*, both to a core group and to the group of their buddy cores, and hence its real core allocation will be twice as large as for the ordinary cool tasks. Note that for hot parallel tasks this applies to all cores it uses, i.e., the effective core allocation of a hot task is twice its nominal allocation. In contrast, cool tasks will only receive their nominal core allocation and be mapped once, as before.

We model this by defining a second task variant $(j,1)$ for each task j. The original version of task j now becomes variant $(j,0)$. There might be more variants of a task, e.g. using a different internal algorithm, but we will not consider them in particular in the sequel. The new variant $(j,1)$ internally employs temperature-dependent alternation among buddy cores as described above, it thus has the double values for minimum and maximum malleability[2], i.e., $w_{j,1} = 2w_{j,0} \geq 2$ and $W_{j,1} = 2W_{j,0}$, and its efficiency parameters can be derived accordingly as $\text{eff}_{j,1}(2q) = \text{eff}_{j,0}(q)/2$ for any $q \geq 1$, which will affect time and E (energy) parameters accordingly, see Sect. 5.1. Thus, a task in variant 1 can simply be mapped by the crown scheduler to a group, and the runtime system alternately uses one half of the group's cores or the other in two succeeding rounds. Variant $(j, 1)$ is to be selected by the scheduler instead of $(j, 0)$ if variant $(j, 0)$ with selected parallelism and DVFS level is considered too hot.

For greater flexibility we will allow also cold tasks to use the alternating variant and hot tasks to use the non-alternating variant, and leave the choice to a global optimizer, which we describe next.

5   ILP Model with Fixed Buddy Cores

5.1   Time and Energy

For a task variant (j, v) running on a core group with q cores at DVFS level k, let $\text{time}(q, j, v, k)$ denote the time and $\text{E}(q, j, v, k)$ denote the overall energy used by the task variant. These model parameter values can either be predicted by a model or obtained by measuring energy for a microbenchmark modeling the task type of task variant (j, v). For example, if sampled or predicted parallel efficiency values for the parallel algorithm used in a moldable task are available, the parallel execution time for the task can be modeled by

$$\text{time}(q, j, v, k) = \text{work}(j, v) / (q \cdot \text{eff}_{j,v}(q) \cdot f_k) . \tag{1}$$

If $Pow(j, v, k)$ is the (average) power consumption of a core when running task variant (j, v) at frequency level k (the dependence on temperature will be captured in Sect. 5.5), then the energy consumption of this task can be modeled by

$$\text{E}(q, j, v, k) = q \cdot \text{time}(q, j, v, k) \cdot Pow(j, v, k) . \tag{2}$$

5.2   ILP Solution Variables

Our ILP model uses binary variables $x_{i,j,v,k} = 1$ iff variant v of task j is selected and mapped to group i at DVFS level k.

5.3   Constraints

Allocation, Mapping and Scaling Constraint. Exactly one variant of each task j must be selected and be mapped to exactly one core group and exactly one DVFS level:

$$\forall j : \sum_{v,i,k} x_{i,j,v,k} = 1 \tag{3}$$

---

[2] Core allocations must be multiples of 2, which is automatically preserved by crown scheduling if $w_{j,v} \geq 2$.

Also, a task variant (j, v) must at least receive its minimum core allocation $w_{j,v}$ and not exceed its maximum core allocation $W_{j,v}$:

$$\forall j, v, k : \ \forall i \text{ where } \text{size}(i) < w_{j,v} : \ x_{i,j,v,k} = 0 \tag{4}$$

$$\forall j, v, k : \ \forall i \text{ where } \text{size}(i) > W_{j,v} : \ x_{i,j,v,k} = 0 \tag{5}$$

Here size(i) denotes the number of cores in core group i. Note that we do *not* add a constraint that forbids hot tasks to use the first (i.e., regular, non-alternating) variant. This also eliminates the need to strictly define some criterion separating hot and cold tasks from each other. In this way we leave it to the optimizer alone to decide by its global view of the problem for which tasks the regular or the alternating variant is more suitable.[3]

In general, the alternating variant of a task will be less energy-efficient than the regular variant because it yields only half the performance from the used resources at otherwise same settings (e.g., same DVFS level), and it will thus only be selected by the optimizer where really necessary to meet the throughput and temperature constraints below.

Throughput Constraint. Each core must complete its assigned tasks within the given deadline M:

$$\forall l : \ \sum_{i \in G_l} \sum_{j,v,k} x_{i,j,v,k} \cdot \text{time}(\text{size}(i), j, v, k) \leq M, \tag{6}$$

where G_l denotes the set of groups core l belongs to.

Temperature Constraint. The *core-local heat load* heat$(l) = $ heat(u, w) of core $l = (u, w)$ is the sum over the energies of its assigned task variants, divided by their accumulated time (in other words, it is the average power of core l over one round):

$$\text{heat}(l) = \left(\sum_{i \in G_l} \sum_{j,v,k} x_{i,j,v,k} \cdot \text{E}(\text{size}(i), j, v, k)/\text{size}(i) \right) / M. \tag{7}$$

The *overall heat load* Heat$(l) = $ Heat(u, w) of core $l = (u, w)$ is given by its local heat load plus the weighted heat differences to its direct neighbor core heat loads, which models nearest-neighbor heat diffusion:

$$\begin{aligned}
\text{Heat}(u, w) = \ &\text{heat}(u, w) \cdot (1 - 4(\alpha + \beta)) \\
&+ \alpha \left(\text{heat}(u{-}1, w) + \text{heat}(u, w{-}1) + \text{heat}(u, w{+}1) + \text{heat}(u{+}1, w) \right) \\
&+ \beta \left(\text{heat}(u{-}1, w{-}1) + \text{heat}(u{-}1, w{+}1) + \text{heat}(u{+}1, w{-}1) \right. \\
&\left. + \text{heat}(u{+}1, w{+}1) \right)
\end{aligned} \tag{8}$$

---

[3] In (rather unlikely) borderline cases it could actually make sense to run even a cold task in alternating mode to make it even colder, so that it can compensate for the heat impact of a hot task on the same core(s) without having to use the more inefficient alternating variant for that hot task.

where $0 \leq \beta < \alpha \ll 1$ are the weights that model the net influx/outflux of heat to/from the core's up to four corner and up to four direct neighbor cores, respectively. For cores located on the chip boundary, i.e., $u = 0$ or $u = q - 1$ or $w = 0$ or $w = q - 1$, the above equation is adapted accordingly as not all neighbor cores exist; for these non-existing neighbors the temperature difference is assumed to be 0. We also note that $\alpha + \beta < 0.25$ because Heat values cannot be negative. Note that, for simplicity, we do not model second-order effects in heat diffusion, i.e., other cores more than one position away in a dimension do not contribute to a core's overall heat.

We require that the overall heat load of a core does not exceed its heat limit:

$$\forall l : \quad \text{Heat}(l) \leq \text{maxHeat} \tag{9}$$

5.4 Objective Function

We minimize the overall energy for the steady state, which is calculated as

$$E = \sum_{i,j,v,k} x_{i,j,v,k} \cdot \text{E}(\text{size}(i), j, v, k) \tag{10}$$

By running the ILP for different settings of the maxHeat parameter, we can explore several thermal design options for a fixed-application embedded system. For instance, a higher maxHeat value could be permitted if employing active air cooling, which however also costs some energy overhead to drive the fan.

5.5 Temperature-Dependent Power Modeling

So far, the heat flow information has only been used to forbid situations where cores may overheat. However, the core temperature also influences the core's power consumption. We use the *Heat* variables to guess the cores' temperatures and classify each core as cold or hot. This is a simplification because the heat flow and thus the temperature may vary over a round, but as the *Heat* variables only provide information summarized over a round, we cannot have more fine-granular information on this basis. The use of only two categories hot and cold is a further simplification, but can be extended to more categories.

According to [3], the temperature mostly influences static power consumption. Thus, the power profile of a core, i.e. power consumption for each operating frequency for a given instruction mix and a core temperature equaling room temperature T_0, is shifted by a temperature-dependent constant $P_{diff}(T)$ when a higher core temperature $T > T_0$ is assumed. Hence, to apply the knowledge about core temperature within the above simplifications, the additional energy for each hot core amounts to $P_{diff}(T_{hot}) \cdot M$.

Thus, we introduce p binary variables hot_l where $hot_l = 1$ iff core l is hot, and adapt the target function by adding a term $\sum_l hot_l \cdot P_{diff}(T_{hot}) \cdot M$.

To set these binary variables, we scale the Heat variables to interval $[0; 1]$ denoted by $sHeat$(see below), and define a threshold $C_{hot} \in [0; 1]$ that distinguishes between hot and cold cores via

$$hot_l \geq sHeat(l) - C_{hot} \tag{11}$$
$$hot_l < 1 + sHeat(l) - C_{hot} \tag{12}$$

Constraint (11) forces hot_l to 1 if $sHeat(l) > C_{hot}$, constraint (12) forces hot_l to 0 if $sHeat(l) \leq C_{hot}$.

After deriving bounds $MinHeat$ and $MaxHeat$ for the scope of variables $Heat$,

$$sHeat(l) = \frac{Heat(l) - MinHeat}{MaxHeat - MinHeat} \cdot$$

6   ILP Model with Arbitrary Buddies

In the ILP model of Sect. 5 we assumed that a fixed, nearest-neighbor core or core group is predefined as the buddy core where buddying is necessary to avoid long-term overheating of a core or core group. This implies that the buddy core group always has the same width as the overheated core group. This restriction can however be relaxed to increase the flexibility for the scheduler: the buddy group could be any group, also narrower or wider than the overheated core group to be offloaded, as long as these two groups do not intersect. In particular, we do no longer request that the buddy cores are direct neighbors, i.e. in one common group in the crown structure. Where a more distant group is selected as buddy group for a task, we charge a certain time penalty for the expected increase in cache misses and/or data movement costs compared to nearest-neighbor buddy selection. Another requirement that can be relaxed is that the idle phase on the buddy core group needs to be equally long as the buddied task—the idle phase could also be shorter if that is already sufficient for cooling down the core.

We present a generalized ILP model that allows such arbitrary buddy selection. To do so, we extend the scope of optimization to two subsequent rounds of the steady-state pattern, where we allow the idle period on the buddy group to be shortened compared to the buddied task's duration by up to a factor $0 < \gamma < 1$ in one round.

We use the following decision variables:

- $x_{i,j,v,k} = 1$ iff task j is executed in variant $v \in \{0, \dots, V\}$ in core group i at frequency level k. Variant 0 is the default variant, variant V is the buddy core variant which is only available for the default variant. Variants 1 to $V - 1$ (if available) are alternative variants for which no buddy variant is necessary.
- $y_{i,j,k} = 1$ iff task j is executed in variant 0 in core group i at frequency level k and buddy cores are employed.

- heatodd(l) is the local heat load for core l in odd rounds.
- heateven(l) is the local heat load for core l in even rounds.
- penalty(i, j) is the penalty for executing task j in the first round in variant 0 in core group i, when task j is executed in variant V, i.e. as a buddy task, in the second round, in a different group i'.

The objective function (13a) is the sum of the energy consumption caused by execution of tasks in two subsequent rounds and penalties for mapping tasks and their buddy tasks to distant buddy cores. In the first (odd) round, buddy variants V of tasks are not executed. In the second (even) round, variant 0 of a task is only executed if the buddy variant V is not chosen. If V is chosen ($y_{i,j,k} = 1$), we therefore subtract energy for variant 0.

The optimization problem then reads as follows:

$$\min \quad \sum_{i,j,v<V,k} x_{i,j,v,k} \cdot \mathrm{E}(\mathrm{size}(i), j, v, k) + \sum_{i,j,v,k} x_{i,j,v,k} \cdot \mathrm{E}(\mathrm{size}(i), j, v, k)$$

$$- \sum_{i,j,k} y_{i,j,k} \cdot \mathrm{E}(\mathrm{size}(i), j, 0, k) + \epsilon \cdot \sum_{i,j} \mathrm{penalty}(i, j) \tag{13a}$$

$$\text{s.t.} \quad \forall j \quad \sum_{i,v<V,k} x_{i,j,v,k} = 1, \tag{13b}$$

$$\forall j \quad \sum_{i,k} x_{i,j,V,k} \leq \sum_{i,k} x_{i,j,0,k}, \tag{13c}$$

$$\forall i,j \quad 1 - \sum_{k} x_{i,j,0,k} \geq \sum_{i' \in F(i),k} x_{i',j,V,k}, \tag{13d}$$

$$\forall j,v \quad \sum_{i:\mathrm{size}(i)>W_{j,v},k} x_{i,j,v,k} = 0, \tag{13e}$$

$$\forall i,j,k \quad y_{i,j,k} \geq x_{i,j,0,k} + \sum_{i',k'} x_{i',j,V,k'} - 1, \tag{13f}$$

$$\forall i,j,k \quad y_{i,j,k} \leq x_{i,j,0,k}, \tag{13g}$$

$$\forall i,j,k \quad y_{i,j,k} \leq \sum_{i',k'} x_{i',j,V,k'}, \tag{13h}$$

$$\forall l \quad \sum_{i \in G_l} \left(\sum_{j,v<V,k} x_{i,j,v,k} \cdot \mathrm{time}(\mathrm{size}(i), j, v, k) \right.$$

$$\left. + \sum_{j,k} x_{i,j,V,k} \cdot \mathrm{time}(\mathrm{size}(i), j, V, k) \cdot \gamma_j \right) \leq M, \tag{13i}$$

$$\forall l \quad \sum_{i \in G_l} \left(\sum_{j,v,k} x_{i,j,v,k} \cdot \mathrm{time}(\mathrm{size}(i), j, v, k) \right.$$

$$\left. - \sum_{j,k} y_{i,j,0,k} \cdot \mathrm{time}(\mathrm{size}(i), j, 0, k) \cdot (1 - \gamma_j) \right) \leq M, \tag{13j}$$

$$\forall i,j \quad \text{penalty}(i,j) \geq \left(\sum_k x_{i,j,0,k} - 1 \right) \cdot \text{LARGECONST}$$

$$+ \sum_{i',k} x_{i',j,V,k} \cdot \text{misscost}(i,i'), \tag{13k}$$

$$\forall i,j \quad \text{penalty}(i,j) \geq 0, \tag{13l}$$

$$\forall i,j \quad \text{penalty}(i,j) \leq \sum_{i',k} x_{i',j,V,k} \cdot \text{misscost}(i,i'), \tag{13m}$$

$$\forall l \quad \left(\sum_{i \in G_l, j, v < V, k} \text{E}(\text{size}(i), j, v, k)/\text{size}(i) \right) /M = \text{heatodd}(l), \tag{13n}$$

$$\forall l \quad \left(\sum_{i \in G_l, j, v, k} \text{E}(\text{size}(i), j, v, k)/\text{size}(i) \right.$$

$$\left. - \sum_{i:l \in i, j, k} y_{i,j,k} \cdot \text{E}(\text{size}(i), j, 0, k)/\text{size}(i) \right) /M = \text{heateven}(l), \tag{13o}$$

$$\forall l \quad (\text{Heatodd}(l) + \text{Heateven}(l))/2 \leq \text{maxHeat}. \tag{13p}$$

We apply the following constraints:

- general constraints:
  (13b): Exactly one variant (either the default or an alternative one) must be chosen for each task, and the task shall be mapped to one core group at one frequency level (except for buddy core variant, see below).
- buddy constraints:
  (13c): The buddy core variant may be used only in conjunction with the default variant 0.
  (13d): The buddy variant must not share cores with the standard variant (i.e. variant 0). Here, $F(i)$ denotes the set of all groups that share a core with group i.
- width constraints:
  (13e): We do not allocate a number of cores greater than the maximum width of a task.
- throughput constraints:
  (13f), (13g), (13h): $y = 1$ iff variant 0 is selected and buddying is enabled, i.e. variant V is also selected.
  (13i): The sum of task runtimes per core must not exceed the deadline in odd rounds, i.e. for execution of the standard variant, where applicable.
  (13j): The sum of task runtimes per core must not exceed the deadline in even rounds, i.e. for execution of buddy core variant, where applicable.
- constraints for penalty terms:
  (13k): If variant 0 is executed in group i and the buddy variant in group i', the penalty is misscost(i,i'), which is a constant that can be derived

from measurements or microbenchmarks[4]. The large constant serves to neutralize the constraint if variant 0 is not chosen.

(13l): The penalty cannot be negative.

(13m): If no buddy variant is planned for the execution of task j, there is no penalty.

- thermal constraints:

(13n), (13o): The core-local heat load is the average power consumption of a core in odd and even rounds, respectively.

(13p): The average overall core heat over odd and even rounds may not exceed the maximum heat threshold. The definitions of Heatodd(l) and Heateven(l) are in analogy to (8), and omitted for the sake of brevity.

7   Evaluation

In order to demonstrate the applicability of the proposed approach, we have conducted experiments with two applications: parallel mergesort and H.263 encode. The mergesort application consists of 15 tasks forming a tree-shaped task graph as shown in Fig. 3 (left). Moving towards the root, the workload is doubled at each level. We assume that the individual tasks are executed sequentially. The H.263 encode application originates from the Dataflow Benchmark Suite (DFbench) [7]. It comprises 9 tasks, the task graph is depicted in Fig. 3 (right). Some edges related to control flow had to be pruned to obtain an acyclic graph. Again, a task itself is assumed to run sequentially.

By experiment, we mean that we compute a schedule by solving an ILP, and consider the energy from the objective function the result of the experiment. Previous experiments on real platforms have demonstrated that the ILP model predicts energy consumption on real machines with sufficient accuracy [8,9]. Thus, we do not perform a system simulation.

For our experiments, the deadline computation is inspired by [18]:

$$M = d \cdot \frac{\sum_j \frac{\lambda_j}{p \cdot f_{max}} + \sum_j \frac{\lambda_j}{p \cdot f_{min}}}{2},$$

where d can be set to various values and thus enables control over deadline tightness, and where $\lambda_j = \text{work}(j,0)$. The second parameter we vary for the experiments is maxHeat, i.e. the per-core heat limit. For the two task sets in question, we have examined all combinations of d and maxHeat for $d \in \{2.2, 2.5, 3.0, 3.5, 4.0\}$ and maxHeat $\in \{0.2, 0.3, 0.4, 0.5, 0.6, 0.7, 0.8, 0.9, 1.0\}$, which amounts to 45 distinct parameter settings in total. Decreasing d tightens the deadline and serves to find the point where normal Crown scheduling is not able to find a feasible schedule while Crown scheduling with buddy cores still is. Similarly, decreasing maxHeat increases sensitivity to overheating, and thus helps to find the point where the cores get too hot to find a feasible schedule with using buddy cores.

---

[4] If the penalty might differ between tasks, then the misscost table could be further indexed by the task index.

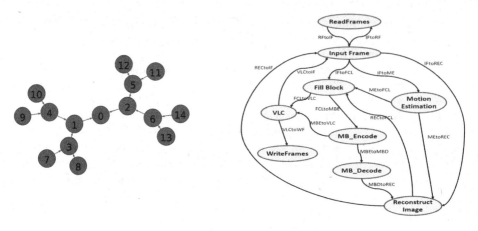

Fig. 3. Left: task graph for the mergesort application. Right: task graph for the H.263 encode application.

For each task set, we compare scheduling with buddying to regular crown scheduling under heat constraints. For the latter case, we add constraints $\forall j$: $\sum_{i,k} x_{i,j,1,k} = 0$ to prohibit the use of buddy cores.

Furthermore, we have performed experiments for two different ways of modeling thermal behavior, which is represented by the values of α and β. We set $\alpha = \beta = 0$ to consider core-local heat only, whereas $\alpha = 0.1$, $\beta = 0.05$ models heat diffusion to neighboring cores. For all experiments, we assume $p = 16$ and an architecture which exhibits the power characteristics of the ARM big.LITTLE, cf. [9]. As we base our experiments on a homogeneous architecture, we adopt the values for the big cores only. We have implemented the ILP in Sect. 5 in Python with the `gurobipy` package and subsequently employed the Gurobi 8.1.0 solver. All scheduling computations were performed on an AMD Ryzen 7 2700X with 8 cores and SMT.

Our primary interest lies in determining whether the buddy core concept enables us to retrieve feasible solutions where otherwise deadlines are too tight or heat constraints too restrictive to produce a feasible schedule. The results for the mergesort task set are displayed in Fig. 4. On the left hand side, only core-local heat is considered, while the results on the right hand side feature heat diffusion to neighboring cores. The plots show for which value combinations of d and maxHeat a feasible solution exists. If feasible schedules exist with and without buddying, both have the same energy consumption. It becomes clear immediately that a significantly wider range of parameter combinations can be covered with the buddy core concept. When looking at core-local heat only, making use of buddy cores leads to successful accommodation of tighter maxHeat constraints for each value of d. In the scenario where heat diffusion to neighboring cores is assumed, there is no need for buddy core execution at longer deadlines for the examined values of maxHeat. This does not come as a surprise since heat diffusion mitigates heat spikes at individual cores, especially when the heat load is distributed heterogeneously among the cores as is the case here due to the number of cores exceeding the number of tasks. A similar behavior can be observed for the H.263 encode task set, cf. Fig. 5, although enabling buddy cores pays off more substantially even in the heat diffusion case, where feasible solutions for more restrictive heat constraints can be found for all but the tightest and the most loose deadlines.

Figure 6 shows corresponding results for an architecture without DVFS, i.e., all tasks run at the same (high) frequency (here, 1.6 GHz). Deadlines and the values for maxHeat correspond to the original experiments in Figs. 4 and 5, respectively. By comparing the diagrams, it is easy to see that the benefit of using buddy cores is strongest in this scenario with no DVFS.

Figure 7 shows that with heat diffusion included in the model (which reduces heat stress on cores due to the cooling effect of their direct neighbors) and flexible buddy selection (cf. Sect. 6) enabled, feasibility is still increased by buddying.

There are cases (such as H.263 encode for deadline factor 2.5 and maxHeat 0.3 or mergesort for deadline factor 2.2 and maxHeat 0.3 or deadline factor 2.5 and maxHeat 0.2) where flexible selection of buddy cores enables a feasible solution when none exists with fixed buddy selection only. In these cases the penalty is accepted in order to select non-neighbored buddy cores and thereby be able to keep the maxHeat constraint.

In an additional set of experiments, we have sought to determine the influence of γ. To this end, we have set $\gamma \in \{0.1, 0.5, 1.0\}$ for both the H.263 encode and the mergesort task set. The smaller γ gets, the more chances the scheduler has to place tasks on the idle buddy core, but this also reduces the time for this core to cool down. The values chosen represent both ends of the spectrum plus a value in-between. Experiments were performed for the same parameter combinations of deadline factor and maxHeat as for the earlier experiments. For both task sets, no difference in the number of feasible solutions could be established. Presumably, this is due to large sequential tasks. The only option is to increase frequency to the maximum. If the deadline is still violated, the value of γ is irrelevant as no other task variants would be mapped to those cores.

In another experiment, we stressed the temperature-aware ILP crown scheduler with a set of $n = 8$ sequential tasks and tight deadline and a 4×4 core CPU with $\alpha = 0.05$, $\beta = 0$, penalty $= 0$. With buddying disabled and the heat limit chosen so that it is just feasible, we obtain a checkerboard mapping, which is expected as it maximizes the self-cooling effect due to unused cores. For a buddying-enabled scenario with $n = 4$ the ILP crown scheduler of Sect. 6 yields an alternating checkerboard schedule with alternation between different white fields in odd and even rounds if tightening the heat limit even more.

As an alternative to the ILP-based approach, we have devised a simple *heuristic algorithm* applying the buddy core concept to a temperature-unaware schedule which turns out infeasible when considering temperature constraints ex-post. The heuristic starts from a schedule generated by converting a scheduler for malleable, pre-emptive tasks and continuous frequencies to moldable tasks and discrete frequencies [15]. Alternatively, it may set out from a temperature-unaware

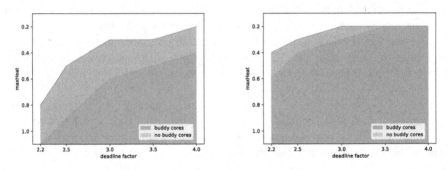

Fig. 4. Value combinations of d and maxHeat for which a feasible solution exists for the mergesort task set. Left: core-local heat only, right: heat diffusion to neighboring cores.

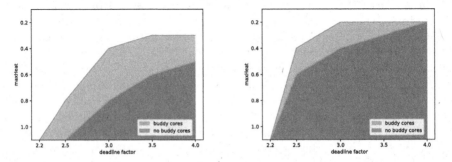

Fig. 5. Value combinations of d and maxHeat for which a feasible solution exists for the H.263 encode task set. Left: core-local heat only, right: heat diffusion to neighboring cores.

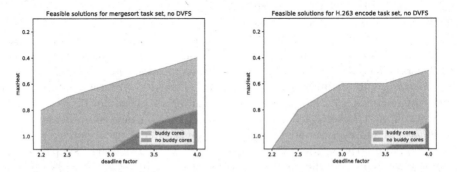

Fig. 6. Value combinations of d and maxHeat for which a feasible solution exists for the mergesort task set (left) and for the H.263 encode task set (right), respectively, on an architecture with no DVFS (i.e., all tasks run at the same frequency, here 1.6 GHz).

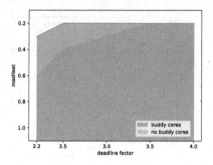
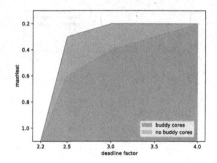

Fig. 7. Value combinations of d and maxHeat for which a feasible solution exists with heat diffusion modeled and flexible buddy selection (Sect. 6) enabled for the mergesort task set (left) and for the H.263 encode task set (right), respectively, with DVFS enabled. Other settings: $\gamma = 1.0$, $\alpha = 0.1$, $\beta = 0.05$, Heat is the arithmetic mean of Heat for odd and even rounds of the steady-state pattern, no penalty is charged for the "natural" fixed buddy cores from Sect. 5.

crown schedule generated by the ILP (or heuristic) described in [18]. The heuristic then applies the temperature model to identify cores that would become too hot. For each such core, it linearly searches for a free core to be used as a buddy resource for all tasks of the overheated core. If at some point there is no free core left although one were required to be designated buddy, the heuristic immediately terminates without a feasible solution. If on the other hand each core in need of a buddy is assigned one, the heuristic again checks whether there remain cores which become too hot. Accordingly, either a feasible solution has been found, or the heuristic did not manage to alter the original solution in such a way that it is ultimately feasible. We have conducted experiments for the mergesort and H.263 encode task sets, with DVFS enabled and $\alpha = \beta = 0$ (i.e. assuming no heat diffusion to neighboring cores). The heuristic encounters a feasible solution in exactly those cases where the ILPs of Sects. 5 and 6 deliver one. This holds true for both kinds of original schedules, the temperature-unaware crown schedules as well as the schedules produced by the heuristic.

Finally, we demonstrate that temperature-aware scheduling may lead to higher energy efficiency compared to temperature-agnostic scheduling when employing a temperature-dependent power model. We set $d = 3$, maxHeat $= 0.4$, and assume $P_{diff}(T_{hot}) = 0.5\,\mathrm{W}$ based on Figure 1 in [10]. Figure 8 shows the energy consumption predicted by the scheduler for temperature-aware and temperature-agnostic scheduling under various hotness threshold values C_{hot}. It can be noted that hotness thresholds have to be rather high (0.7 for the mergesort task set and 0.9 for the H.263 encode task set) for energy efficiency not to improve when performing temperature-aware scheduling. What is more, lower values of C_{hot} may decrease energy consumption by up to 43.8% (H.263 encode) or 57.8% (mergesort) with regard to temperature-agnostic scheduling.

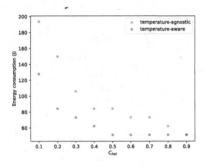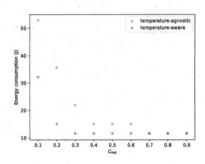

Fig. 8. Predicted energy consumption under various hotness threshold values. Left: H.263 encode task set, right: mergesort task set.

8   Conclusion and Future Work

We addressed the problem of deadline-constrained, energy-efficient temperature-aware scheduling of moldable tasks on a many-core CPU with a 2D mesh geometry. We introduced the buddying technique as an additional, software-only configuration option for tasks to control energy and temperature of cores. We integrated the buddying technique into heuristic and (crown-)optimal schedulers for moldable tasks. Our experimental results indicate that buddying adds flexibility to the scheduler to significantly improve the chances for finding a feasible solution in temperature-constrained scenarios, compared to temperature-unaware scheduling. Future work will comprise experiments with further streaming task graphs and validations by execution on real platforms, as well as extensions of the buddying concept to heterogeneous platforms and e.g. by allowing task and buddy task to use different task variants.

Acknowledgments. C. Kessler acknowledges partial funding by ELLIIT, project GPAI.

References

1. Alkabani, Y., Koushanfar, F., Potkonjak, M.: N-version temperature-aware scheduling and binding. In: Proceedings of the International Symposium on Low Power Electronics and Design, San Francisco, CA, USA, pp. 331–334. ACM, August 2009
2. Bampis, E., Letsios, D., Lucarelli, G., Markakis, E., Milis, I.: On multiprocessor temperature-aware scheduling problems. In: Snoeyink, J., Lu, P., Su, K., Wang, L. (eds.) AAIM/FAW -2012. LNCS, vol. 7285, pp. 149–160. Springer, Heidelberg (2012). https://doi.org/10.1007/978-3-642-29700-7_14
3. Bao, M., Andrei, A., Eles, P.I., Peng, Z.: Temperature-aware task mapping for energy optimization with dynamic voltage scaling. In: 11th IEEE Workshop on Design and Diagnostics of Electronic Circuits and Systems, pp. 44–49 (2008)

4. Bao, M., Andrei, A., Eles, P.I., Peng, Z.: Temperature-aware idle time distribution for energy optimization with dynamic voltage scaling. In: Proceedings of the Design, Automation, and Test in Europe Conference and Exhibition (DATE 2010), pp. 21–26 (2010)

5. Chantem, T., Hu, X.S., Dick, R.P.: Temperature-aware scheduling and assignment for hard real-time applications on MPSoCs. IEEE Trans. Very Large Scale Integr. Syst. 19(10), 1884–1897 (2011). https://doi.org/10.1109/TVLSI.2010.2058873

6. Coskun, A.K., Rosing, T.S., Whisnant, K.: Temperature aware task scheduling in MPSoCs. In: Proceedings of the DATE 2007 (2007)

7. Eindhoven Technical University, Electronic Systems: Dataflow Benchmark Suite (DFbench) (2010). http://www.es.ele.tue.nl/dfbench/

8. Eitschberger, P.: Energy-efficient and fault-tolerant scheduling for manycores and grids. Ph.D. thesis, FernUniversität in Hagen, Germany (2017)

9. Holmbacka, S., Keller, J.: Workload type-aware scheduling on big.LITTLE platforms. In: Ibrahim, S., Choo, K.-K.R., Yan, Z., Pedrycz, W. (eds.) ICA3PP 2017. LNCS, vol. 10393, pp. 3–17. Springer, Cham (2017). https://doi.org/10.1007/978-3-319-65482-9_1

10. Hällis, F., Holmbacka, S., Lund, W., Slotte, R., Lafond, S., Lilius, J.: Thermal influence on the energy efficiency of workload consolidation in many-core architectures. In: 24th Tyrrhenian International Workshop Digital Communications-Green ICT, pp. 1–6 (2013)

11. Jaja, J.: An Introduction to Parallel Algorithms. Addison Wesley, Boston (1992)

12. Jayaseelan, R., Mitra, T.: Temperature aware scheduling for embedded processors. J. Low Power Electron. 5(3), 363–372 (2009)

13. Kahn, G.: The semantics of a simple language for parallel programming. In: Proceedings of the IFIP Congress on Information Processing, pp. 471–475. North-Holland (1974)

14. Kessler, C., Litzinger, S., Keller, J.: Static scheduling of moldable streaming tasks with task fusion for parallel systems with DVFS. IEEE Trans. Comput.-Aided Des. Integr. Circuits Syst. (TCAD) 39(11), 4166–4178 (2020)

15. Litzinger, S., Keller, J.: Influence of discretization of frequencies and processor allocation on static scheduling of parallelizable tasks with deadlines. PARS-Mitteilungen 35(1), 95–108 (2020)

16. Lu, S.J., Tessier, R., Burleso, W.: Reinforcement learning for thermal-aware many-core task allocation. In: Proceedings of the GLSVLSI 2015. ACM, May 2015

17. Melot, N., Kessler, C., Eitschberger, P., Keller, J.: Co-optimizing core allocation, mapping and DVFS in streaming programs with moldable tasks for energy efficient execution on manycore architectures. In: Proceedings of the 19th International Conference on Application of Concurrency to System Design (ACSD 2019) (2019)

18. Melot, N., Kessler, C., Keller, J., Eitschberger, P.: Fast crown scheduling heuristics for energy-efficient mapping and scaling of moldable streaming tasks on manycore systems. ACM Trans. Archit. Code Optim. 11(4), 1–24 (2015)

19. Pierson, J., Stolf, P., Sun, H., Casanova, H.: MILP formulations for spatio-temporal thermal-aware scheduling in cloud and HPC datacenters. Clust. Comput. 23(2), 421–439 (2020). https://doi.org/10.1007/s10586-019-02931-3

20. Rajan, D., Yu, P.S.: Temperature-aware scheduling: When is system-throttling good enough? In: Proceedings of the 9th International Conference on Web-Age Information Management (WAIM 2008), Zhangjiajie, China, pp. 397–404. IEEE Computer Society, July 2008

Scheduling Challenges for Variable Capacity Resources

Chaojie Zhang[1] and Andrew A. Chien[1,2(✉)]

[1] University of Chicago, Chicago, IL, USA
chaojie@uchicago.edu
[2] Argonne National Lab, Chicago, IL, USA
achien@cs.uchicago.edu

Abstract. Datacenter scheduling research often assumes resources as a constant quantity, but increasingly external factors shape capacity dynamically, and beyond the control of an operator. Based on emerging examples, we define a new, open research challenge: **the variable capacity resource scheduling problem**. The objective here is effective resource utilization despite sudden, perhaps large, changes in the available resources.

We define the problem, key dimensions of resource capacity variation, and give specific examples that arise from the natural world (carbon-content, power price, datacenter cooling, and more). Key dimensions of the resource capacity variation include dynamic range, frequency, and structure. With these dimensions, an empirical trace can be characterized, abstracting it from the many possible important real-world generators of variation.

Resource capacity variation can arise from many causes including weather, market prices, renewable energy, carbon emission targets, and internal dynamic power management constraints. We give examples of three different sources of variable capacity.

Finally, we show variable resource capacity presents new scheduling challenges. We show how variation can cause significant performance degradation in existing schedulers, with up to 60% goodput reduction. Further, initial results also show intelligent scheduling techniques can be helpful. These insights show the promise and opportunity for future scheduling studies on resource volatility.

Keywords: Resource variability · Data center · Batch scheduling · Power limits

1 Introduction

The extensive research studies on job scheduling and resource management generally focus on problems where the quantity of resources is fixed or constant. In this paper, we define a new, open research challenge: **the variable capacity resource scheduling problem**. That is, in data centers or clusters of the

© Springer Nature Switzerland AG 2021
D. Klusáček et al. (Eds.): JSSPP 2021, LNCS 12985, pp. 190–209, 2021.
https://doi.org/10.1007/978-3-030-88224-2_10

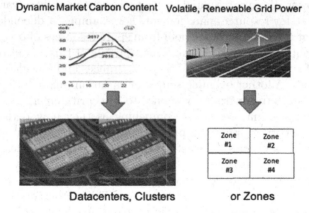

Fig. 1. Management to minimize carbon emissions or power cost combined with power grid, power markets, and renewable generation producing variable capacity. This is because changing power level directly affects the available computing resources [17,34].

future it will be common to have variable capacity, and that capacity determined by external factors. Changing resource capacity is a challenge for job schedulers and resource managers because of the *uncertainty* about future resource capacity. On one hand, this means that even if job runtime is known at start time, the resources may not be available long enough to complete it. On the other hand, resources can increase rapidly, challenging the availability of workload to utilize them.

A wide variety of sources can produce variable resource capacities. For example, power limits are constraining the scale of world's largest supercomputers [6] and already define datacenter size. With the largest supercomputers approaching 50 megawatts, and predicted to grow well beyond 150 megawatts by 2025 [43]. These limits make dynamic power management for cost, cooling, sharing, or simply to be a good citizen in a fluctuating or stressed power grid a source of variable capacity for datacenters. At another level, carbon emission management can give rise to dynamic capacity. Concerned about climate, governments around the world have adopted policies to reduce carbon emissions whenever possible at the same time hyperscale cloud operators (e.g. Amazon, Microsoft, Google, etc.) are growing rapidly, accelerated further by exploding popularity of machine learning [19,36]. This means that they must reduce datacenter power, perhaps on a dynamic basis in concert with use of renewable generation [27,29,32].

The importance of power and carbon as both a limit and a key cost has spawned a large and vibrant body of research on synergizing use and load with the grid (ZCCloud with renewables and low price [8,42]) or with the availability of local renewables [12,16,20]. These approaches all suggest that future data centers will have variable capacity, determined by external factors such as the general (grid-wide) or local (on site) availability of renewable generated power.

Beyond power, there are a number of other scenarios where variable capacity is of interest for resource management. For example, a dependent cloud (a meta-cloud that forms its resource pool from spare resources of others) typically experiences frequent capacity change. One example of this would be the meta-cloud formed from a collection of AWS spot instances and Google's preemptible virtual machines. Another example source of variation might include partition-shutdowns for software upgrades, response to a security emergency, and so on. The latter examples may seem less compelling as they may perhaps be more controllable in theory. However, in practice they may not be controllable.

These varied scenarios suggest clusters, availability zones, scheduling domains, even entire data centers will have variable capacity, driven by external factors such as power allocation, market prices, or even general (grid-wide) or local (on-site) availability of renewable energy. This is the core motivation for the variable capacity resource scheduling problem. As shown in Fig. 1, an external factor such as varying power creates variation in capability/capacity and the resource manager must effectively manage this varying capacity as it changes over time, as in Fig. 2(b).

Today's resource management systems and schedulers generally assume full knowledge of resource capacity, and presume that it is stable going forward. While resource managers have dealt with the addition and removal of resources, these have typically been rare events with either unpredictable (failures) or simply structured (upgrade) [11]. Further, these are typically small-scale compared to cluster size. In contrast, many of the sources of variation we consider are continually varying, have complex correlation with external factors (e.g. weather), and have large-scale effect on cluster resources. It is not known how to achieve high goodput (useful throughput) in the face of continual resource capacity variability.

To define the problem, in subsequent sections we first define the key dimensions of resource capacity variation. With this framework of dynamic range, frequency, structure, and foresight in place, an empirical trace can be characterized, abstracting it as a generic problem. Second, we give several specific examples in the natural world (carbon-content, power price, datacenter cooling, and more) that give rise to variation. We illustrate how varied and challenging these examples are. Third, we present simulation results that show that variable resource capacity presents new scheduling challenges. Without change, current schedulers suffer significant performance loss, up to 60% goodput degradation. Finally, we present initial studies which show that intelligent scheduling techniques can be helpful.

Specific contributions of the paper include:

- Formal definition of a new scheduling problem, variable capacity resource management in datacenters
- Examples of and empirical traces of sources that lead to resource capacity variability
- Study of variable capacity that show today's schedulers suffer significant performance degradation

– Study of scheduler improvements shows that intelligent scheduling techniques are promising in regaining performance loss.

The rest of the paper is organized as follows. In Sect. 2 we formally define the scheduling problem of variable resource capacity. In Sect. 3, we discuss some empirical examples and cover metrics in Sect. 4. In Sect. 5, simulation results show how resource variability impacts scheduler performance and scheduling techniques that can mitigate performance degradation. We discuss some future directions and opportunities in Sect. 6 and related work in Sect. 7. Finally, we summarize in Sect. 8.

2   Scheduling Problem with Resource Capacity Variations

2.1   Scheduling Problem Definition

We formally state the job scheduling problem as follows. In a data center or cluster, let M denote the number of total machines, where each machine m has $r(m)$ resources. We want to schedule a set of jobs J on M machines. Each job $j \in J$ has submission time $s(j)$, resource requirement $r(j)$ and execution time $t(j)$. The data centers need to decide j_{mt}, which is the decision variable of running job j on machine m at time t. In traditional systems, such placements are subject to each machine's resource constraint:

$$\forall t \in T, \forall m \in M, \sum_{j \in J} j_{mt} \times r(j) \leq r(m) \tag{1}$$

where the left hand side calculates the number of active resources that are processing jobs on each machine.

However in the new scheduling problem with resource capacity variations, the available resource capacity is a function of time t, denoted as $R(t)$ where $R(t) \leq M$. Hence, all job placements are now subject to a time-varying resource capacity constraint at each time slot t:

$$\forall t \in T, \forall m \in M, \sum_{j \in J} j_{mt} \times r(j) \leq r(m)$$

$$\text{subject to}$$

$$u_{mt} = 1 \iff \exists j \in J \ s.t. \ j_{mt} = 1 \tag{2}$$

$$\sum_{m \in M} u_{mt} \times r(m) \leq R(t)$$

This constraint ensures that the total number of machines which have active running jobs do not exceed current resource capacity $R(t)$, where u_{mt} indicates whether a machine is active or not.

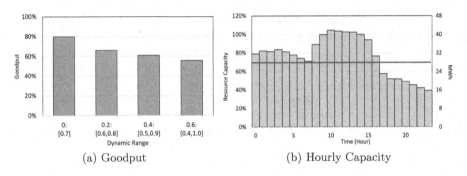

Fig. 2. Scheduler goodput for a batch HPC workload under variable capacity (a); as dynamic range increases, performance degrades. Example of hourly capacity variation (b), assuming with enough capacity headroom.

2.2   Challenges of Job Scheduling

When resource capacity varies, even if the average capacity does not change, significant losses in system goodput(useful resource utilization based on total available resources) can result. In Fig. 2(a), we present the resulting system goodput under dynamic capacity, even when a state-of-the-art scheduler [9] is used! As the dynamic range of variation increases from 0 to 0.6 (around an average capacity of 0.7), goodput decreases by 30%. Results are shown for capacity variability with random walk structure with stepsize of one-fourth the dynamic range. Figure 2(b) shows an example of capacity variation based on constant hourly carbon emissions from the Germany electricity market on 12.03.2020 [15]. The quantity of compute resources available $R(t)$ can vary significantly and on short time scales compared to job runtimes.

What accounts for this degradation in goodput? Traditional schedulers assume constant resource capacity. Based on the assumption that current capacity will continue, these schedulers make decisions that commit resources into the future. Because they have been designed to maximize goodput, they strive to fill as much of this capacity as possible. So if resource capacity decreases, expressed as $R(t) < R(t-1)$, the schedule reflects an overestimate, and the resource capacity constraint in Eq. 2 can be violated. This results in that some scheduled jobs may have to be terminated (fail) to release the machine. If resource capacity increases, the situation is a little better. No jobs need to be disturbed, but the schedule reflects an underestimation, and the scheduler has missed an opportunity to increase goodput (Fig. 3).

In this new world, key open research questions include:

1. How do current schedulers respond to capacity variation?
2. How can scheduler performance be improved in these challenging situations?
3. How should we best limit or shape capacity variability for performance and other benefits?

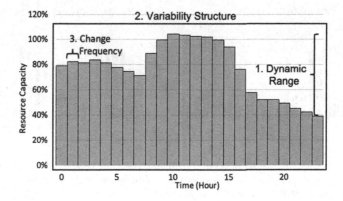

Fig. 3. Modeled dimensions of capacity variation include (1) dynamic range, (2) variability structure and (3) change frequency (temporal granularity) on a time-sequence of datacenter capacity from Fig. 2(b).

2.3 Approach

To characterize the challenge to conventional schedulers under dynamic resource capacity, we study workloads and schedulers drawn from both HPC and commercial environments. These workloads are well-known exemplars of their respective environments. For each workload, we use a system model that varies the resource capacity available to the scheduler and evaluate performance. Constant resources is a simple model; variable resources can have many different dimensions of variation. We consider three:

- Dynamic range: minimum to maximum capacity
- Variability Structure: random uniform, random walk
- Change Frequency: frequency of capacity variation

We consider these key dimensions as abstract framework, where specific examples can be characterized and generalized. Dynamic range captures the distance over which resource capacity varies – from a low to high watermark and back. It is the most foundational element of resource capacity change. Variability structure reflects how capacity is constrained to change from one time period to the next. Such constraints often reflect the realities of physical systems - inductance, momentum, inertia and more – that prevent large instantaneous change. Change frequency reflects our choice to model time discretely – capacity varies only at time period boundaries – so change frequency reflects the size of those periods. In a real system, periods could be defined by external structures (power markets), datacenter physicals (cooling and power sharing control systems), or other factors.

Using these workloads and schedulers, we execute a set of scheduler experiments that explore this multi-dimensional capacity change space, characterizing scheduler performance. In effect, each experiment explores scheduler performance when actual resource capacity diverges from the scheduler's simple fixed

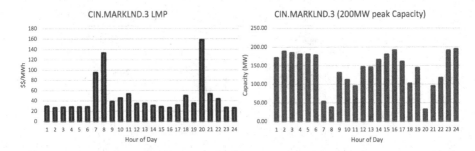

Fig. 4. Power price ($/MWh) (left) and resulting resource capacity for a 200 megawatt datacenter (right), using constant cost purchase approach. Exemplar 24-hour day from MISO January 9, 2018, CIN.Marklnd grid node.

estimate of stable resources. Our goal is to understand the capabilities of existing state-of-the-art schedulers. With a broad characterization of the negative impacts of capacity variation, we explore several scheduling ideas for how to mitigate performance degradation due to capacity variability.

3   Resource Capacity Variations from Empirical Traces

We focus on a few such factors that give rise to variable resource capacity and derive variable resource traces from them that can be used to evaluate scheduling systems. For each of these sources, we produce a set of sample traces of one-year duration with a variety of temporal resolutions (spanning 5 min to hourly). These exemplar capacity traces are generated based on several simple policies, e.g. constant (hourly) carbon budget.

3.1   Variation from Price

In order to manage a supply cost (e.g. power), a common strategy is to constrain expenditures to a constant rate for an operating period. In datacenters or many types of machinery, this couples dynamic market price to resource capacity as illustrated in Fig. 4, showing capacity variation of 5-fold [0.2,1.0] or more. Variation can be large over time periods as short as 5-minutes, and with very low (even negative) prices variable capacity may be limited by physical capacity.

3.2   Variation from Carbon Emissions

Concern is increasing about climate change, and thereby associated carbon emissions with power consumption. Carbon budgets must be managed against power grids with large fluctuations in carbon content. A basic strategy is a constant carbon budget for each time period as shown in Fig. 5. Carbon emissions often vary not only daily, but also with patterns that differ by month of the year. Note that workload SLOs such as "catchup by end of day" can have difficult interactions with the shape of variation curves.

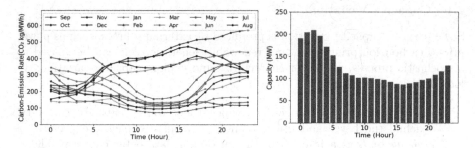

Fig. 5. Carbon-emissions rate (mT/MWh) (left) and resulting resource capacity at Constant Carbon purchase approach (December 2019, right).

3.3 Variation from Stranded Power

A different approach to lower carbon emissions is stranded renewable power [8,42], where excess renewable energy (power with zero-marginal carbon) can be used to power datacenters intermittently. This excess case may be important for combatting climate [42,43], and produces a nearly binary on-off resource capacity (Fig. 6, ERCOT), while operating at zero carbon emissions. The graphs illustrate 15-minute intervals, and reflect variation over a weeklong period. The power availability variation is day-to-day, week-to-week, and also by season of the year.

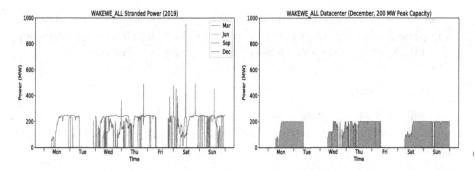

Fig. 6. Stranded Power (curtailed and negative priced power) in 15-minute intervals for a node in the ERCOT power grid (left, each line is a different week), and the resulting resource capacity for a 200 megawatt datacenter for the week in December (right).

4 Metrics

In this section, we discuss the metrics for resource capacity variation and measuring system performance.

4.1 Capacity Variation

Since resource capacity variation is produced by external sources, such as power prices, carbon footprint rates, and renewable generations, it can be viewed as a stochastic process. To better characterize and explore capacity variation, we look at three dimensions:

- **Dynamic range**: the range over which the resource capacity can vary. We define the lower and upper bound of resource capacity, expressed as *lbound, ubound*, as a fraction of the maximum datacenter capacity. Therefore, $R(t)$, the resource capacity at any time t, will be within the dynamic range, $lbound \leq R(t) \leq ubound$.
  We consider variation ranges of 0 (constant), 0.2, 0.4 and 0.6 as a fraction of maximum datacenter capacity. To normalize average capacity at 0.7, this produces dynamic ranges and intervals: 0: [0.7], 0.2: [0.6, 0.8], 0.4: [0.5, 0.9], and 0.6: [0.4, 1.0].
- **Variability Structure**: defines how much the capacity can change between adjacent time periods. *Random Uniform:* Resource capacity can be any level within the dynamic range at each interval and is drawn from a uniform distribution $\mathcal{U}([lbound, ubound])$, and *Walk:* Resource capacity can be any level within the dynamic range, but can only change by a maximum of *stepsize* in adjacent time intervals. Stepsize is one-fourth of the dynamic range.

$$R(t) = \begin{cases} \mathcal{U}([lbound, ubound]), & \text{if Random Uniform} \\ R(t-1) \pm stepsize, & \text{if Random Walk} \end{cases}$$

- **Temporal Granularity** represents the length of each time slot t. Between any time t and $t-1$, the capacity is constant. We vary the change frequency from 0.25 per hour (every 240 min) to 4 per hour (every 15 min).

4.2 Performance

Scheduling performance is measured by a group of widely-adopted metrics. Here we formally define these metrics which address system expectation and user experiences.

- **Goodput** is a measure of useful cluster utilization. It is calculated as total completed work divided by total available resource capacity: $\frac{\sum_{j \in J_{completed}} r(j)}{\sum_{t \in T} R(t)}$.
- **Failure Rate** represents the percentage of jobs that fail to complete due to resource capacity changes. It is calculated as $\frac{|J_{failed}|}{|J_{completed}| + |J_{failed}|}$.
- **Average Job Wait Time** measures the average of interval between job arrival time in the queue and job start time, which can be expressed as $\frac{\sum_{j \in J} START_j - ARRIVAL_j}{|J|}$.
- **SLO Miss Rate** represents the percentage of jobs that fail to complete before Service-Level-Objective (SLO) required deadline. For each job j, SLO miss $SM(j)$ is true if $FINISH_j - ARRIVAL_j - t(j) \geq X\% \times t(j)$, where X%

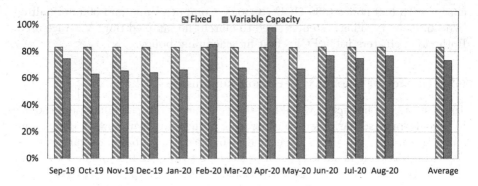

Fig. 7. Goodput for 12 exemplar days, comparing fixed and variable capacity.

is a threshold and usually set to 10%. The total SLO miss rate is therefore calculated as $\frac{\sum_{j\in J} SM(j)}{|J|}$.

There are many other widely-used metrics targeting different goals, such as response time and slowdown for cloud workloads and scheduling fairness. In addition to metrics, there are also various constraints that a system must consider. For example, "catch-up" constraint that bound the maximum start time of jobs, and hardware constraints that limit system's ramping capabilities or headroom limits that constrain system's maximum capacity.

5   Example Studies of Variable Resource Capacity Data Centers

5.1   Experiment Methodology

We considered a variety of publicly available workloads. While all of them are relevant and useful to study, we pick a few examplars that are widely-studied with distinct characteristics to understand new scheduling challenges. We use a month-long production trace from ALCF/Mira with a full range of job runtimes and large parallelism as the exemplar of large-scale HPC workload [5]. We pick Azure [10], Borg V2 traces [33] as node-sharing commercial cloud workload. Compared to Azure, the Borg trace has more small and short jobs, as well as significant load from long-running jobs.

For the Mira workload, we study the corresponding Cobalt [9] scheduler with the Mira supercomputer, a 10-petaflops IBM Blue Gene/Q system, deployed at the Argonne Leadership Computing Facility. Mira contains 49,152 nodes (786,432 cores) and 760 TB memory [28]. We model an Azure commercial cluster with 1,250 nodes (20,000 cores) and 160 TB of memory. This system is a close match in scale in resource utilization to the Mira system. We also model a Borg cluster with 630 nodes (336 GCU - Google-Compute-Unit) and 300 normalized bytes of memory. This system is sized to match the sampled Borg V2 trace used. Both cloud clusters use a FCFS first-fit scheduling policy.

5.2 Impact of Capacity Variation Dimensions

To illustrate the impact of variable resource capacity on scheduling performance in a real-world scenario, we consider a hypothetical 40-megawatt datacenter, which dynamically acquires power and resource capacity based on carbon emission rate, operating in the German Power Market [15]. Because the power market varies every day, and has a strong seasonal structure, we pick a set of exemplar days from the 12 most recent months (Sept 2019 - August 2020). When using constant carbon emissions per hour, they have power variation such as shown in Fig. 5. These twelve days have 24-hour capacity increases from 6% to 16% with an average of 11%.

We use an HPC Mira workload, Mira system, and Cobalt HPC schedulers. For reference, we include a baseline mode (fixed power), comparing the variable capacity resulting from constant hourly carbon emissions, and showing the resulting goodput in Fig. 7. Each blue bar depicts the results for a single exemplar day. Shifting from fixed to variable capacity produces a large drop in goodput as large at 24% on some days and 12% on average.

To further understand the impact on scheduling performance, we systematically vary the variability dimensions of dynamic range, structure, and change frequency while keeping average available capacity constant to understand how features of capacity variation affect scheduler performance, so we can highlight what is most important to address with scheduling techniques.

Dynamic Range. First, let's consider how resource capacity variation impact varies as we increase dynamic range. In Fig. 8, we first consider random walk structure (blue, left), comparing to no variation (patterned). The x-axis shows different dynamic ranges, and stepsizes are always one-fourth of the dynamic range. As the dynamic range increases, the scheduler performance degrades, and with the largest range, 0.6: [0.4,1.0], the goodput has declined by 25–45%.

Variability Structure. We consider two variability structures, random walk and random uniform. Now we compare random uniform (yellow, right in Fig. 8). The resource schedulers experience goodput degradation as much as 35% (for a total degradation of 55%). This is because random uniform allows large jumps in capacity, disrupting the job schedule with terminations or wasted resources. It appears variation structure can be as important as dynamic range in degrading scheduler performance.

Change Frequency. Change frequency is another dimension of capacity variation, so we start with a low rate (0.25 changes/hour), and increase to a high

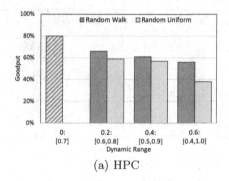

(a) HPC

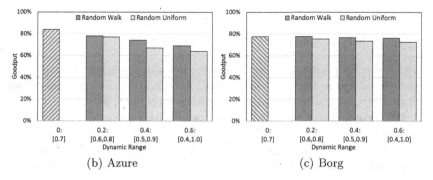

(b) Azure

(c) Borg

Fig. 8. Scheduling performance with random walk and random uniform resource variability structure, varying dynamic range.

rate (4 changes/hour). Note that all prior experiments used a change frequency of 1 change/hour. We focus on dynamic range of 0.6: [0.4, 1.0] with stepsize of 0.15 first. In Fig. 9, significant goodput drop is observed across all structures and workloads as frequency increases. For HPC workload, goodput has fallen by as much as 50%. For Azure workload, higher change frequencies cause clear degradation in goodput (up to 30% overall, but 15% attributable to frequency); Borg V2 exhibits clear, but lesser degradation. These commercial workloads are less sensitive to resource variation because of their lower parallelism and shorter duration.

We combine change frequency with the other parameters (dynamic range and structure), putting it all together in Fig. 10. With very low change frequency of 0.25 changes/hour, performance approaches the fixed capacity case. The negative impact of increasing change frequency on goodput remains but less extreme across all dynamic ranges.

We find that resource capacity variation can have a large impact on goodput, reducing it by up to 60%. Goodput in HPC and both commercial resource models are particularly sensitive to dynamic range, structure (and stepsize), and change frequency.

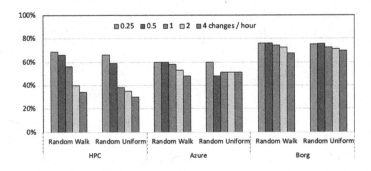

Fig. 9. Goodput versus change frequency (dynamic range 0.6: [0.4, 1.0]).

5.3   Scheduling Potential for Improvement

To show there is opportunity, we examine scheduling policies to mitigate performance degradation from capacity variation. When capacity decreases below the scheduled workload, to meet the capacity constraint, jobs must be terminated (fail). We explore how to choose the jobs for termination with the goal of maximizing goodput. Selective terimination or preemption is frequently adapted while facing mis-estimates based on priority or resource consumption [30, 38]. Here we consider three policies:

– **Random**: Select a node randomly, terminate the associated job, and free its resources.
– **Least Wasted Work (LWW)**: Select the job whose termination wastes least work (smallest $nodes \times (t - start\,time)$, where t is the current time) and free its resources.
– **Least Fraction Done (LFD)**: Terminate the job which is least fraction completed (minimum $\frac{(t - start\,time)}{runtime_j}$, where t is the current time) and free its resources.

For each policy, we repeat until the desired (lower) resource level is reached. For the HPC workloads, we use the requested runtime to compute LFD; for the commercial workloads we use the trace information for actual job length. However in production, this information is not generally available. We compare the termination policies, using scheduler performance metrics of goodput and failure rate.

Broadly, Fig. 11 presents goodput results for a variety of dynamic ranges and variability structures. The results show that intelligent termination policies make a big difference. For HPC both intelligent termination algorithms improve performance, but best performance is achieved with LWW (rightmost, gray). The goodput achieved by LWW approaches the stable resource capacity, and is an average of 44% improvement over Random. For Azure and Borg V2 workloads, the algorithm preference is similar, with LWW producing highest goodput, but with smaller benefits.

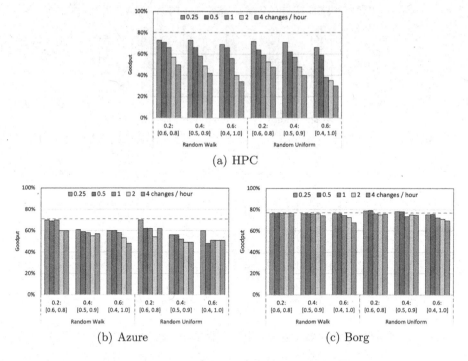

(a) HPC

(b) Azure   (c) Borg

Fig. 10. Goodput versus change frequency, varying dynamic range and structure of capacity variation.

These policies show that scheduling strategies can provide improvement, and in this case increase performance to match the fixed-resource scenario (no variation), increasing goodput by 30% on average. These results show that intelligent scheduling techniques are of interest in variable capacity data centers.

6   Further Directions and Opportunities

While we have outlined the core aspect of the open scheduling problem variable capacity, where resource capacity changes under external control on time scales shorter than many scheduled jobs. There are several dimensions that significantly broaden the space of interesting research.

Complex SLO Requirements. Many workloads have complex dependencies amongst jobs and tasks that constrain scheduling, and correlate task failures [37]. Complex dependence structures make variable capacity scheduling challenging. Further, service-level objectives for jobs and tasks create further constraints on scheduling and opportunities for improvement. For example, a 24-hour time shifting model might have an asymmetric "catch-up" constraint.

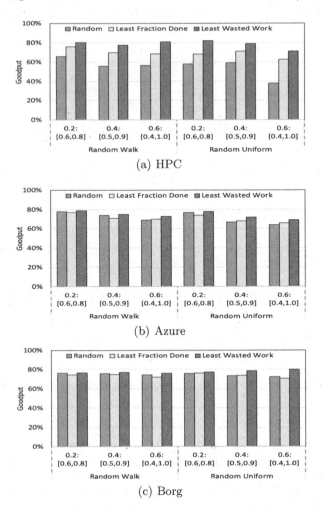

Fig. 11. Goodput versus termination policy, varying dynamic ranges and structures

More Sources of Variability and Correlation. Another dimension of challenges comes from different sources of variability. Beyond power management, weather can produce variation in time and space, power availability and cooling efficiency (external temperature or humidity). Variation can be correlated across space and time – cloud cover can be correlated with weather, affecting solar and wind and temperature. Power grid element failures have correlated, cascading effects, and load changes can spill over from one cloud network to another. Unlike local failures, resource capacity variations coming from various external factors can be informed, estimated, or predicted through other correlated information. Power grid carbon-content can be correlated with price, and power availability can depend on competition.

Resource Heterogeneity. The addition of heterogeneity to the variable capacity problem creates new challenges. Variants include fixed ratios, dictated ratios, partially controlled, or even fully controlled ratios of each type as capacity changes. All of these problems represent interesting challenges, both creating more complex and changing scheduling problems or in some cases added new critical decisions such as to invest the power relative to the potential heterogeneity.

Complex External Metrics; e.g. "Overall Cost Optimization", Overall Carbon Optimization. One more additional dimension is the notion that metrics might depend on the input metrics that cause variation. Such a dependence not only affects the assessment of success, but therefore may also affect the scheduling strategies used. For example, power costs might be passed through to cloud users, and likewise responsibilty for carbon-emissions. Combinations of these metrics combined with traditional time-based techniques – 5s at high carbon, but overnight latency at low carbon – might make sense for some applications.

7   Related Work

We study resource management for both supercomputer and datacenter scenarios responding to capacity changes that could arise from carbon-emission-aware dynamic power acquisition. Other potential sources of resource capacity variation include cluster, datacenter, and site power management [34] or power grid dynamics [8,22,42]. While many other scheduling studies have also dealt with variations and uncertainty, they mainly focus on fluctuation of the load and job information [14,18,35]. It is an open question how well these techniques apply to the variation that is our focus, and perhaps more interesting if they can be adapted to cope better by exploiting the properties of the variation.

Burstable Instances and Turbo Modes. In several cloud environments, virtual machines can have variable performance [1], but the resource consumption is typically controlled by the application. Bursting credit is accumulated over time and expended as the application demands. Turbo modes are similar, where heat capacity is akin to credit. This differs from variable capacity where resource constraint is enforced on the workload/resource manager.

Resource Revocation. Many systems have volatile resource management (e.g. PC's in desktop grids [7,26], and more recently AWS Spot Instances [3] and Google Preemptible VM's [4]), employing checkpointing and a range of statistical techniques to achieve high throughput through revocations [39,40]. Commercial versions include [2,21]. Most of these systems are application-oriented, and deal with collections of single-node jobs. The capacity variation problem is large-scale resource-oriented, and formulated for a job scheduler managing a workload with complex mixes of co-run, run-before, and other kinds of task dependencies in the face of a rich set of service-level objectives (SLO's).

Meta-schedulers. There have been some systems that do this, but they typically manage batch queue delay (Condor Glideins with known durations). These systems schedule revocable resources, but the focus has traditionally been on managing across several resource pools and assumes new resources can be immediately obtained while revocations happen, not the scheduling efficiency within one (our focus here).

Power Capping and Large-scale Power Management. Power capping generally limit power, a fixed capacity. Then, the challenge is managing the performance of the applications within a fixed cap [13,23,31]. Large-scale power management, power oversubscription, and power capping is common in commercial datacenters to improve power efficiency (e.g. Facebook's Dynamo [41], IBM's CapMaestro [25], and Google [34]). These studies do not model schedulers, and interestingly suggests that smaller and therefore more variable power pools may be preferrable, suggesting variable capacity.

Green Scheduling. Researchers have also explored the use of local renewables or integration of grid demand-response with job scheduling [16,24]. Local renewables are a simpler instance of the variable capacity scheduling problem – many variants exist. The grid demand-response examples are also related – but deal with rare circumstances (e.g. 4 h a year). Our formulation of the variable capacity problem admits a rich, general externally imposed variation. It can vary at many time scales, with correlation or dependence across sites, and focuses on typical performance, but could perhaps include rare events.

8   Summary

We have proposed a new scheduling challenge: the variable resource capacity scheduling problem. We have defined the key dimensions (dynamic range, frequency, and structure) of resource capacity variations and provided empirical traces of such variation from several real-world scenarios. Using real HPC and commercial workloads, our results show that the negative impact of resource variability on goodput can be severe – as much as 60%, and 30% on average.

Further, we find that intelligent scheduling techniques such as job termination policies can reduce goodput losses for both workloads. These results not only show that variable resource capacity imposes new challenges, but also suggest that intelligent scheduling solution is of benefit. And we look forward to both exploring this space, and exploring the coupling of these studies with the complex systems which are also producing capacity changes [22,34].

References

1. Amazon burstable instances (2019). https://docs.aws.amazon.com/AWSEC2/latest/UserGuide/burstable-performance-instances.html
2. Amazon spot fleet (2019). https://docs.aws.amazon.com/AWSEC2/latest/UserGuide/spot-fleet.html
3. Amazon spot instance (2019). https://aws.amazon.com/ec2/spot/
4. Google preemptible VMs (2019). https://cloud.google.com/preemptible-vms/
5. Allcock, W., Rich, P., Fan, Y., Lan, Z.: Experience and practice of batch scheduling on leadership supercomputers at Argonne. In: Klusáček, D., Cirne, W., Desai, N. (eds.) JSSPP 2017. LNCS, vol. 10773, pp. 1–24. Springer, Cham (2018). https://doi.org/10.1007/978-3-319-77398-8_1
6. Bourzac, K.: Supercomputing poised for a massive speed boost. Nature (November 2017). https://www.nature.com/articles/d41586-017-07523-y
7. Chien, A., Calder, B., Elbert, S., Bhatia, K.: Entropia: architecture and performance of an enterprise desktop grid system. J. Parallel Distrib. Comput. **63**(5), 597–610 (2003)
8. Chien, A.A., Yang, F., Zhang, C.: Characterizing curtailed and uneconomic renewable power in the mid-continent independent system operator. AIMS Energy **6**(2), 376–401 (2018)
9. Cobalt: Component based lightweight toolkit (2019). https://github.com/ido/cobalt, iBM Commercial Job scheduler for Mira, JuQueen, and other Blue Gene systems
10. Cortez, E., Bonde, A., Muzio, A., Russinovich, M., Fontoura, M., Bianchini, R.: Resource central: understanding and predicting workloads for improved resource management in large cloud platforms. In: Proceedings of the 26th Symposium on Operating Systems Principles, pp. 153–167. ACM (2017)
11. Curino, C., et al.: Hydra: a federated resource manager for data-center scale analytics. In: NSDI, pp. 177–192 (2019)
12. Derin, O., Ferrante, A.: Scheduling energy consumption with local renewable microgeneration and dynamic electricity prices. In: First Workshop on Green and Smart Embedded System Technology: Infrastructures, Methods, and Tools, vol. 12, pp. 1–6 (2010)
13. Ellsworth, D.A., Malony, A.D., Rountree, B., Schulz, M.: Dynamic power sharing for higher job throughput. In: SC 2015: Proceedings of the International Conference for High Performance Computing, Networking, Storage and Analysis, pp. 1–11 (2015)
14. Feitelson, D.G., Tsafrir, D., Krakov, D.: Experience with using the parallel workloads archive. J. Parallel Distrib. Comput. **74**(10), 2967–2982 (2014)
15. Electricity market data: Generations, prices, power (2020). https://www.smard.de
16. Goiri, Í., Katsak, W., Le, K., Nguyen, T.D., Bianchini, R.: Parasol and greenswitch: managing datacenters powered by renewable energy. In: ACM SIGPLAN Notices, vol. 48, pp. 51–64. ACM (2013)
17. Google: White paper: Moving toward 24x7 carbon-free energy at Google data centers: Progress and insights. Technical report, Google (October 2018)
18. Gupta, V., Harchol-Balter, M., Wolf, A.S., Yechiali, U.: Fundamental characteristics of queues with fluctuating load. In: Proceedings of the Joint International Conference on Measurement and Modeling of Computer Systems, pp. 203–215 (2006)

19. Hao, K.: Training a single AI model can emit as much carbon as five cars in their lifetimes. Technology Review (June 2019)
20. Haque, M.E., Goiri, I., Bianchini, R., Nguyen, T.D.: Greenpar: scheduling parallel high performance applications in green datacenters. In: Proceedings of the 29th ACM on International Conference on Supercomputing, pp. 217–227. ACM (2015)
21. Harlap, A., Chung, A., Tumanov, A., Ganger, G.R., Gibbons, P.B.: Tributary: spot-dancing for elastic services with latency slos. In: 2018 USENIX Annual Technical Conference (ATC 2018), pp. 1–14 (2018)
22. Kim, K., Yang, F., Zavala, V., Chien, A.A.: Data centers as dispatchable loads to harness stranded power. IEEE Trans. Sustain. Energy **8**(1), 208–218 (2016)
23. Le, K., Bianchini, R., Zhang, J., Jaluria, Y., Meng, J., Nguyen, T.D.: Reducing electricity cost through virtual machine placement in high performance computing clouds. In: Proceedings of 2011 International Conference for High Performance Computing, Networking, Storage and Analysis, pp. 22:1–22:12. SC 2011, ACM, New York, NY, USA (2011). https://doi.org/10.1145/2063384.2063413, http://doi.acm.org/10.1145/2063384.2063413
24. Le, T.N., Liu, Z., Chen, Y., Bash, C.: Joint capacity planning and operational management for sustainable data centers and demand response. In: Proceedings of the Seventh International Conference on Future Energy Systems, pp. 1–12 (2016)
25. Li, Y., et al.: A scalable priority-aware approach to managing data center server power. In: 2019 IEEE International Symposium on High Performance Computer Architecture (HPCA), pp. 701–714. IEEE (2019)
26. Litzkow, M.J., Livny, M., Mutka, M.W.: Condor-a hunter of idle workstations. Technical report, University of Wisconsin-Madison Department of Computer Sciences (1987)
27. Megerian, C., Panzar, J.: Gov. Brown signs climate change bill to spur renewable energy, efficiency standards. Los Angeles Times (September 2015)
28. Mira-ALCF: MIRA: A 10-Petaflop, 4 MW IBM Supercomputing at Argonne (2019). https://www.alcf.anl.gov/mira
29. New York State Energy Planning Board: The energy to lead: 2015 New York state energy plan (2015). http://energyplan.ny.gov/Plans/2015.aspx
30. Park, J.W., Tumanov, A., Jiang, A., Kozuch, M.A., Ganger, G.R.: 3Sigma: distribution-based cluster scheduling for runtime uncertainty. In: Proceedings of the Thirteenth EuroSys Conference, pp. 1–17 (2018)
31. Patel, T., Tiwari, D.: Perq: fair and efficient power management of power-constrained large-scale computing systems. In: Proceedings of the 28th International Symposium on High-Performance Parallel and Distributed Computing, pp. 171–182. HPDC 2019, Association for Computing Machinery, New York, NY, USA (2019). https://doi.org/10.1145/3307681.3326607
32. Penn, I., Kang, I.: California today: A move to mandate 100% carbon-free electricity. New York Times (August 2018)
33. Reiss, C., Wilkes, J., Hellerstein, J.L.: Google cluster-usage traces: format+ schema. Google Inc., White Paper, pp. 1–14 (2011)
34. Sakalkar, V., et al.: Data center power oversubscription with a medium voltage power plane and priority-aware capping. In: Proceedings of the Twenty-Fifth International Conference on Architectural Support for Programming Languages and Operating Systems, pp. 497–511 (2020)
35. Schroeder, B., Harchol-Balter, M.: Web servers under overload: how scheduling can help. ACM Trans. Internet Technol. (TOIT) **6**(1), 20–52 (2006)
36. Strubell, E., Ganesh, A., McCallum, A.: Energy and policy considerations for deep learning in NLP. arXiv preprint arXiv:1906.02243 (2019)

37. Tirmazi, M., et al.: Borg: the next generation. In: Proceedings of the Fifteenth European Conference on Computer Systems (2020)
38. Verma, A., Pedrosa, L., Korupolu, M., Oppenheimer, D., Tune, E., Wilkes, J.: Large-scale cluster management at google with Borg. In: Proceedings of the Tenth European Conference on Computer Systems, p. 18. ACM (2015)
39. Wolski, R., Brevik, J.: Providing statistical reliability guarantees in the aws spot tier. In: Proceedings of the 24th High Performance Computing Symposium, pp. 1–9 (2016)
40. Wolski, R., Brevik, J., Chard, R., Chard, K.: Probabilistic guarantees of execution duration for amazon spot instances. In: Proceedings of the International Conference for High Performance Computing, Networking, Storage and Analysis. ACM (2017)
41. Wu, Q., et al.: Dynamo: facebook's data center-wide power management system. ACM SIGARCH Comput. Archit. News 44(3), 469–480 (2016)
42. Yang, F., Chien, A.A.: Zccloud: Exploring wasted green power for high-performance computing. In: 2016 IEEE International Parallel and Distributed Processing Symposium (IPDPS), pp. 1051–1060. IEEE (2016)
43. Yang, F., Chien, A.A.: Large-scale and extreme-scale computing with stranded green power: opportunities and costs. IEEE Trans. Parallel Distrib. Syst. 29(5), 1103–1116 (2017)

GLUME: A Strategy for Reducing Workflow Execution Times on Batch-Scheduled Platforms

Evan Hataishi[1], Pierre-François Dutot[2] , Rafael Ferreira da Silva[3] ,
and Henri Casanova[1([⊠])]

[1] Information and Computer Sciences, University of Hawaii, Honolulu, HI, USA
{evanhata,henric}@hawaii.edu
[2] Univ. Grenoble Alpes, CNRS, Inria, Grenoble INP, LIG, Grenoble, France
pierre-francois.dutot@univ-grenoble-alpes.fr
[3] Information Sciences Institute,University of Southern California,
Marina Del Rey, CA, USA
rafsilva@isi.edu

Abstract. Many scientific workflows have computational demands that require the use of compute platforms managed by batch schedulers, which are unfortunately poorly suited to these applications. This work proposes GLUME, a strategy for partitioning a workflow into batch jobs. The novelty is that these jobs are explicitly constructed to minimize overall workflow execution time. Experimental evaluation via simulation of production batch workloads and workflows shows that our heuristic is more effective than previously proposed strategies when executing workflows with moderate to high computational demand.

Keywords: Batch scheduling · Workflows · Task clustering

1 Introduction

Workflow applications are mainstream in the sciences and often require High Performance Computing platforms. Most such platforms run Resource and Job Management Software (RJMS) that implements batch scheduling. Batch scheduling was designed for workloads in which users submit moderate numbers of large, long-running, and loosely dependent parallel jobs. It is thus poorly suited to workflows. Workflow scheduling on batch-scheduled platforms can be attacked at the RJMS level [1,9,18] or at the application level [23,24,27,28]. Both kinds of solutions have drawbacks: RJMS-level solutions face adoption challenges while application-level solutions are impeded by constraints imposed on batch jobs.

We proposes an application-level strategy for minimizing workflow execution time, or *makespan*. This requires answering two questions. First, how should a workflow be partitioned into batch jobs? At one extreme is a one-job-per-task approach. This approach is problematic for workflows with long tasks (due to cascading wait times) and/or with many tasks (due to per-user caps on the number of running jobs). The other extreme, a workflow-as-a-single-job approach, is

© Springer Nature Switzerland AG 2021
D. Klusáček et al. (Eds.): JSSPP 2021, LNCS 12985, pp. 210–230, 2021.
https://doi.org/10.1007/978-3-030-88224-2_11

also problematic as large jobs suffer from long wait times. Second, when should workflow batch jobs be submitted? Submitting a job only once the previous job has completed is inefficient, but aggressively overlapping wait times and run times can lead to job expirations. To the best of our knowledge, the only previous work that provides non-trivial answers to these questions is that in [28]. The strategy therein uses wait time estimates to submit sets of consecutive workflow levels as batch jobs. We make the following contributions:

- The authors in [28] did not compare their proposed strategy to a baseline workflow-as-a-single-job approach that uses wait time estimates. We find that this simple approach can outperform that in [28] significantly.
- We propose a new strategy, GLUME, which, unlike that in [28], explicitly aims at minimizing makespan.
- We compare GLUME to the strategy in [28] and to baseline strategies in simulation, and find that GLUME is more effective than its competitors for workflows with moderate to high computational demands.

2   Related Work

Some authors have proposed RJMS that are well-suited to workloads that include workflows. The RJMS in [1] uses a hierarchical design to ensure that scheduling decisions can be made quickly even when the workload includes workflows with thousands or even millions of possible short-running tasks. In [18], the authors propose to augment the Slurm RJMS [26] to make it workflow-aware, ensuring that a workflow's jobs are positioned in adjacent positions in the batch queue. The approach in [9] inserts a RJMS between the application and the platform's native RJMS so as to allocate resources to workflow applications elastically.

In this work, we propose an application-level approach that can be used with non-workflow-aware, standard RJMS. Also, it can benefit RJMS-level solutions that execute workflows one level at a time [9,18], making it possible to decide how to aggregate consecutive levels judiciously. The workflow scheduling literature is enormous but in this work we target batch-scheduled platforms, for which only a few approaches have been proposed. Some authors have proposed submitting each workflow task as a single job [23,24,27] Given high wait times incurred by the one-task-per-job approach in practice with current RJMS implementations [18], a few authors have proposed to group workflow tasks together into batch jobs. A commonly used baseline approach is to execute each workflow level as a single batch job [9,18]. To the best of our knowledge, the only work that goes further is [28], which we detail and evaluate in Sect. 5.

Our approach, like those in [27,28], relies on wait time estimates. Wait times are notoriously difficult to predict. In this work, instead of predictions, we rely on wait time *estimates* as provided by production batch schedulers (see Sect. 3).

3   Problem Statement

We consider a cluster of homogeneous compute nodes, or *nodes*, managed by a RJMS that implements batch scheduling, i.e., a *batch scheduler*. The batch scheduler provides job wait time estimates based on currently running and pending jobs, assuming that all job run times are exactly as requested upon submission. Virtually all production batch schedulers provide "start time estimates" for pending jobs (e.g., `--start` option of Slurm's `squeue` command). They can thus in principle provide wait time estimates speculatively. This is possible, for instance, in MOAB/Torque (with the `showstart` command). One source of inaccuracy of these estimates is that jobs terminate earlier than expected since users specify conservative time bounds [11]. Early job completions create *backfilling* opportunities, causing some jobs to start earlier than expected, and wait time estimates for these jobs were then pessimistic. Another source of inaccuracy is that backfilling may increase the wait times of other pending jobs, making wait time estimates for these jobs optimistic. This is the case with *aggressive backfilling* [13]. By contrast, *conservative backfilling* [15] guarantees that backfilling will not delay any pending job. This leads to fairer schedules, possibly at the expense of lowered resource utilization, and makes wait time estimates more accurate. Several popular production batch schedulers implement conservative backfilling [16,26]. In this work we only consider conservative backfilling.

On the cluster we wish to execute a static workflow, i.e., a directed acyclic graph of compute tasks, where each task executes on a single compute nodes, and where edges denote task dependencies. Although emerging workflows are dynamic and include parallel tasks, static workflows of non-parallel tasks are commonplace in today's production scientific applications [12,14,20]. We assume that for each task we have an accurate estimate of its run time, including computation and I/O. This is a common assumption in the literature, justified in production settings in which the same workflow applications are executed repeatedly, and previous executions can serve as benchmarks for future executions. The objective is to minimize *makespan*, i.e., the wall clock time between the first job submission and the last job completion.

4   Experimental Methodology

In this work we compare different strategies for executing workflows on a batch-scheduled cluster. These comparisons must be for a given workflow instance submitted at a given time to a batch-scheduled cluster subject to some background workload (i.e., other users submitting competing batch). It is impossible to perform these comparisons fairly on real-world systems, as back-to-back workflow executions would face different competing workload conditions. For this reason, like most previous works, we use simulation. We have implemented a simulator in C++ using the WRENCH [7] simulation framework and Batsched [6], a batch scheduler simulator. WRENCH provides the necessary high-level simulation abstractions for implementing the workflow scheduling algorithms we consider in this work. Batsched, which is a component of the Batsim simulator [8], implements the necessary batch scheduling algorithms.

Our simulator takes as input (i) a number of nodes; (ii) a workload trace file with competing job submissions; (iii) a workflow description file that specifies task run times and dependencies; (iv) the date at which the workflow execution begins (i.e., when the first task can be submitted for execution); and (v) a workflow scheduling strategy to use. The simulator outputs an execution log and the workflow makespan. The source code for our simulator is publicly available [21].

4.1 Workflow Configurations

Using a popular generator [19], we instantiate workflow configurations from these four applications: EPIGENOMICS (bioinformatics; many independent multi-level-fork join patterns with a single final a 3-task chain), SIPHT (bioinformatics; many independent 31-task structures whose first level consists of 23 independent tasks), CYBERSHAKE (earthquake engineering; sets of independent and massively parallel 2-level fork-join patterns), and MONTAGE (astronomy; a moderately parallel phase followed by a massively parallel phases, followed by a 6-level chain of sequential or moderately parallel phases). We refer the reader to [25] for more details about these workflows. For each application we generate workflows with $50, 250, 500 \pm 5$ tasks. The ± 5 is because the generator cannot produce a (realistic) configuration for any arbitrary workflow size. We generate workflows with sequential run times (i.e., sum of task run times) of $100, 500, 1000 \pm 3$ hours. The ± 3 is because the generator draws task execution times from random distributions. The 36 generated workflow configurations have overall and per-task computational demands that vary by orders of magnitude. We name each workflow x-y-z, where x denotes the application (E, S, C, or M); y denotes the number of tasks; and z denotes the sequential execution time (short, medium, or long). For instance C-250-short denotes a $\sim$ 250-task CYBERSHAKE workflow with sequential run time of $\sim$100 h.

4.2 Batch Scheduling and Workloads

Table 1. Batch logs used to drive simulations

Workload	#nodes	#jobs	duration	utilization
KTH	100	$\sim$28,000	11 months	$\sim$70%
SDSC	128	$\sim$60,000	24 months	$\sim$83%
HPC2N	100	$\sim$203,000	42 months	$\sim$60%
CTC	338	$\sim$77,000	11 months	$\sim$85%

We configure our simulator to use conservative backfilling, using arrival times as job priorities. We simulate background workload by replaying job submission logs from production systems, as available in the Parallel Workloads Archive [17] (see Table 1). All simulations include a one day "warm-up" period, after which we simulate workflow execution when submitted on the half-hour for 6 days, for a total of $(48 \times 6) + 1 = 289$ different submission times. We simulate the execution of jobs in the background workloads with either accurate or real job requested run times. For the former, we replace each job's requested run time by its actual run time. For the latter, we instead use the job's actual requested time from the log, which is known to be conservative [11]. Although unrealistic, we include the former method as a way to compare the merit of scheduling algorithms in ideal conditions w.r.t. wait time estimates. When discussing results we specify which method is used (either "accurate" or "real" estimates).

It is typical to cap the number of jobs a user can run simultaneously (e.g., setting the MaxSubmitJobsPerAccount for Slurm [22]). Taking the Argonne Leadership Computing Facility as an example: the recently decommissioned Mira system allowed users to have at most 5 running jobs per batch queue [3]; The Cooley and the Theta systems allow both for up to 10 running jobs [2,4]. Surveys of the Oak Ridge Leadership Computing Facility, the National Energy Research Scientific Computing Center, and the Texas Advanced Computing Center yield similar observations, with most batch queues imposing low caps (i.e., below 20 and often below 10). As the caps can have a large impact of workflow executions we present results for different cap values.

5   The Algorithm by Zhang et al.

5.1   Overview

The algorithm proposed by Zhang et al. [28], which we call ZHANG, is invoked repeatedly to decide which workflow tasks should be submitted as batch job next. It considers the workflow as a sequence of *levels*, where each level comprises the tasks that have the same top-level (i.e., the same maximum distance from entry tasks). When all tasks in a level have been executed, all tasks in the next level can begin execution as it is guaranteed that all their parents have been executed. When invoked, ZHANG always submits a sequence of consecutive workflow levels as a single job to the batch scheduler, starting with the next level to be executed. A heuristic decides how many levels should be included in each job as follows.

Let l_{start} be the first yet-to-be-executed level of the workflow and l_{end} be the workflow's last level. The heuristic iteratively considers the option of scheduling all levels from level l_{start} to level l_i, for $i = end, start, start + 1, \ldots, end - 1$. Submitting all remaining tasks as a single job ($i = end$) is considered first as a "safe" baseline option. The iteration stops prematurely whenever a current option is deemed worse than the previously considered option. More precisely, at each iteration i ZHANG considers executing all tasks in levels l_{start} to l_i as a single job, requesting a number of nodes equal to the maximum width of these levels (in number of tasks) and a sufficiently long run time to execute all tasks in these levels. A wait time estimate is obtained from the batch scheduler and the ratio of the wait time to the run time is computed. If the ratio computed at the previous iteration, if any, was lower, then the iteration stops, the option evaluated at the previous iteration is selected, and the corresponding job is submitted to the batch scheduler. However, if $i = end$ (i.e., the first iteration) is selected, and the estimated wait time is more than twice the run time, then each task is submitted as an individual job. The rationale is that if wait time is much larger than run time, the one-job-per-task strategy is preferable as many small jobs may benefit from backfilling.

To overlap run times and wait times, whenever a submitted job begins execution ZHANG is re-invoked for the yet-to-be-executed workflow levels. Thus it is possible that the next job would start "too soon." This leads to unsatisfied task dependencies, causing the job to idle before being able to execute its tasks. These tasks may then fail to complete within the job's requested run time. Whenever a job expires with uncompleted tasks, any subsequent job that had been submitted is canceled, and ZHANG is re-invoked. To reduce the number of job expirations and re-executions, ZHANG uses a *leeway*, i.e., an extra requested amount of time to ensure that all tasks in the job can complete even if the job starts too early. Consider a job that starts execution at time 0 and will complete at time t. At time 0 ZHANG is invoked to submit a new job for execution. Say that this new job has run time r and (estimated) wait time $w < t$. A naive leeway would be $t - w$, i.e., requesting $t - w + r$ time for this new job, making sure that all its tasks will complete successfully in spite of the job starting too early. This leeway is naive because requesting the extra time will change the wait time. Since the leeway both depends on and changes the wait time, ZHANG computes the leeway using a simple iterative approach. However, given non-determinism in the batch queue behavior, a job could still expire before completing all its tasks.

Figure 1 shows an example execution in which ZHANG splits a workflow execution into four jobs. It is first invoked at time t_1 and submits job #1, which executes all the tasks in a first set of consecutive workflow levels. At time t_2, this job begins execution, and ZHANG is invoked again and submits job #2 (which comprises the tasks in the next set of consecutive levels). In this example, the run time of job #1 overlaps perfectly with the wait time of job #2; thus, job #2 can begin executing tasks as soon as it starts. At time t_3, ZHANG is invoked again and submits job #3. As shown in the figure, the wait time of job #3 is insufficient to completely overlap with the run time of job #2, so ZHANG adds a leeway to job #3's run time to ensure that job #3 can complete all its tasks successfully. Job #3 begins its execution at time t_4 but must wait for job #2 to complete. This lost time is made up with the leeway, and tasks in job #3 begin executing at time t_5. Although job #3 is idle until t_5, ZHANG is still invoked at time t_4 and submits job #4. But the wait time of job #4 is longer than the run time of job #3, so between times t_6 and t_7 no workflow task is being executed.

We found two issues with the algorithm as described in [28]. First, it aborts if the workflow's width is greater than the number of available compute nodes. Since workflows can be very wide in practice, we have modified the algorithm so that jobs can execute on arbitrary numbers of nodes. This is done via a standard list-scheduling approach (which greedily schedules the ready task that can complete the earliest). Second, the pseudocode in Fig. 5 in [28] contains a potentially infinite loop for the leeway computation. We have modified this loop to ensure that it terminates (and computes the leeway as intended). From here on, by ZHANG we mean the algorithm in [28] with these two modifications.

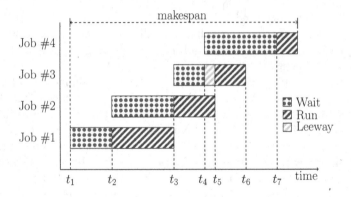

Fig. 1. Example workflow execution with 4 batch jobs using ZHANG.

5.2   Evaluation Results

We compare ZHANG to three baseline competitors: ONEJOBPERTASK, ONE-JOB, and LEVELBYLEVEL. ONEJOBPERTASK submits each task as a single job. ONEJOB submits the entire workflow as a single job. To determine the number of nodes to request, ONEJOB exhaustively considers all possibilities (from 1 to the maximum parallelism of the workflow or the maximum number of nodes in the platform, whichever is smaller). For each, it estimates the workflow run time (using list-scheduling for scheduling tasks on nodes) and obtains an estimate of the wait time. It then submits the workflow as a single job, requesting the number of nodes that leads to the shortest (estimated) makespan. This strategy is not considered as a competitor in [28]. Instead, the authors consider a version that always requests the maximum number of nodes. It is thus a much weaker competitor than ONEJOB since requesting fewer nodes typically achieves a better trade-off between wait time and run time. Finally, LEVELBYLEVEL is a standard approach that submits each workflow level as a single job [9,18]. This strategy was not considered as a competitor in [28]. Like ONEJOB, it determines the best number of nodes for each job based on wait time estimates. The job for a level is submitted only after the job for the previous level has completed. Finally, the results in [28] are only for wait times, while we instead consider overall makespan (which includes wait time) since this is the main metric of interest to users. Given all the above, it is not straightforward to make a direct comparison between the results hereafter and those in [28].

We simulate the execution of the *-250-* workflow configurations for the KTH batch workload for our 289 different submission times, assuming accurate requested job run times (see Sect. 4.2). We set the cap on the number of running workflow jobs to 128, which, for these workflow configurations, means that ONEJOBPERTASK is never limited. For each workflow submission we compute the percentage improvement in workflow makespan achieved by ONEJOBPER-TASK, ONEJOB, and LEVELBYLEVEL relative to ZHANG. Positive values thus correspond to cases in which ZHANG is outperformed by a baseline competitor.

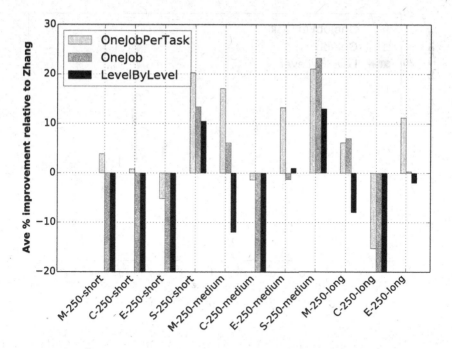

Fig. 2. Average percentage improvement relative to ZHANG for ∗-250-∗ workflows on the KTH workload (number of simultaneously running workflow jobs capped at 128).

Figure 2 shows average relative improvements for the 12 workflow configurations. When comparing ZHANG to ONEJOBPERTASK, we find that ZHANG leads to better results for only 3 workflow configurations (by 5.1%, 1.39%, and 15.29%). For the other 9 workflow configurations, ONEJOBPERTASK leads to relative improvements of 11.16% on average and up to 21.06%. ZHANG, which can default to ONEJOBPERTASK, does so in these results in 23.79% of the cases. When it does not default to ONEJOBPERTASK, it outperforms it in less than 30% of the cases. Overall, we find that although ZHANG can outperform ONE-JOBPERTASK, in the vast majority of the cases ONEJOBPERTASK is preferable to ZHANG (and it is trivial to implement). The second baseline competitor, ONE-JOB, is similar to or outperforms ZHANG on average for 6 of the 12 workflow configurations. As expected, ONEJOB fares better for workflow configurations with higher total run times (even though there are some exceptions, e.g., the C-250-long configuration). This is because for workflows with long tasks, ONE-JOBPERTASK and ZHANG, when it defaults to ONEJOBPERTASK, suffer from cascading task wait times: while a set of (long) one-task workflow jobs are executing, many other (background workload) jobs arrive, causing longer queue wait times for the next set of one-task workflow jobs. By contrast, because of the use of conservative backfilling, at submission time ONEJOB "locks in" a slot in the batch queue that will never be delayed by future job arrivals. The third baseline

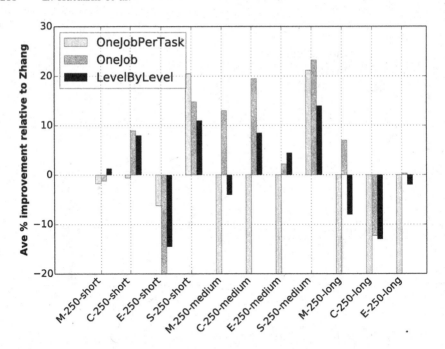

Fig. 3. Average percentage improvement relative to ZHANG for ∗-250-∗ workflows on the KTH workload (number of simultaneously running workflow jobs capped at 16).

competitor, LEVELBYLEVEL, does not perform well. It can outperform ZHANG, but is always outperformed by ONEJOB. This is because, unlike ONEJOB, it does not "lock in" a slot in the batch queue.

The results in Fig. 2 correspond to a best case for ONEJOBPERTASK (and thus for ZHANG when it defaults to ONEJOBPERTASK) as the number of ongoing workflow jobs is not capped. As discussed in Sect. 4.2, many platforms impose low caps on per-user numbers of running jobs. Figure 3 shows results when this cap is set to 16. In these results, ONEJOB outperforms ZHANG on average for 9 of the 12 workflow configurations (losing by 22.45%, 1.21%, and 12.29% in the other 3 workflow configurations). Expectedly, ONEJOBPERTASK leads to the worst results, losing to ZHANG for 9 of the 12 workflow configurations. ZHANG can default to ONEJOB, and in these results it does so in 48.32% of the cases. When it does not default to ONEJOB, ZHANG outperforms ONEJOB in 52.53% of the cases. Here again, LEVELBYLEVEL does not perform well. When it outperforms ZHANG significantly, it is itself outperformed by ONEJOB. Results for other workloads show similar trends (see [10] for full results).

5.3 Discussion

The takeaway from our evaluation of ZHANG is: (i) when the cap on the number of running workflow jobs is not a limiting factor, ONEJOBPERTASK typically outperforms ZHANG; (ii) when this cap is a limiting factor, ONEJOB typically outperforms ZHANG; and (iii) although used in practice, LEVELBYLEVEL does not compare well to its competitors. Importantly, ZHANG does not consistently outperform all the baseline competitors. This is unlike the results presented in [28], and is due to our considering more sound competitors and using the overall makespan as our performance metric. We experimented with three possible improvements to ZHANG, namely: (i) exhaustively examine all options for grouping levels together; (ii) pick the best number of nodes for each job based on wait and run time estimates; and (iii) compute better leeways via a true binary search. We have found that these improvements only lead to marginal improvements (see [10] for all details).

We hypothesize that ZHANG's disappointing results are because it does not explicitly seek to minimize the makespan. Instead, it strikes a compromise between wait time and run time for the next set of workflow levels to be executed, with the hope that these local decisions will reduce the makespan.

6   Proposed Algorithm

In this section, we describe GLUME (Group Levels Using Makespan Estimates), a new strategy that explicitly aims at reducing workflow makespan. The pseudocode in this section is written for best readability rather than for best complexity.

6.1   Intuition and Overview

Like ZHANG, GLUME is invoked repeatedly throughout workflow execution to decide on the next set of consecutive, yet-to-be-executed workflow levels to submit as a single job. But while ZHANG greedily optimizes the wait time to run time ratio of the next job to be submitted, instead GLUME attempts to minimize the makespan directly. Given a workflow with n levels, GLUME considers all possible ways to partition the levels into two jobs: a first job to execute levels 0 to i and a second, subsequent, job to execute levels $i + 1$ to $n - 1$, for $i = 0, 1, \ldots, n - 1$ (the second job could be empty). From here on, we refer to the first job (levels 0 to i) as J_i and to the second job (levels $i+1$ to $n-1$) as J_i'. Figure 4 shows an example workflow execution, where J_i' is submitted as soon as J_i begins executing, and where J_i''s wait time overlaps with J_i's execution. Like ZHANG, the overlap is achieved using a leeway mechanism. In case of a premature job expiration, we use the same approach of canceling any subsequent job that has already been submitted and invoking GLUME again.

For each $i = 0, \ldots, n - 1$, GLUME computes the best job configuration (a number of nodes and a requested run time) for J_i and J_i', i.e., the job configurations that minimize the estimated makespan. The i that leads to the lowest estimated makespan is chosen. J_i is then submitted to the batch scheduler, but J_i' is not. When J_i begins execution, GLUME is invoked again on the remaining yet-to-be-executed workflow levels, possibly leading to partitioning these

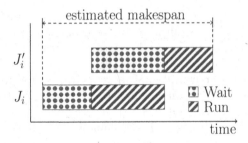

Fig. 4. Example execution of the J_i and J_i' jobs by GLUME.

levels into yet another two groups. In other words, every invocation of GLUME assumes a two-job execution but only submits the first job; thus, the execution of a workflow with n levels can entail up to n jobs. Unlike ZHANG, GLUME never defaults to the one-job-per-task approach. It is thus never impacted by per-user caps on numbers of running jobs (since at most two workflow jobs are in the system at a time).

GLUME estimates the wait times and run times of J_i and J_i' for every possible number of nodes so as to pick the configuration that minimizes the (estimated) makespan. Run time is estimated based on task schedules computed using list-scheduling (since workflow levels can have more tasks than the number of requested compute nodes), and wait time estimates are obtained from the batch scheduler. This is similar to the approach used by the ONEJOB algorithm (see Sect. 5.2). The one difficulty here is obtaining wait time estimates for J_i'. GLUME obtains this estimate "now", but J_i' would be submitted in the future. By then, the state of the batch queue will have changed, further decreasing the accuracy of the wait time estimate. Nevertheless, given no knowledge of the future, GLUME uses this estimate as a best effort.

6.2   Detailed Description

The pseudocode for GLUME is shown in Algorithm 1. GLUME is invoked at the beginning of and repeatedly throughout workflow execution whenever a previously submitted job begins execution. GLUME takes as input a workflow (G) and a duration in seconds ($delay$). G only contains un-executed tasks (already executed tasks are ignored). $delay$ corresponds to an amount of time before the next job to be submitted, as decided by this invocation of GLUME, should begin executing. It is used to overlap the execution of a job with the wait time of the next job. Specifically, the first time GLUME is invoked, $delay$ is zero, as the first job should be submitted immediately. For each subsequent invocation, i.e., each time a previously submitted job begins executing, $delay$ is this job's requested run time. Each invocation of GLUME returns a level (l), a number of nodes (n), and a duration in seconds (t). Based on this output, a job is submitted to the batch scheduler that requests n nodes for t seconds to execute all tasks in levels 0 to l (inclusive) of G.

Algorithm 1. GLUME($G, delay$)

1: $last \leftarrow$ (number of levels in G) $- 1$
2: let $A[0..last]$ be a new array   ▷ Allocations
3: let $M[0..last]$ be a new array   ▷ Makespans
4: $A[last] \leftarrow$ PICKBESTALLOCATION($G, delay, 0, last$)
5: $M[last] \leftarrow A[last].wait + A[last].leeway + A[last].run$
6: **for** $l \leftarrow 0$ **to** $last - 1$ **do**
7:     $M[l] \leftarrow \infty$
8:     $A[l] \leftarrow$ PICKBESTALLOCATION($G, delay, 0, l$)
9:     **if** $A[l].leeway > 0.1 \times A[l].run$ **then**
10:         *continue*
11:     **end if**
12:     $delay' \leftarrow A[l].leeway + A[l].run$
13:     $a' \leftarrow$ PICKBESTALLOCATION($G, delay', l + 1, last$)
14:     **if** $a'.leeway > 0.1 \times a'.run$ **then**
15:         *continue*
16:     **end if**
17:     $t \leftarrow A[l].wait + a'.wait + a'.leeway + a'.run$
18:     **if** $t < M[last]$ **then**
19:         $M[l] \leftarrow t$
20:     **end if**
21: **end for**
22: $l \leftarrow \text{argmin}(M)$
23: **return** $(l, A[l].nodes, A[l].leeway + A[l].run)$

Line 1 of the algorithm sets variable $last$ to the index of the last level of the workflow. Line 2 declares an array A, where $A[i]$ holds the best computed allocation for J_i. This allocation stores the job's wait time ($A[i].wait$), run time ($A[i].run$), leeway to be added to the run time ($A[i].leeway$), and number of nodes ($A[i].nodes$). Line 3 declares an array M, where $M[i]$ holds the estimated workflow makespan for J_i.

As mentioned in Sect. 5.1, submitting the entire workflow as a single job is a safe choice: once this job is submitted its wait time is bounded (provided the batch scheduler uses conservative backfilling), and thus also the workflow makespan. Therefore, we consider executing the entire workflow as a single job as a baseline. This is done at lines 4 and 5. Line 4 computes the best allocation (procedure PICKBESTALLOCATION is described later in this section) for executing the entire workflow, and Line 5 computes the corresponding makespan (which is just the sum of the wait time, the leeway, and the run time).

The for loop at lines 6–21 iterates over all i, $0 \leq i < last$, to search for the best way to partition the workflow levels, i.e., for the best J_i and J_i' pair. Line 7 sets the makespan for J_i, $M[i]$, to infinity. Line 8 calculates the best allocation for J_i, $A[i]$. This allocation has a certain leeway, and lines 9–11 are used to remove the current partition from consideration (i.e., leave $M[i]$ as infinity) if the leeway is more than 10% of the run time. This is a heuristic for avoiding resource waste (since all nodes are idle during the leeway period). Assuming that J_i is submitted to the batch scheduler, then, as soon it begins executing, J_i' will be submitted to the batch scheduler. The algorithm then calculates the allocation for J_i'. The delay for J_i', $delay'$, is computed at Line 12 as J_i's total run time (the sum of its leeway and its run time). The best allocation for J_i' is computed at Line 13. As explained in the previous section, this allocation is computed using a wait time estimate obtained "now", even though the job would be submitted in the future. Lines 14–16 apply again the heuristic to ensure that the leeway for J_i' is not more than 10% of the run time. The overall workflow makespan is then estimated at Line 17, accounting for the overlap of J_i's run time with J_i''s wait time. Lines 18–21 simply updates the workflow makespan for this considered partition, but only if it is shorter than the baseline ONEJOB option. At Line 22 the algorithm computes the index of the partition, l, that leads to the shortest makespan (the argmin notation denotes the index of the minimum element in an array). The algorithm finally returns its decision that workflow levels 0 to l should be submitted to the batch scheduler as one job that requests $A[l].nodes$ nodes and $A[l].leeway + A[l].run$ seconds of run time.

Algorithm 2. PICKBESTALLOCATION $(G, delay, l_{start}, l_{end})$

1: $n \leftarrow$ PICKBESTNUMNODES$(G, delay, l_{start}, l_{end})$
2: $run \leftarrow$ ESTIMATERUNTIME$(G, n, l_{start}, l_{end})$
3: $leeway, wait \leftarrow$
     PICKBESTLEEWAY$(G, delay, n, l_{start}, l_{end}, run)$
4: **return** $(n, run, leeway, wait)$

The pseudocode for PICKBESTALLOCATION is shown in Algorithm 2. It takes as input a workflow (G), a duration in seconds $(delay)$, a start level (l_{start}), and an end level (l_{end}). It returns a number of nodes (n), a run time (run), a leeway $(leeway)$, and a wait time $(wait)$. These are computed so that executing levels l_{start} to l_{end} as one job that requests n nodes for $run+leeway$ seconds would lead to the earliest completion time, incurring a wait time of $wait$ seconds. n is computed at Line 1 via a call to PICKBESTNUMNODES (described hereafter). run is computed at Line 2 by invoking helper function ESTIMATERUNTIME (pseudocode not shown), which estimates the run time for executing all tasks in levels l_{start} to l_{end} on n nodes. This is, once again, done using list-scheduling as for ONEJOB (see Sect. 5.2). At Line 3, another helper function, PICKBESTLEEWAY (pseudocode not shown), is called that returns $leeway$ and $wait$. PICKBESTLEEWAY computes the leeway (and the resulting wait time) in the interval $[0, delay]$ using binary search.

The pseudocode for PICKBESTNUMNODES is shown in Algorithm 3. PICKBESTNUMNODES takes four inputs: a workflow (G), a duration in seconds $(delay)$, a start level (l_{start}), and an end level (l_{end}). PICKBESTNUMNODES returns the best number of nodes to request for a job that executes levels l_{start}

to l_{end} of G. At Line 1, it computes the maximum number of nodes that can be used, $maxnodes$. It is simply the minimum of the number of nodes in the platform and of the maximum width of levels l_{start} to l_{end} in G. At Line 2, we declare an array M, where $M[n]$ will be the estimated makespan when using n ($n = 0, \ldots, maxnodes$) nodes. These makespans are computed in the loop at Lines 3–7. The run time (run) is computed at Line 4 using the previously described ESTIMATERUNTIME helper function. The wait time ($wait$) is estimated at Line 5 based on a wait time estimate obtained from the batch scheduler for a job that requests n nodes for run seconds. $M[n]$ is then computed at Line 6. The first term accounts for the overlap of the execution of the currently running job (which will last $delay$ seconds) with the wait time of the job that is to be submitted (which will last $wait$ seconds). Finally, at Line 8, the index of the shortest makespan, i.e., the best number of nodes to use, is returned.

Algorithm 3. PICKBESTNUMNODES $(G, delay, l_{start}, l_{end})$

1: $maxnodes \leftarrow$ maximum usable number of nodes
2: let $M[1..maxnodes]$ be a new array   ▷ Makespans
3: **for** $n \leftarrow 1$ **to** $maxnodes$ **do**
4:     $run \leftarrow$ ESTIMATERUNTIME$(G, n, l_{start}, l_{end})$
5:     $wait \leftarrow$ queue wait time estimate for a (n, run) job
6:     $M[n] \leftarrow \max(delay, wait) + run$
7: **end for**
8: **return** $\operatorname{argmin}(M)$

GLUME has polynomial time complexity $\mathcal{O}(N \cdot T \cdot M^2)$, where N is the number of workflow levels, T is the maximum number of tasks per level, and M is the number of compute nodes. Each invocation of GLUME requests $\mathcal{O}(M \cdot T + \log D)$ queue wait time estimates from the batch scheduler, where D is the maximum workflow job duration. The logarithmic term accounts for the leeway computation via binary search (in practice the complexity of this binary research is much lower since the leeway upper bound is much lower than D). Different batch schedulers may implement different algorithms for computing queue wait time estimates, which thus may have different complexities. This said, a batch scheduler must maintain an efficient data structure that describes the current schedule and that allows it to make scheduling decisions with low complexity. This same data structure is used for obtaining queue wait time estimates (simply find the first "hole" in the schedule where a job could fit, but not actually insert that job in the schedule). In the experiments described in the next section, we employ a simulator that uses an implementation of a batch scheduler that provides queue wait time estimates. Computing all necessary queue wait time estimates for each invocation of GLUME requires at most a few seconds on a single 2.5GHz core.

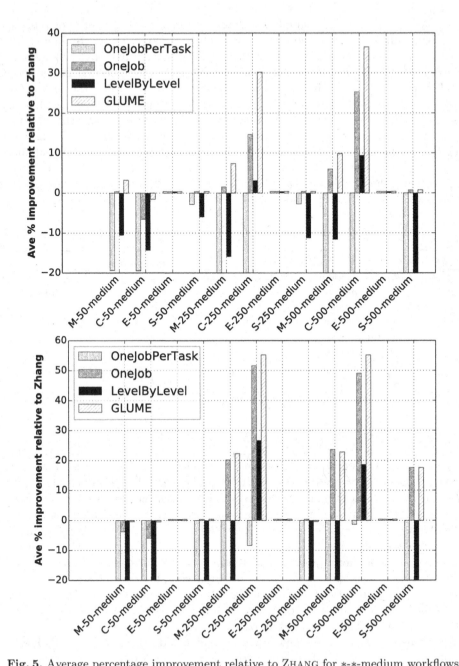

Fig. 5. Average percentage improvement relative to ZHANG for *-*-medium workflows on the KTH (top) and SDSC (bottom) workloads, with the number of simultaneously running workflow jobs capped at 16 and assuming accurate job requested run times.

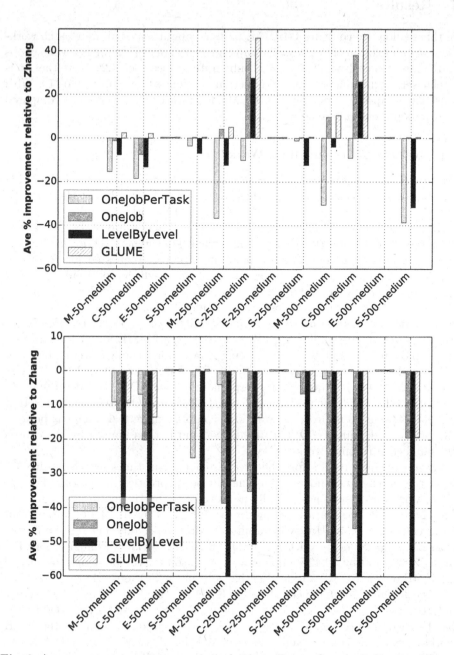

Fig. 6. Average percentage improvement relative to ZHANG for *-*-medium workflows on the KTH (top) and SDSC (bottom) workloads, with the number of simultaneously running workflow jobs capped at 16 and realistic job requested run times.

7   Results

In this section, we compare GLUME to its competitors for all four batch work-loads. In all experiments we fix the cap on the number of running workflow jobs to 16, based on real-world platform configurations (see Sect. 4.2). Note that 16 is a relatively high value as many production systems set the cap to 5 or 10. With these lower cap values results for GLUME are further improved when compared to results presented hereafter.

7.1   Results for *-*-medium Workflows

We discuss results for the *-*-medium workflow configurations and the KTH and SDSC workloads. We picked these results because results for the HPC2N and CTC workloads are similar to that for the KTH workload, unlike results for the SDSC workload. Also, results for the short and long workflow configurations are more clear-cut and thus easily summarized (see the next section).

Figure 5 shows results obtained assuming accurate requested job run times (see Sect. 4.2). Positive values correspond to cases in which a particular strategy outperforms ZHANG. For the KTH workload, ZHANG beats GLUME for 2 of the 12 configurations (by at most 1.5%), while GLUME beats ZHANG for 8 of these configurations (by up to 36.6% and by 10.6% on average). For the SDSC workload, results are similar, with ZHANG beating GLUME for 3 configurations (by at most 0.5%), and GLUME beating ZHANG for 9 configurations (by up to 55.1% and by 26.6% on average). ONEJOBPERTASK and LEVELBYLEVEL fare poorly, while ONEJOB fares better, especially for the SDSC workload, but not as well as GLUME. The performance of GLUME and ONEJOB relative to that of ZHANG tends to improve as workflows comprise more tasks. This is because ZHANG often defaults to ONEJOBPERTASK and is thus limited by the cap on the number of running workflow jobs.

Figure 6 shows results for when requested job run times are taken directly from the batch logs, and are thus inaccurate in practical situations. For the KTH workload, results are actually improved : GLUME beats ZHANG for 9 of the 12 workflow configurations (by up to 47.6% and by 16.2% on average) but is never beaten by it. However, results are drastically different for the SDSC workload: ZHANG beats GLUME for 11 of the 12 workflow configurations (by up to 55.3% and by 22.42% on average). A reason for the poor performance of GLUME on the SDSC workload is that jobs in the SDSC workload request on average 3h20m more than needed. In the KTH workload, jobs request on average only 1h01m more than needed. As a result, wait time estimates provided by the batch scheduler are less accurate for the SDSC workload than for the KTH workload, which can negatively impact GLUME. This said, in the HPC2N and CTC workloads jobs request on average 4h27m and 3h56m more than needed, respectively. And yet, results with those workloads are consistent with those obtained with the KTH workload. There is thus some feature of the SDSC workload, which we were not able to pinpoint, that makes wait time estimates less accurate, which in turns penalizes GLUME. Although ZHANG also uses wait time estimates, in these results it often defaults to ONEJOBPERTASK, and is thus less impacted by inaccurate wait time estimates.

7.2   Overall Results

Table 2 summarizes results across all four workloads and 36 workflow configurations, assuming accurate (left hand-side) and real (right-hand side) requested job run times in the workloads. Each cell in the table shows the number of wins and losses of GLUME vs. one of its competitors for a given workflow computational demand (short, medium, and long). Each cell aggregates results over 48 experimental scenarios (4 workloads, 4 workflow types, 3 workflow sizes in number of tasks). Boldface is used for cells in which GLUME records more wins than losses. We define a "win", resp. "loss", as an average makespan decrease, resp. increase, by more than 5% when compared to a competitor. Otherwise, we declare a draw. Without this threshold, the table would include many wins and losses for cases in which two competitors achieve results that would make little difference to end users. We pick 5% arbitrarily, but note that different values (say between 1% and 10%) lead to similar conclusions from the results.

Table 2. Wins/losses of GLUME against competitors, aggregated for each worklow computational demand, assuming accurate (left) and real (right) requested job run times.

	Accurate requested run times			Real requested run times		
	Worklows			Workflows		
	short	medium	long	short	medium	long
ONEJOBPERTASK	14/18	**40/0**	**37/0**	18/19	**27/8**	**37/0**
LEVELBYLEVEL	**22/6**	**36/1**	**35/0**	**21/10**	**33/1**	**34/0**
ONEJOB	**9/4**	**10/1**	**5/0**	**17/6**	**17/1**	**9/0**
ZHANG	5/18	**17/1**	**9/0**	13/20	10/11	**14/0**

Let us first consider the left-hand side of the table, i.e., assume that requested job run times in the workloads are accurate. GLUME outperforms LEVEL-BYLEVEL across the board, which was already noted in the previous section. GLUME clearly outperforms ONEJOBPERTASK for medium and long workflows, but as expected does not fare as well for short workflows. GLUME outperforms ONEJOB as well, although not as drastically as it does LEVELBYLEVEL and ONEJOBPERTASK. Finally, GLUME outperforms ZHANG for medium and long workflows, only recording one loss for one medium workflow configuration. For short workflows, GLUME is outperformed by ZHANG. This is because for these configurations ZHANG often defaults to ONEJOBPERTASK after executing only a few levels of the workflow, which turns out to be a winning strategy.

The results in the right-hand side of the table are for actual requested run times. While one might expect GLUME to perform worse since it should be more sensitive to wait time estimate inaccuracies, trends are similar. The one glaring difference is for medium workflow configurations, where GLUME experiences 11 losses to ZHANG. 10 of these losses are seen in Fig. 6 (right-hand side) and are for the SDSC workload, as discussed in Sect. 7.1).

Our main conclusion is that GLUME beats its competitors provided work-flow computational demands are high enough, and even with inaccurate queue wait time estimates as provided by batch schedulers in practice. The way in which GLUME partitions workflow levels into jobs is more effective than that of ZHANG, allowing it to outperform the baseline ONEJOB approach. Note that our "medium" workflow configurations only correspond to 500 h of computation, which is at best modest given current workflow and platform trends [1]. It is thus only for very short workflows that GLUME loses to the approach that consists in running at most a few workflow levels as a single job before devolving to ONEJOBPERTASK. For these workflows it is difficult to beat this approach as it can benefit from backfilling opportunities without suffering from cascading wait times. Note, however, that current trends make it clear that longer work-flows are more broadly relevant to current practice in most scientific application domains [5].

8   Conclusion

We have proposed GLUME, a strategy for reducing the makespan of workflow executions on batch-scheduled platforms. Like the strategy in [28], GLUME partitions workflow levels into batch jobs, but its key novelty is that its explicit objective is to minimize the makespan. Simulation results show that GLUME outperforms the strategy in [28] as well as baseline strategies, provided workflow computational demands are moderate to high. GLUME relies on queue wait time estimates provided by batch schedulers and achieves good results in spite of the inaccuracy of these estimates.

There are three broad future directions for this work. The first is to allow GLUME to default to ONEJOBPERTASK so that it can be effective even for very short workflows. This will require the development of a heuristic for decid-ing when to default to ONEJOBPERTASK, which should take into account the platform's per-user cap on the number of running jobs. The second is to account for other metrics besides the makespan and, in particular, resource utilization. A straightforward enhancement to GLUME would be to enforce that each work-flow job achieves a minimum, user-provided resource utilization (by reducing the number of nodes allocated to the job until an acceptable resource utiliza-tion is guaranteed). Much more challenging would be to consider a bi-objective makespan/utilization scheduling problem. The third is to augment GLUME so that it can partition workflows vertically as well as horizontally, e.g., splitting a single level into multiple jobs. This would be useful for cases in which a sin-gle workflow level would already be a large job relative to the target platform and would thus experience long wait time. Ultimately, our goal is to implement GLUME as part of a software tool for executing workflows on platforms man-aged by standard batch schedulers.

Acknowledgments. This work is partially funded by NSF contracts #1923539 and #1923621: "CyberTraining: Implementation: Small: Integrating core CI literacy and skills into university curricula via simulation-driven activities", and the H2020-EU.2.1.1.2. project REGALE (grant ID: 956560).

References

1. Ahn, D., et al.: Flux: overcoming scheduling challenges for exascale workflows. In: Proceedings of the IEEE/ACM Workshop on Workflows in Support of Large-Scale Science (WORKS), pp. 10–19 (November 2018)
2. Cooley Batch Scheduling Policies (2020). https://www.alcf.anl.gov/support-center/cooley/job-scheduling-policies-cooley
3. Mira Batch Scheduling Policies (2019). https://www.alcf.anl.gov/support-center/miracetusvesta/job-scheduling-policy-miracetusvesta, page cached at https://webcache.googleusercontent.com/search?q=cache:4NqDg5gNq6MJ:www.alcf.anl.gov/support-center/miracetusvesta/job-scheduling-policy-miracetusvesta+&cd=1&hl=en&ct=clnk&gl=us&client=firefox-b-1-d
4. Theta Batch Scheduling Policies (2020). https://www.alcf.anl.gov/support-center/theta/job-scheduling-policy-theta
5. Atkinson, M., Gesing, S., Montagnat, J., Taylor, I.: Scientific workflows: past, present and future. Futur. Gener. Comput. Syst. **75**, 216–27 (2017)
6. Batsim-compatible algorithms implemented in C++ (2017). https://gitlab.inria.fr/batsim/batsched
7. Casanova, H., et al.: Developing accurate and scalable simulators of production workflow management systems with WRENCH. Future Generation Comput. Syst. **112**, 162–175 (2020). https://doi.org/10.1016/j.future.2020.05.030
8. Dutot, P.F., Mercier, M., Poquet, M., Richard, O.: Batsim: a realistic language-independent resources and jobs management systems simulator. In: Proceedings of the 20th Workshop on Job Scheduling Strategies for Parallel Processing (2016)
9. Fox, W., Ghoshal, D., Souza, A., Rodrigo, G.P., Ramakrishnan, L.: E-HPC: a library for elastic resource management in HPC environments. In: Proceedings of the 12th Workshop on Workflows in Support of Large-Scale Science, pp. 1–11 (2017)
10. Hataishi, E.: Efficient Execution of Scientific Workflows on Batch-Scheduled Clusters. Master's thesis, University of Hawai'i at Mānoa (2020)
11. Lee, C., Schwartzman, Y., Hardy, J., Snavely, A.: Are user runtime estimates inherently inaccurate? In: Proceedings of the 10th international conference on Job Scheduling Strategies for Parallel Processing, pp. 253–263 (2004)
12. Liew, C.S., Atkinson, M.P., Galea, M., Ang, T.F., Martin, P., Hemert, J.I.V.: Scientific workflows: moving across paradigms. ACM Comput. Surv. **49**(4), 1–39 (2016)
13. Lifka, D.A.: The ANL/IBM SP scheduling system. In: Feitelson, D.G., Rudolph, L. (eds.) JSSPP 1995. LNCS, vol. 949, pp. 295–303. Springer, Heidelberg (1995). https://doi.org/10.1007/3-540-60153-8_35
14. Liu, J., Pacitti, E., Valduriez, P., Mattoso, M.: A survey of data-intensive scientific workflow management. J. Grid Comput. **13**(4), 457–493 (2015)
15. Mu'alem, A.W., Feitelson, D.G.: Utilization, predictability, workloads, and user runtime estimates in scheduling the IBM SP2 with backfilling. IEEE Trans. Parallel Distrib. Syst. **12**(6), 529–543 (2001)

16. The OAR Scheduler (2020). http://oar.imag.fr
17. Parallel Workloads Archive (2020). https://www.cs.huji.ac.il/labs/parallel/workload
18. Rodrigo, G.P., Elmroth, E., Östberg, P.O., Ramakrishnan, L.: Enabling workflow-aware scheduling on HPC systems. In: Proceedings of the 26th International Symposium on High-Performance Parallel and Distributed Computing, pp. 3–14 (2017)
19. Ferreira da Silva, R., Chen, W., Juve, G., Vahi, K., Deelman, E.: Community resources for enabling and evaluating research on scientific workflows. In: 10th IEEE International Conference on e-Science, pp. 177–184. eScience 2014 (2014)
20. Ferreira da Silva, R., Filgueira, R., Pietri, I., Jiang, M., Sakellariou, R., Deelman, E.: A characterization of workflow management systems for extreme-scale applications. Futur. Gener. Comput. Syst. **75**, 228–238 (2017)
21. Task-Clustering Batch Simulator (2020). https://github.com/wrench-project/task_clustering_batch_simulator
22. Slurm Resource Limits (2020). https://slurm.schedmd.com/resource_limits.html
23. Sonmez, O., Yigitbasi, N., Abrishami, S., Iosup, A., Epema, D.: Performance analysis of dynamic workflow scheduling in multicluster grids. In: Proceedings of the 19th ACM International Symposium on High Performance Distributed Computing, pp. 49–60 (2010)
24. Tovar, B., et al.: A job sizing strategy for high-throughput scientific workflows. IEEE Trans. Parallel Distrib. Syst. **29**(2), 24–253 (2017)
25. Pegasus Workflow Gallery (2020). https://pegasus.isi.edu/workflow_gallery/
26. Yoo, A.B., Jette, M.A., Grondona, M.: SLURM: simple linux utility for resource management. In: Proceedings of the 9th International Workshop on Job Scheduling Strategies for Parallel Processing, pp. 44–60 (June 2003)
27. Yu, Z.F., Shi, W.S.: Queue waiting time aware dynamic workflow scheduling in multicluster environments. J. Comput. Sci. Technol. **25**, 864–873 (2010)
28. Zhang, Y., Koelbel, C., Cooper, K.: Batch queue resource scheduling for workflow applications. In: Proceedings of the IEEE International Conference on Cluster Computing, pp. 1–10 (2009)

Author Index

Printed in the United States
by Baker & Taylor Publisher Services